PAUL GOODMAN was born in New York City in 1911, and died in 1972. He received his doctorate in humanities from the University of Chicago, and taught and lectured at various schools, including Sarah Lawrence and Black Mountain College. A novelist, social commentator, poet, literary critic and psychologist, he was consistently controversial and thought-provoking. Goodman's writings have appeared widely, and his best-known books include *Growing Up Absurd, The Empire City, Compulsory Mis-education*, and *Gestalt Therapy*.

Creator Spirit Come!

WEAPONS

THAT

DO

NOT

WEIGH

ONE

DOWN

CREATOR SPIRIT COME!

THE LITERARY ESSAYS OF

Paul Goodman

EDITED BY TAYLOR STOEHR

CREATOR SPIRIT COME!: The Literary Essays of Paul Goodman

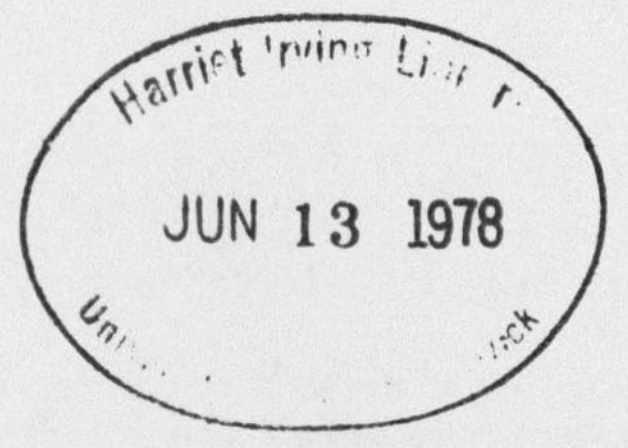

First Edition

Published 1977 by
FREE LIFE EDITIONS, INC.
41 Union Square West
New York, New York 10003

Library of Congress Number 77-71942
ISBN 0-914156-19-5

Book Design by Sidney Solomon
Jacket Design by Elliot Kreloff

Acknowledgments

The editor and publisher wish to thank the following for permission to reprint material included in this book:

Colt Press—for Preface to *The Grand Piano*. Reprinted from Colt Press.

Dissent—for "Reflections on Literature as a Minor Art." Reprinted from *Dissent*, Summer, 1958.

5 x 8 Press—for "The Drama of Awareness." Reprinted from *Stop-Light*, 5 x 8 Press, 1941.

Horizon Press—for Preface to *Our Visit to Niagara*. From *Our Visit to Niagara*, copyright © 1960 by Paul Goodman, by permission of the publishers, Horizon Press, New York.

Kulchur—for An Interview on *The Empire City*. First published in *Kulchur* 18:

Midstream—for "The Real Dream." Reprinted from *Midstream*, Winter 1959.

The Nation—for "Obsessed by Theatre." Reprinted from *The Nation*, November 29, 1958.

New York Times Book Review—for "Wordsworth's Poems." Copyright © 1969 by the New York Times Company. Reprinted by permission.

Poetry—for "The Chance for Popular Culture." Reprinted from *Poetry*, June 1949;—"Between the Flash and the Thunderstroke." Reprinted from *Poetry*, March 1956;—for "The Abundance." Reprinted from *Poetry*, December 1958.

Politics—for "Occasional Poetry." Reprinted from *Politics,* March-April 1947.

Random House—for "Dieses Ist Das Tier Das Es Nicht Gibt." Copyright © 1972, 1973 by the estate of Paul Goodman;—for "Let me praise rapid speech." Copyright © 1967 by Paul Goodman;—for "At the San Remo Bar." Copyright © 1972, 1973 by Paul Goodman;—for "The Empire City." Copyright © 1972, 1973 by Paul Goodman. Reprinted from *Collected Poems* by Paul Goodman, edited by Taylor Stoehr, by permission of Random House, Inc.

Acknowledgments

Random House—for "New Theatre and the Unions." Copyright©1959 by Paul Goodman;—for "'The Crime of Our Century'." Copyright©1957 by Paul Goodman;—for "Wingless Wandervogel." Copyright©1958 by Paul Goodman. Reprinted from *Growing Up Absurd* by Paul Goodman, by permission of Random House, Inc.

Random House—for "An Apology for Literature";—for "The Sweet Style of Ernest Hemingway." Copyright©1971 by Paul Goodman. Reprinted from *Speaking and Language: Defence of Poetry* by Paul Goodman, by permission of Random House, Inc.

Random House—for "Some Problems of Interpretation." Copyright©1958 by Paul Goodman;—for "Notes on a Remark of Seami." Copyright©1958 by Paul Goodman;—for "Advance-Guard Writing in America." Copyright© 1951 by Paul Goodman;—for "Good Interim Writing." Copyright©1955 by Paul Goodman;—for "Underground Writing." Copyright©1960 by Paul Goodman. Reprinted from *Utopian Essays and Practical Proposals* by Paul Goodman. Reprinted by permission of Random House, Inc.

University of Chicago Press—for "On A Poem of Catullus." Copyright©1954 by Paul Goodman. Reprinted from *The Structure of Literature*, by permission of University of Chicago Press.

Vanguard Press—for Preface to Kafka's *Metamorphosis*. Copyright©1946 by the Vanguard Press, Inc.; renewed©1973 by Sally Goodman. Reprinted by permission of the Vanguard Press, Inc.

Contents

Preface

This selection attempts to bring together Paul Goodman's best and most characteristic thought, from among the hundreds of things he wrote over a long and prolific career. Before the decade of his fame much of his writing was published in out of the way places and went unnoticed; even some of the more celebrated essays have been out of print since their first appearance. Although he rescued two or three volumes of miscellaneous pieces during his lifetime, they represented what he had on hand more than any retrospective view. This is the first attempt to collect his work systematically.

Goodman's favorite genre was the occasional poem. In prose too he always kept his eye on the present moment ("the kind of books these are, you're talking about the cases which are in *The New York Times,* no?"), so it is remarkable how well his work has held up. I have made no effort to prune the texts of dated material, but aside from a few references to other contributors in a symposium, other speakers from a platform, the reader will find little to remind him that these thoughts were not written yesterday. The issues he addressed are still with us, and his radical solutions are all the more appropriate as the problems persist and multiply. This applies to his literary as well as his social criticism; they were not so different.

Since this edition is meant for use, not for the record, its priorities vary from those of the usual "standard edition." Instead of the last text corrected by the author, for example, I have picked the fullest, strongest and most characteristic version whenever more than one exists. To preserve rather than muffle their occasions, I have chosen to handle the texts as lightly as possible, letting idiosyncracies of time, place and manner of publication stand. The inconsistencies (some magazines changed *tho* to *though, thru* to *through,* others didn't) reflect the tastes of editors, easy enough to live with. For similar reasons I have not worried about the few cases where Goodman borrowed whole paragraphs from one essay to use in another; it is interesting to see what he thought bore repeating. In short, the individual essays have not been trimmed, nor the speeches tidied up, except for punctuating a few tape-recorded sessions.

For the most part I have avoided reproducing much from Goodman's famous books—*Growing Up Absurd*, *Communitas*, *Gestalt Therapy*, *The Structure of Literature*—because they are still in print and likely to be widely available for a long time to come. Moreover, although readily excerpted, these books have a certain integrity and are best *read through.* Rather than a sampling of classics, I have striven after some sense of the range and development of his thought over several decades, with emphasis on the way he lived the intellectual life—his commitment to ideas. Whenever it has been possible, I have chosen writings that give a personal turn to the issues; and some selections have been included because you can hear Goodman's voice there, still sounding with his lively idiom.

For their suggestions and counsel I thank my fellow literary executors Sally Goodman, George Dennison, and Jason Epstein. Others too have been invaluable sounding boards for me as I wrote the introduction, especially Geoffrey Gardner and Ruth Perry. Maurice and Charlotte Sagoff made reading proof a pleasure, and Chuck Hamilton has proved what an advantage it can be to have a publisher who is an enthusiast.

T.S.

Introduction

When Goodman cried, as he often did in poems, "Creator Spirit Come!" he meant to invoke his muse. Like Milton calling upon his "Heav'nly Muse," Goodman wanted to stand in the light of both the classical and Judeo-Christian traditions, so his "Creator Spirit" is sometimes "Father," and many of his poems are "prayers." Most poets invoke the muse at the outset of poems; Goodman more often called upon him at the end, when one might think it was too late to do any good—for poetry. But it was not quite inspiration that Goodman was asking for, and poetry was not *what* the Creator Spirit sustained so much as *how* succor came. In personal suffering and confusion Goodman counted on poetry helping, so that many of his poems end by saying that writing about it has eased the pain. But when it didn't, he knew that his case was desperate—and *then* he sometimes calls upon the Creator Spirit, who has failed him. Late in life, when he turned from peace politics back to poetry, disillusioned and in ill health, he often found himself at this extremity. What he wanted was consolation, not the art-work. Art-works fell away from him like chips from the strokes of an axe; his "little prayers" were the refuse of his soul-work, a means of self-communing. "To say deliberately just how it is with me is apparently how I pray."

So this was what he meant by the Creator Spirit: sometimes, especially "in moments of impasse," he addressed the Spirit in himself as if outside himself; at other times, "in the best pages, I am not writing, but the Spirit in me." He was not the maker of his best works, any more than the rest of the Creation was made by man. He was the vehicle or conduit through which the Spirit spoke. And at the same time he was the man invoking the Spirit, calling for light in darkness.

This was Goodman's sense of what it meant to be an artist, and it was what he thought all great artists believed and did. When he wrote, and when he considered his art, he always thought of himself as part of this tradition. "On the advice of Longinus, I 'write it for Homer, for Demosthenes' and other pleasant company who somehow are more alive to me than most of my contemporaries." Some of his contemporaries found this attitude pretentious—"Imagine!" one them said to me, "he compared himself to Erasmus!"—while the truth is that Goodman was quite above such petty egotism when he spoke of his heroes of art and philosophy. He sometimes did give way to competitiveness or spite, but always on the level where his detractors were too much at home to notice—back-biting and snubs and scrambling for the public eye—far from the timeless company of the great. The Western Tradition was sacred to Goodman, the Spirit breathed in it, and when he felt it living in him he was as far as possible from measuring himself against anyone.

I do not raise the question of his egotism merely to dismiss his enemies, but to draw attention to a source of difficulty in appreciating his work. We are none of us used to this high seriousness, least of all perhaps those of us who teach literature or practice criticism in the schools. "Academic" has not come to mean "of no real importance" for nothing. Even the selflessness of the best teachers, the disinterestedness of the best critics, can be as fatal to literature as hustling for tenure or a place in the *New York Review,* because all such stances assume that something—the young, the facts, a livelihood, profession, or self—is more important that the Creator Spirit.

For Goodman nothing was more important. He was not infallible of course, and sometimes he forced the Spirit, thought he heard it when he did not, or despaired of it altogether. Often it was his assurance that seemed desperate. The intensity of his longing was itself in the way. Like most of America's great writers—Melville, Whitman, Thoreau, Twain, to name only indisputable cases—he worked at the limits of his ability and drew heavily on his reserves; he was daring, obsessed, tempted to leaps of faith as often disastrous as sublime.

In American society it has not been possible to dedicate oneself to art without such a passionate abandonment of all else. (That "all else" returns to haunt the artist, in his subject matter, in his audience, in his own moments of weakness and defeat—but that is another question.) The great American writers have all been romantics in this way, laying themselves open to the accusation of self-indulgence, for the sake of making contact with the deepest movements of Spirit. Goodman was also a romantic, but more like Thoreau than Melville or Twain, he was a classicist too. His university training did not deaden the Creator Spirit in him. On the contrary, it may have been the quickening of it, the source of his faith in it, just as the solitary reading of Shakespeare was inspiriting to Melville, and Twain was transfigured when he spoke the common speech of his boyhood. However it was with them, Goodman's belief in himself was scarcely distinguishable from belief in his tradition, and this made him seem shameless to some, glorious to others.

Goodman used to call himself a "man of letters," by which he meant that he was a public thinker, whose subject was Man and whose medium was language. He was primarily an artist, but he was that kind of artist, he insisted, who could not create unless he was also doing "his citizenly duty," whatever that seemed to be at any moment. One might compare him to Matthew Arnold, Coleridge, Dr. Johnson, Dryden, or Sidney: he took it as a matter of course that his views of society and human nature were of interest and importance. In America he was most of all the descendent of Emerson, poet and public moralist.

His training was classical—not, perhaps, as rigorous as Emerson's or Thoreau's, but unusually broad and deep for our time. His French was fluent. He was a good Latinist; at City College he learned his Catullus by heart and was on the way to a philological career when Morris Raphael Cohen snared him for philosophy. He later studied with Richard McKeon, first as an illegal auditor of classes at Columbia that he could not afford, then as a paid teaching assistant at the University of Chicago, where McKeon found a job for him when he became dean. He taught himself Greek and German, read not only philosophy but also literature, psychology, and history. His Ph.D. exam in "Literature" covered four fields: History of Criticism, Practical Criticism (Shakespeare's plays and the nature of genre), Theory of Knowledge, and Kant's Aesthetics. His dissertation, "The Formal Analysis of Poems," was a major undertaking in the theory of genre.

He was a university man in the best sense, and proud of it. He never collected books (too poor), but he read everything. He was unsuited to the protocols and decorums of present-day academic life, but he loved the intellectual virtues and he taught as a matter of course—one might almost say compulsively—in whatever company he happened to find himself. His self-image was of the poor scholar, ragged but learned, able to philosophize with newsboys as well as clerics. This created problems. By the end of his life a dozen schools had had a strong dose of him, and either he or they always called it quits after a semester or two. Only the University of Chicago held onto him longer; his three years of exile from New York were tolerable because he happened to fall in love.

At the same time that he was pursuing his studies, he was writing a tremendous amount of fiction, poetry, plays. Between 1931, when he graduated from City College, and 1940, when he finished at Chicago, he wrote two novels, a dozen plays, fifty or sixty short stories, who knows how many thousand poems—not to mention various articles and essays on architecture, cinema, philosophy, and literature. Mostly it was the essays that got published, at least until he came back home in 1940 and began the second phase of his career, as a member of the New York City intelligentsia.

During this next period he wrote most of his literary criticism, partly as a "follow-through" from his Chicago years, partly as his continuing effort to understand and place his own creative work in the tradition. Some of his literary criticism was merely a written-down version of his teaching, a spelling-out in detail of the analysis that he did in the classroom when he dealt with specific texts. His dissertation "The Formal Analysis of Poems" was nothing but a collection of separate studies that he had worked up for courses called "Introduction to the Theory and Practice of Criticism" and "Exercises in the Analysis of Ideas." Later, when he turned it into *The Structure of Literature* most of the new material that he added had also originated in academic occasions—thoughts on Kafka he had broached in the night school at NYU, Shakespeare studies he had made during his summer at Black Mountain.

All this was formal analysis, more or less in the Aristotelian camp of McKeon, R.S. Crane, and others, who later became identified as "The Chicago School" of criticism. It is not clear how much the Chicago School influenced Goodman, or how much he influenced it. Viewed closely, each man seems to worship his own Aristotle, though from the distance of Berkeley or New Haven it might have appeared there was a single challenge flung at the New Criticism. The Chicago critics did meet together formally over a period of years (they discussed the *trivium*), and their work was certainly concerted; but it is hard to see much more than bare compatibility among the methodological passions of McKeon, the obsessive plot summaries of Crane, the logic-chopping of________. What they chiefly shared, aside from their formalist orientation, was a certain taste for polemics.

Goodman knew them all, as teachers or fellow students. McKeon was his mentor, Crane was his boss. Yet he was not invited to join their club. Perhaps he was too disputatious even for them. None of them ever considered their enterprise indebted to him, though most of them thought he was brilliant in his own eccentric way. On the other hand, Goodman imagined (at least he said so, later) that his ideas had been significant in the development of the Chicago School. Obviously someone was mistaken.

Since the school was much less homogeneous than it appeared to outsiders, one might immediately say that Goodman's claim to have influenced it cannot be taken too seriously, unless one understands by that only the evident impact that he made on those in the group with whom he had regular intellectual dealings, chiefly McKeon and Crane. Certainly he did not *invent* the formal analysis of poems; Aristotle did. It must also be recorded that Goodman did not learn formal analysis at Chicago, but brought it with him when he came, for the initial chapter of his dissertation—an amplification of Aristotle's remarks on plot in the Poetics—was already in a first draft by February 1935, more than a year before he left New York City. Since he was auditing McKeon's seminars at Columbia in 1933 and 1934, he might have begun to think along these lines then. I do not know. It may at least be said that Goodman was part of the Chicago School in the way that Kenneth Burke was, that is, vaguely. The interest in formal analysis was common, but no one else asked the questions Goodman did about the *meanings* of characteristic forms. What are the literary genres and how do their structures suit their contents? How do they grow out of the needs of a writer and his culture? How do the formal means—spectacle, diction, plot, character—convey thought and feeling?

The Structure of Literature is far and away Goodman's most important book of literary criticism, the equivalent of *Communitas* in community planning, *Gestalt Therapy* in psychotherapy, or *The Empire City* in letters. But it is not quite so representative of his range within that discipline as those others are in theirs. It *is* marked by his Chicago training. In the criticism of the Forties, *Kafka's Prayer* or the literary essays of *Art and Social Nature,* his own startling voice begins to come through, for which the term "range" is almost beside the point. His essay on "The Method of Abstraction in Literature" is a good example of this later quality, because it shows his formalist analysis applied to questions that also engaged him crucially as a writer of fiction.

For some years (since 1936) Goodman's stories had been evolving a new manner, which at first he merely called "prose composition" and finally identified as "literary cubism." The cubist trick was, as he said in a preface written for a proposed collection of them, to allow the formal means an "emphasis and independent development" so that "the relations of the characters, thoughts, and acts will seem to be partly advanced by the mere literary handling, apart from their natural or imaginary relations." This gave "a literary, formal quality to the subject-matter which is to my taste excellent." How intimately his creative work and his criticism were tied! it turns out that his fiction is itself another chance for formal analysis!

At the same time his own fiction provided him with material for analysis, so that in his essay on literary abstraction he invents a little plot about an architect-turned-camoufleur, which he sketches out first as a naturalistic story, then a cubist tale, and finally an abstract prose-poem—to show the formal nature of three literary methods or manners. Moreover, having borrowed the circumstances of his plot from life (his architect brother Percival was a partner in a camouflage company), Goodman went on to use the same idea in the second volume *The Empire City,* where he finds a manner somewhere in between the naturalistic and the cubist—"expressionistic naturalism"—to match his current attitude toward the subject.

This is a remarkably tight knot of creative acts and critical observations: human circumstances becomes material for art, art becomes example for criticism; the criticism focuses on the relation of circumstance to rendering, as revealed in structure; and the rendering itself is critical commentary, on both circumstance and art, in its playing with the formal means. Even the subject—the architect-turned-camoufleur—repeats the concern, for she (the architect is a woman in all versions) is an expert in formal means, and the plot shows how she discovers, first, that she had drawn attention to precisely her own house in camouflaging the city, and then, from a plane, that she has been successful after all—the joy in her artistic feat being immediately succeeded by despair, "for there is no satisfaction of the heart in nothingness."

The order of these acts and observations is important. Although they seem to round upon one another in a chain of interrelations, in fact their beginning is in the creative moment. Goodman's criticism followed his art—sometimes right on its heels, but always attendant. One can see in some of his applications for Guggenheim fellowships (he never got one) that he usually had a good idea of what he was trying to create and how to go about it, and if one looks closely his plans are seen to grow out of some already realized work, the analysis of which has determined the next step. It is therefore a little unsettling to read rapidly through these fellowship applications—1942, 1943, 1945, 1946, 1947—for the career unfolds too fast, novels and plays conceived, brought forth (midwife or not), and autopsied, like animated cartoons. Perhaps this haste was anxiety, the result of having no audience to justify his art. Just as likely, it was the other way around, his eagerness to explain himself cost him that larger audience. His experiments in cubist and expressionist forms always seemed too didactic to the few critics who paid any attention at all, and he was likely to reveal something else along the way that completely alienated them. None of its handful of reviewers had anything to say of the literary essays in *Art and Social Nature*; they couldn't maintain their composure past the encouragement of childhood sexuality and draft-dodging in "The May Pamphlet."

But in spite of deliberation and self-awareness, Goodman's writing rarely seems programmatic. When he gave advice to the young writers in his class at Black Mountain, he had one inalterable rule: write from the heart. Everything depended on being honest, all else followed naturally. He had other principles too, of course, but there was no deeper belief in all his aesthetics—or, for that matter, in his anthropology, psychology, and politics. A single human nature unites us all, and that nature is the source of all human achievement and value. Culture is rooted in it, institutions feed on it, heroes and saints exemplify it. A writer must write from it. The assurance that the Creator Spirit moved in him, and in his tradition, was grounded in this doctrine, which he found in all his teachers, Aristotle and Kant, Freud and Reich, the early Marx and Kropotkin. Of course it is possible to betray our nature, and to construct a social order that systematically thwarts it, but since all energy and creative force can only arise in nature, such bondage can never be complete or permanent; its own dissolution is entailed. As Goodman loved to say, Nothing comes from nothing.

This view can be seen in his most unique contribution to literary criticism, the theory of literary methods or manners. His essay "Literary Method and Author-Attitude" was written at just the juncture of his own career and world history to bring the view into the strongest light. By early 1942 his own creative work was at last being published—two books from small presses, numbers of stories and poems collected in several New Directions Annuals, regular appearance in the *Partisan Review*—and at the same time the United States had just entered the war. Already the War Spirit began to smother his little success: a writer who published a collection of Noh plays a week after Pearl Harbor, or an anti-war novel like *The Grand Piano* during the Bataan Death March, could not expect to be popular, however much he might write from the heart. In these circumstances, personal and global, Goodman had perforce a new set of topics for structural analysis, for he uses the history of his own growing alienation, as revealed in his stories, to show the different literary manners and how they arise in "author-attitude." He describes the manners that he found himself working in, 1931-1942, according to the relations he was able to maintain with a world going from bad to worse:

Naturalism—"I was willing to regard the scene and the society as *my* scene and my society, rich in interest, still possessing the potentiality of life, worth transcribing with fidelity. . . ."

Symbolism—"It is intolerable that this scene should be merely what it seems, it must have also some other meaning."

Expressionism—"Now the scene was not even admitted to be *my* scene. . . . I was impatient to present anything but its schematism, which I analyzed and abstracted with the more ferocity in order to put it in *its* place, and what had that to do with me?" This last manner is one of several (*cubism, abstraction,* etc.) all of which are examples of "the expression of artistic confidence under the conditions of alienation."

Intent on his own plight in 1942, Goodman made no attempt in this little lexicon to show how such an analysis might be of use in understanding literary history, but one need only think of the difficulties in identifying and distinguishing the literary manner of Defoe and Dreiser—accounting for the two naturalisms, each at the edge of symbolism, separated by two centuries—to be aware of important possibilities.

In the fall of 1942 he proposed to the Guggenheim Foundation to write a book on the subject of literary manner. It was a curious plan, somewhat on the model of his essay on abstraction in literature except that now he planned to dispense with critical apparatus altogether, and write a novel that would illustrate the different literary manners. The plan was to retell Balzac's novel *Les Illusions Perdues* in four different manners (with interludes reflecting the possibilities of further combinations), so that the result would be "a kind of Art of the Novel" couched entirely in fiction.

This is one of the few projects he proposed to the Guggenheim

Foundation that their failure to support seems to have cancelled. He wrote almost everything else, even though no help was forthcoming. Perhaps this means his heart was not really in it, and we should thank the Committee for its habitual frown upon Goodman's exuberance. But it seems to me that the idea (not necessarily the way he proposed treating it) was his major discovery in literary theory, and I deplore its long languishing in the unread back pages of *Art and Social Nature* while Northrup Frye's jejune *Anatomy of Criticism* led a generation of graduate students round and round the maze of post-Chicago School formalism. Goodman's "Literary Method and Author-Attitude" and "The Method of Abstraction in Literature" contain the germ of a treatise on manner that would have been more important even than the book on genre he did write, *The Structure of Literature.*

It may seem strange to ask why the author of over 30 books, including three or four classics in as many fields, did not bother to write another one. Goodman himself would have thought it a good question though. Aside from *The Structure of Literature*—which was finally rewritten and published in 1954 (but bore the impress of Chicago still)—the literary criticism he wrote after the middle Forties seems to have been concerned with very different matters. Like his social criticism, its focus shifted with the times and Goodman's own case. *Kafka's Prayer* was written during his first, disturbing experience of psychotherapy, as one might have guessed from its religious subject and psychoanalytic method. In all his social and philosophic thought Goodman's gift was for structural analysis, so that he never loses sight of the formal means and pattern of parts and whole, but his motives in reconstructing Kafka's existential plight were far from the academic aims of literary theory or history. He was looking for the spiritual meaning, the foundations of faith that one writer may sometimes pass on to another. Of course that is what "Literary Method and Author-Attitude" is really all about. The point is, he now brought that question to the forefront of subject matter; he is asking for a faith, a manner to write in. It was a fateful moment in the history of his relations with the Creator Spirit when Goodman began to doubt himself.

Not so surprisingly, the next literary theory he wrote was the chapter in *Gestalt Therapy* called "Verbalizing and Poetry," where he speaks of literature and language from a new point of view, addressing himself to the pathologies of modern speech. There is a poignant parallel in Goodman's inner life at the same time, in the long unpublished essay "On Being a Writer" which he wrote for his fortieth birthday—a chilling account, half invented, half cold truth, of his systematic self-balking in the midst of his great prolificness and facility. He sensed a certain side of his imagination drying up. As he began to practise psychotherapy himself in the early Fifties, he wrote essays on significant special interests, "A Writer's Block" and "The Intellectual Inhibition of Explosive Grief and Anger." Even his survey of "Advance-Guard Writing: 1900-1950," a psychoanalytic exploration of his own literary backgrounds and confrères, was written more as if from the perspective of one who is finished with all that, than from the engaged stance he took in "Literary Method and Author-Attitude" eight years earlier. The literary essays and reviews he produced during the Fifties continued to emphasize structural analysis directed at the psyche of the author, or the psychopathology of the period, or the psychodynamics of the relation of author to audience, but there was an important change in the overall thrust of his criticism. The orientation became increasingly social or political rather than literary or philosophic. There are exceptions to be made—much of his reviewing, especially of poetry—but it is important to notice that during this period he wrote far less fiction than he had averaged for the last two decades. Whatever one is to make of it, there is certainly some correlation between the falling off of his narrative impulse (for he still wrote many poems and plays) and the shifting of focus in his literary criticism, to issues less personally grounded, and now always framed in polemically psychoanalytic terms. It is impossible to say which came first, the fading of the imaginative life or the burgeoning of the analytic; somehow they implied one another.

Another way of saying the same thing would be to suggest a line of development in Goodman's critical writings that begins in the late Thirties with formal literary theory; then moves to self-analysis energized by an outburst (how else to describe it?) of creative work, and also by a new sense of social and political pressures during the War; next entering a phase of *crise* in which the very source of his artistic impulse is touched, and likely wounded, as he struggles to adopt psychoanalysis as his own religious discourse; and finally, in the Fifties, the solidifying of this drift in a doctrine or tool of analysis, no longer turned on his own work or career but sharp for the anatomy of his times. He was ready to write *Growing Up Absurd.*

The next ten years were as prolific as the Forties had been, but in a different vein. Goodman's social criticism fills a long shelf. Here and there in this more popular and familiar outpouring of dissent and schemes for change, there are glimpses of the years of experience in analytic modes of thought, philosophic, literary, and psychoanalytic, for he never left these interests or principles behind: they were the "weapons that do not weigh one down," as he said at the end of *The Empire City*. It would not be far afield to read through his entire work of the Sixties as a kind of literary criticism applied to social problems.

I mean this quite literally. At the end of the decade, when the Movement had soured for him, had turned away from its populist and grass-roots anarchism (as he saw it) to violence and power-fantasies (again, as he saw it), Goodman went back to two abiding interests, one might almost say addictions: literary criticism and poetry. He knew he was dying, and in both now there was a strong autobiographical flavor, not self-assessment so much as final testament. His last book, *Little Prayers and Finite Experience*, contained chiefly his religious poetry, combined with a sort of apologia that said how he found himself in the world, "how I think." The book before that was *Speaking and Language*, which he intended as a major work, comparable to *Gestalt Therapy* or *The Structure of Literature*, presenting his views of the new linguists and linguistic philosophers, and still another *apologia,* his own "Defense of Poetry" in the tradition of Sidney and Shelley.

Speaking and Language may not be the classic treatment of the subject that he wanted it to be, but it is a stunning book, and it shows more vividly than anything else I could name just why it makes sense to speak of his social thought as somehow a version of his literary criticism. The bulk of the book is a discussion of human speech from the point of view of a literary man. He finds himself, as he says, "steering a middle course between the dogmatic phenomenologists on the one hand and the dogmatic linguists and scientists of Communications on the other. This gives me the genuine pleasure of being able to affirm platitudes that all others are denying.'' Now this may seem at first very curious—it certainly did to me, and I had been urging him to write this book for ten years—for here is the formalistic critic, the Aristotelian champion of structural analysis, taking the position that the modern linguists and philosophers, of whatever camp, have falsified language and human speech in their rigorous effort to ''break the code'' and reveal the true and eternal structure behind all sayings. To their formulas and methodologies Goodman presents no alternatives, as surely he would have done thirty years earlier when he was as young as these young Turks of the schools; rather he systematically pokes holes in their theories, shows how language is not ultimately susceptible to positivist analysis at all, and leaves the subject without even bothering to pick up the pieces and stack them according to some tentative theory of his own. The book ends with his ''Apology for Literature,'' essentially a defense of his own career and practice in the arts.

Even in argument he refuses to build a position in the way he did in *Kafka's Prayer* or *The Structure of Literature*. His method is like that he developed in the Sixties for his polemical speeches and essays, a series of quick examples that do not add up to a ''case'' so much as they incisively sketch in the range of alternatives to a hardened status quo he is trying to dismantle. But the piecemeal approach is not what links this book to his social criticism. Rather it is the homely truth he opposes to the linguists' elegant theories. His argument begins with a different premise from theirs, for they are after the rules and essential forms of language, where he is concerned with the endless variety and lively possibilities of human *uses* of language. In short, they are interested in grammar as a science, he is interested in style. This difference is crucial not only to linguistic theory but also to social and political thought. It is the equivalent in linguistics of his anarchism in politics, or Gestalt Therapy in psychoanalysis. Linguistics, politics, and psychoanalysis are dangerously liable to ideology and dogmatism, and are best kept open and alive with reminders that nothing is so important as the potential for ''novelty, excitement and growth'' (the sub-title of *Gestalt Therapy*).

So far as I know there was only one book that Goodman did not live to write; he used to talk about someday writing an Ethics. But I wonder whether he did not finally regard *Speaking and Language* as that book, as well as his final attempt at literary criticism. Long before, in the spring of 1955, when he was reading Otto Jespersen with much admiration, Goodman jotted the following thoughts in his journal:

> Complex-words that compel feeling & action are the premisses in ethics. This justifies the carryings-on in the literary reviews. It is the only possibility for an intrinsic ethics—as contrasted to the "prescriptive commands + deduction" of the positivists. Poems & rhetoric give premisses—the implications must be drawn out by criticism. (So Scriptures are this interpretation.) Much simplicity or precision is not to be hoped for.

Ten years later when he revised this passage for publication in *Five Years*, he made it clearer that what he meant by "complex-words" was poems, literature, and reminded us that Arnold had said that literature was "the criticism of life." In *Speaking and Language* the chapter called "Complex Words and Poetry" does not repeat the argument (though Jespersen is again prominent), yet his entire book is now a demonstration of that view of language, literature, and criticism. This is what accounts for the piecemeal approach, the emphasis on style rather than grammar, and the resistance to the positivist side of Chomsky and the linguistic philosophers. One sees how his literary criticism always lay behind his social thought —literally. And why the long service of the Sixties, in the politics of dissent, was finally not wasted or alien to his Creator Spirit. He kept writing his poems, the ethics that "state the relations in the soul between how I am in the world and what I command myself to do." And he persisted in the next step too, drawing out the implications, by criticism.

Taylor Stoehr

Dieses ist das Tier das es nicht Gibt.—Rilke.

Lose yourself of thoughts and fears.
Your face will fade out of the looking-glass.
You breathe a mist of sighs, they slowly pass,
your heart is empty when the mirror clears.
What's in *there? what's to come? what of art?*
—this void no natural animal can breathe.
Stifle the clouds that from your nostrils wreathe
now eagerly.

Ah! the light-curtains part,
appears the Unicorn with his light step
and the breath of roses curling from his teeth.
He wants to speak. "I am not fed on corn
but on the chance of being." *His white horn*
silently shatters the barrier with its tip
and he emerges between life and death.

I

LITERATURE, CULTURE, AND TRADITION

Western Tradition and World Concern

Now that in technique, economy, and government the world is fast becoming a unity, a unity not only of great ideas like the brotherhood of mankind or of great movements like Christianity or social revolution, but of daily habits and manners—at such a time a self-conscious artist who is aware of the sources of his style and his themes is faced with a terrible dilemma. Either he abandons the western tradition he has been brought up in and patiently absorbed, and tries, a late-learner, to adopt a new outlook (but what outlook and how to absorb it?); or he persists in his ways and feels that he is somewhat parochial (but a conscious sense of parochialism is fatal to high seriousness or high comedy, for these are incompatible with any suspicion of merely relative value). The following reflections spring from my own awareness of this dilemma; but unfortunately they do not solve the problem.

I.

How can we speak more precisely of the "western tradition" or the "oriental tradition"? Let us use as an earmark the following consideration: to have a literary tradition means that in thinking of the most basic human relations and human conflicts, a writer pictures them dramatically to himself in a few ancient exemplary stories. The most basic relations are those of child and parent or other exemplar, of kin and friends, of ruler and subject, of sexual love, of death, of man and God. In the western tradition these are conceived fundamentally as Greek and Biblical stories, to which are added a few medieval national cycles. Thus, the tragedy of the family is the story of Oedipus or Orestes, the murderer is Cain, the dominant father is Abraham expelling Ishmael and sacrificing Isaac, the lover is Phaedra, the poet-king is David, the premier among peers is Arthur. Then, the tradition is alive when in each generation these stories are retold: not simply told again, but revived, dreaming through the old story to the moral of the current wisdom. In the past thousand years the Greek and Biblical stories have always been so revived, and the authors include, of course, the greatest names in western letters. On this criterion we see how Goethe, for example, is the very embodiment of the western tradition—so that he is almost a myth himself:—whereas Shakespeare is less so, but also in the tradition. (The reason is that Shakespeare did not pose to himself the basic problems as such, but started from current theatrical excitement.) Further, when a radical social and historical change brings people to consider a new human relation as basic, as basic as the other continuing basic relations, then an occasional new story is added, e.g., Tristan or Faust. From a sophisticated point of view we may consider that the new relation, e.g., sex-death, is not really fundamental but is a secondary perversion; but it is preferable to consider it as basic in the socio-psychological situation into which the people have been maneuvered.

Psychologically there is no mystery about the fact of such a continuing tradition, revived and revised from generation to generation. A small child is instructed and entertained with stories, and these are the stories. Then grown-up, when he is face to face with the expression and interpretation of his deepest thoughts, the old stories recur to him as compelling formulae because they are energized by the thoughts of childhood which were unconscious in childhood. (To be sure, only stories with a certain formal greatness can carry such energies to begin with, and this is why a tradition is long in developing, for it requires the inheritance of stories already greatly told.)

It follows that if, as we find today, these stories are no longer told to children—I mean the Bible stories and the Tale of Troy—then the tradition must lapse, no matter how deep and accurate the comparative literature may become. By "comparative literature" I mean the adult collation of great stories not necessarily energized by the thoughts of childhood. In fact the situation is fast becoming as follows: (a) There ceases to be a large public aware of the stories. (b) The learned and intellectual poets to whom the stories are deeply meaningful cling to them all the more closely and defiantly. (c) But their handling becomes increasingly private and hectic, lacking the centrality of common wisdom, for it is only a common standard that can keep a story clear and grand in form. (d) What was originally human fate comes more and more to be the private case history of the poet. (e) And the larger public, having not yet learned other stories, now has no basic stories at all, but is condemned to shallow literature.

Every step of the way could be easily demonstrated by examples.

II.

Now we are entering a time of world awareness and world concern, in politics, economy and communications. What is the deepest possible relation between the western tradition and this world concern? for it is obviously not possible in every way both to use the traditional culture to communicate one's new concern to vast new audiences, and at the same time to have a simple and integral style. But we must seek for the deepest possible relation, because only a deep memory can invent humane letters.

It must be pointed out at once that the expansion from a western to a world concern is not analogous to the expansion from a national to a Great-European point of view. For intrinsically the Great-European point of view is culturally prior to the separate national cultures; it is everywhere apparent in the great national works; even in the most limited political meaning, it is a late historical phase of the western tradition, not something added to that tradition. Is there any sense in which world awareness is similarly apparent in the western tradition?[1]

I do not think that there are important world stories in the sense that there are important western or far-eastern stories. On the contrary, it seems that the same fundamental human problems have been pre-empted in the different cultures by precisely different classic stories, with corresponding differences in style. For the most part, in the west the eastern stories have been employed exotically; sometimes, as we shall discuss at once, they have been handled with deep earnestness; but there are no positive world stories. If the world concern is to be related integrally to the western tradition, it cannot be on the basis of the myths directly, but in some way on the attitude and handling.

During the Enlightenment and in the time of Goethe, great western writers, interesting themselves in the near-eastern and far-eastern traditions, drew the inspiring moral of universal brotherhood: namely that it is the same human nature that speaks out in different stories. Among the *philosophes* this meant generally a thinning out of their own stories into rational fables, and no profound intuition of the eastern stories. But in Goethe the western dreams are told with undiminished depth, and he does not misread the foreign dreams, for he saw both that all the traditions belong to one humanity and that they differ in the most radical way possible in style. A few Great-Europeans of the 19th Century, e.g. Nietzsche, likewise reached beyond the European tradition without losing all tradition whatsoever and degenerating into comparative literature, philology and history. What a beautiful *ambassadorial* role these poets had! imposing nothing, but communicating the universal philosophy and natural science that by definition belong to all intellect.

World concern has developed beyond this ambassadorial relation of mutual respect and communication: first, into the imperialism of the west over the east, and then into the present stage of either superficial tolerance or international social revolution.

[1] Yes, perhaps just in the negative stories of calamity and irreparable exclusion, like the Tower of Babel; or in the Hellenic awareness, proud and guilty, of the existence of Barbarians. And in the Mission of Paul to the Gentiles we read how one such irreparable breach was healed.

III.

The classic pattern of imperial culture (when once it is beyond the stage of brutal parochial imposition) is the amalgam of traditions, tolerant of all, and lightly blurring differences in style to facilitate urbane intercourse among the literary masters. Soon there ceases to be any fundamental tradition at all, yet superficially nothing is lost and a great master either can invent a hybrid story (which often becomes classic: for the mixture also, e.g., Christianity itself, may be fundamentally humane); or he can return to a sophisticated purity of tradition, with the appropriate audience. One aspect of the Paris International Style of the twenties was just such an amalgam; but, as we shall see, it had also a profound and traditional aspect. But there are strong reasons why just the Americans could be the leaders of such an imperial amalgam: (a) Having aborted their national culture into a technology, they have weaker ties to the western tradition. (b) Their history has given them a cultural humility, the guilt or conversely the boasting of major American writers at having cut loose from Europe in 1776; but now they can joyously atone, in new circumstances, as the literati of the world: the Americans would be quick to adopt any number of styles if once they could learn to read. (c) And they have the wealth to finance a world academy. On a vaster scene they could repeat the relation of Rome to Greece and Syria.

The chief American locus of this tolerant amalgam, so shiny to think of, is not in the seaport cosmopolitanism of New York, but in the cornfed cosmopolitanism of the west coast. The Californian (*homo californiensis*) could become the perfect variety to bear such a broad culture vitaminized, for the first time, with a universal high standard of living. Radiant in body, accustomed to material success, without idiosyncracy, acquainted with the ideas of the two worlds but unembarrassed by the cultural lag that comes only from trouble or vocation, and impenetrable by any earnest word. A remarkable beginning has already been made there by the best type of refugees (academicians and Nobel Prize winners) who seek out the climate.

Against this (but unfortunately exploited by it) is the world-wide communication of the ideals of social revolution: humane labor, physical security and freedom, mutual aid; and among more thoughtful revolutionaries, the humanizing of technology and the ethical measure of production and consumption. These social ideals are simple and integral, not an amalgam; they are close to every concern and causally grounded in the universal spread of the techniques and economy; but of course they are not yet fundamentally cultural at all. It is only in the fantasies of the political press that they even make such a pretension. They are largely concerned with secondary relations; they are as yet aimed at overt action, rather than profound practice or thought; they do not even recognize the simple psychological sources of their own energies—and fiascos. Nevertheless, such as they are, they are compatible with the humane culture of the world and they partake of its spirit, though no master has made them part of its content. The notion that as merely mass ideals they will continue to blank out our deep personal and social concerns is mere desperation; it comes from the cultural accident (no historical accident)[2] that the generation of world concern happens to be the generation distraught by a technical revolution.

It is in this direction that the Americans can make a true contribution. The heirs, through the Dissenters and Franklin and Jefferson, of the English and French political philosophers, they have had the historical chance to make many great experiments in what an independent man can do with material resources. (But we see that this living line is sidetracked into sociolatry and Lincolniana.)

IV.

One aspect of the Paris International Style was the amalgam of cultures that we have already referred to; bringing together all times and places as if these things were neighborly here and now. But another aspect was the concentration on literary method, the abstraction from the content, everything that goes by the name of

[2] I say a "cultural accident" simply because it is logically conceivable that America, for instance, could have completed its technical revolution (it had the inventions and the resources) before going overseas; but historically, of course, the technical revolution, and its economy, and going overseas, are all causes and effects of each other.

the Revolution of the Word. And this development, it seems to me, has been the greatest achievement thus far (a) within the stream of western tradition, and (b) towards the integral culture of the world.

If we return a moment to the 19th Century masters, we see that there is a curious contrast between the Parisian way and the national ways of being a Great-European writer. Byron, Tolstoi, Nietzsche, Ibsen, Dostoievski were Great-Europeans; the ideas they represented and their powers of expression overrode the national boundaries (even when they were nationalists!) in a way that the works of equally great writers such as Keats or Gogol, did not. But with the French, surprisingly, we find that Flaubert, Mallarmé, or even Zola have a European importance quite beyond the scope of their ideas. Their power, of course, is that they are the inventors of literary methods, and these methods carried their fame and spirit abroad wherever a young writer made use of what had been invented. It was not necessary for them, in order to achieve the most humane communication, to have a philosophic or revolutionary content, for they at once touched the deepest possible of meanings, a new style. In the nature of the case, however, a literary society that habitually seeks such a level, soon ceases to be France or any other country, and becomes—precisely—Paris.

Artistic method, when it is the grappling of the artist with his attitude toward the subject-matter, is his most integral act qua artist; it is his way of neutralizing the ego and drawing freely on the common immortal energies of life. To say it again: artistic methods, e.g., naturalism, expressionism, or cubism, are fundamental theories of the universe, the perception of it, the place of personality in it; and they are proved by the successful creation of the unity of a work, for you cannot create a work with a false attitude. Now such an increased self-consciousness of method and style is not a break with tradition so long as the author does not and cannot forsake his fundamental stories, but is driven by the refinement of the habit of art and by skepticism of those stories that he still cannot but believe, to get behind those very stories to express what is more humane still. But there *is* a break with tradition in so-called experimental writing, which is preoccupied with technique as such, apart from the analysis of the stories. I am referring in poetry to exactly the contrast in painting between abstraction and non-objectivism: abstraction is traditional; non-objectivism is exotic.

At the same time, however—and this is the capital point—abstraction and every other self-conscious method are potentially traditional in several traditions; for they are a passage beyond the stories themselves to the artist in every man universally; they are a passage to the fundamentals of feeling and perception that all men share as brothers. Thus it seems to me that in the abstract handling of his deepest stories learned in childhood, the traditional poet contributes also to a world culture. His *deepest* stories, because only these have the tension of the most humane feeling and perception; and *abstract* handling, in which he is most free. But thus we have come to the hackneyed aphorism that classic art is universal, for classic art has been always just this self-conscious expression of fundamental stories, where neither the expression nor the story calls attention to itself alone and nothing can be added or omitted, for it is like nature.

Consider lastly such a work as *Finnegans Wake*—I say "such a work" as if there were another such!—where there is not only a stubbornly abundant invention of method, perfecting whatever was invented in Paris for 100 years and in England for 500, but also an exploration beneath the stories themselves toward the sources of image, myth and language. These sources are of course a more universal content than the western stories, just as the dictionary of inherited dreams (if these exist) is more universal than a man's dream. But the enormous complexity of Joyce's detail follows from the unlucky naturalism with which he starts ("unlucky" relatively, in that naturalism belongs toward the end of a tradition, not toward the beginning); but no doubt with a different method to start with, similar primordial stories will be presented more simply, and be like the images of Picasso or Klee.

First published in *Art and Social Nature (1946)*, this essay was written in the winter of 1943-4, when Goodman was a teacher at Manumit, a progressive school in New York State.

The Meaning of Abstraction in Literature

In the argument over abstraction, we find that the abstract musicians and painters aim to avoid in their work anything which is, as they say, "literary." In music the essential and ancient problem has to do with song and dance—the later question of "program" or "absolute" music is along the same lines but more superficial—and now for three hundred years abstract music has established itself firmly in the west, though how far this music is abstracted from emotion and a kind of wordless drama is always a lively issue. In painting the arguments date back only fifty years and have to do with carrying the program of Cubism to its logical conclusion, namely: having reduced the objects and their space to their colors, solidity, and planes, to reduce these in turn to what is two-dimensional and nothing but the canvas-space itself. In literature, however, the issue has hardly been raised at all and exists for the most part only in the disguise of debates on "form" and "content."

Now what the absolute-musicians and abstract-painters call "literary" is not specific to literature at all, and this can be shown by the analysis of *abstract literature*. If the other artists would understand the nature of abstract literature, the quarrels among the arts would certainly be eased; and the general theorist could better approach the far-reaching problem facing all arts alike.

I. WHAT IS "LITERARY"?

A painter has said, "Literature cannot be abstract in the sense that painting can be, because words have associations. If I say 'blue,' we think of the color, of colored objects, the sky, etc. If I put a patch of blue on canvas, however, there need be no associations *outside* the canvas, so long as in composing I employ only the painting-relations of the patch, namely its hue, shade, value, extension."

To this the abstract-writer should reply, " 'Blue' certainly has associations; but an *adjective* need have no associations outside the literary passage. What association has a phrase as such, or a simile, or a syllogism, or a dilemma?"

The abstract literary elements are to be found, not in the significations and their associations, but in the means of signifying; they are not the denotations and connotations, but the parts of speech.

Literary signifying is of course broader than logical signifying. Starting with a situation to describe or narrate, a literary-man may signify it in many ways: by a complex of isolated phrases of immediate sensation or feeling; or by allusions and associations; or by a structure of definitions and a sorites; or by a dramatic action, etc., as well as the combinations of these.

The choice of the means of signifying is not irrelevant to the significant situation, *nor is it completely determined by it.* The artistic content, what is called the subject-matter of the work, is already the effect of this selection; it is that in the natural situation which the particular artist habitually observes or treats, according to his artistic habits of signifying. Most of the words and much of their arrangement are usually given by the subject-matter. When the artist lays unusual stress on the words and structures of signifying, and on the choosing and manipulating of the other words, the work becomes "stylized," what I shall here call cubist. When he lays all his stress on signifying, reducing the subject-matter to the act of describing or narrating itself, the work is abstract.

Natural situations—I everywhere mean physical, social, and psychological nature—are common to the literary man and painter; they are the pictorial appearances of the latter, as we say a painter sees pictures everywhere. But since they are held in common, a painting in which such a subject-matter is an important principle of arrangement comes to be called "literary"! This is absurd. In fact, the *essential* literary structures, the structures that give a passage its character of being description, or proof, or narration, are impossible to paint directly and extremely difficult to paint indirectly, no matter how "literary" the painter is willing to be. The argument over abstraction in painting, therefore, is: What is the relation between painting and objective and subjective nature? It is not, what is the relation between painting and literature. And in literature itself a similar argument may be raised.

There is an important sense in which by analogy a consonance may be called a syllogism of music or a harmonizing ground behind two hues a syllogism in painting; and so with many other abstract elements of literature. But in such cases, where the *abstract* elements of different arts express each other, we are no longer in the field of the poetics of the arts, but in general aesthetics, a branch of metaphysics; we are discussing such topics as "unity," "probability," or "necessity."

II. METER AND SIGNIFYING

On the analogy of music, it has sometimes been thought that abstraction in literature would consist in reducing a passage to its sounds, its rhythm, timbre, tone, and accent. Such a view is unsatisfactory. For not sound, but signification, is the essential property of spoken and written language.

Indeed, it seems to me that most of the classic treatment of meter is off-center on this point. (I do not mean that it is in error.) Except with reference to setting verses to music, there is no cause to begin a discussion of poetic meter by counting and weighing the syllables. The fundamental rhythm of a passage—this must be evident to any reader—lies not in the quantities of the sounds, but in the quantities of the signifying parts. The most fundamental count is the count of the phrases or moments of thought or acts of verbal-signifying; and the most fundamental weight is the weight of the significance. Other things being equal, a phrase is a unit, and a noun or verb has more accent than a connective. Thus, in analyzing the rhythm of the line "I put my hat upon my head," it is more relevant to say that there is one moment of thought with perhaps two little phrases than to say, more definitely, that there are four iambs; and the weight of "hat" and "head," despite their short vowels, is heavier than "I" or "my" (they are accented in conversation just because their significance is heavier). Further, if we say that "I put my hat upon my head"[1] has two little phrases of meaning, we are in a position to see the comic beauty of the line

whose hat was in his hand,

for here "in," far from being a weak word like "upon" in "upon my head," has a strong meaning by contrast. This change is where the joke lies. (The metrical probablity of the joke, of course, if I may be allowed to dot the i's, lies in the fact that the alliteration in the first line forces us to read four iambs in defiance of all sense, that is as doggerel. It would follow that counting the syllables is the immediate theory of doggerel.)

Starting from musical quantities, Sidney Lanier, a classical prosodist, makes concessions to "pronunciation accent" and "logical accent." When the exceptions become too numerous he declares that the passage is rhythmic prose, and he is willing to class "Shakespeare's later verse among that noble and free species of verse which is really a prose throughout which some secondary rhythm (iambic) is consistently carried." But about the *form* of this "prose" he then has nothing to say except that it has agreeable variation, which it certainly has. Would it not have been wiser, however, to look for his fundamental idea not in music but in what he calls the "phrasing," which is something that Shakespeare and other poets have in common?

What I am saying here is of course nothing more novel than the metric "system" of Coleridge, which operated by beats of

[1] I put my hat upon my head
    and walked into the strand,
and there I met another man
    whose hat was in his hand.

thought, counting off the feet by the caesuras. It is interesting that Lanier interprets this system by counting off the lengths of the rests at the caesuras, rather than counting off the beats themselves. (He is not in error here, but what he proves is not that Coleridge is rhythmic but that his rhythm is also musical. Further he unintentionally demonstrates that the silences are significant.)

The counting of syllables is of the first importance, but its importance does not lie in musical beauty which, in the end, must be regarded as an embellishment. *The importance of the syllables is that, being readily countable, they can furnish the measure for an average normal signifying part;* thus, a pentameter might be a clause-length, an heroic couplet an antithesis, the octave of a sonnet a pair of premises; then some particular meaning gains added significance *either by agreeing with the norm or by violating it,* as an overflowed or truncated pentameter expresses fulness or abruptness of thought, etc.

But I have introduced this vast subject only to show that it is not in the patterns of meter or of sound that abstract literature is to be found; on the contrary, even syllabic meter is a means of signifying, unless it is doggerel.[2]

III. ABSTRACTION

In abstract literature the attempt is made to organize a signifying whole of signifying parts abstracted in the highest degree from any signified subject-matter; and as in any work of art, the whole is organized according to the possibilities of combination of the parts. (I say "the attempt is made" rather than something more definite for two reasons: in the first place, it seems to me theoretically impossible, in literature, painting, or any *art,* to abstract completely from subject-matter—the reason for this is a long psychological argument of no especial importance; therefore it is the tendency rather than the achievement that labels a work abstract. But secondly, it is likely that to attain magnitude and

[2] Obviously I have omitted entirely the *second* principle of significant metrics: that language is significant by *convention.* Thus, it is by convention that "constitution" is accented on the penult.

power an abstract structure must incorporate subject-matter in a subordinate way; if true, this is very important and we must return to it.)

The terms and structures of verbal signifying are the familiar ones found in treatises of grammar (such as comparative degrees of adjectives), rhetoric (such as simile), logic (such as paralogism), poetics (such as peripety); in manuals of punctuation and editorial usage; and most ambitiously in the history of literary styles and approaches (such as the conceited style or the attic style, and realism or symbolism).

As signifying becomes more abstract, just those syntactical and attitudinal words which are unaccented in ordinary speech and writing, become prominent, the "and" 's "but" 's and "it seems" 's. It is the same process by which the modern logic, aiming at abstraction from all sciences, throws into such high relief the little notion "or." Cummings lays great stress on commas and Capital letters. Stein relies with remarkable persistence on the abstract attitude of insistence, so that often her entire formal aim is to reduce experiences and propositions to a word, and that word an adverb, for instance "regularly." (She and Cummings are of course cubists, where he is not an imagist.)

Besides this strangeness, another accidental effect of abstract handling is to awaken the sentiment of vast meanings expressed with more than Heracleitan reticence. This is because the simplest auxiliaries and mere conjuctions like "be" and "if" are associated with the most cosmic and universal subject-matter; exactly the same occurs when we wonder what the feelings in a piece of music are feelings about: Destiny itself seems to be always involved.

Still another effect is that the abstract passage seems to be a comically reticent statement of any subject-matter that leaps to the mind; it may, for instance, be taken for pornography on the principle of *Mother Goose Censored.* This is equivalent to seeing an abstract painting as a grotesque portrait of a woman.

IV. AN EXAMPLE OF THE PROCESS OF ABSTRACTION

Conceive of a real-life or imaginary situation of the following sort:

1. An architect who has planned and built a village is commissioned to camouflage it against air-attack. He finds he has a different frame of mind as architect and as camoufleur.

(In the nature of the case, since I am writing an essay, this is already signified, but conceive of it as not signified.)

This situation was conceived as a *story,* that is it occurred to the author in scenes employing literary devices, somewhat as follows:

2. (The architect is a woman in order to make it conventionally plausible for her to speak of the plan as a reflection of her heart.) She directs the camouflage, leaving her own elegant house for the last. At the Local Board, she tries to resign because the work is distasteful to her and because she fears that she will unconsciously invite destruction by including visible proportions. (The destruction is spoken of as "destruction from the Sky.") She wants to return to her earlier occupation of painting easel-pictures. The Chairman of the Board, a parson, upbraids her arrogance. Camouflaging her own house, she sees it is just the most glaring landmark; and then she sees that it, and every other house, is a prison, and that all are in a sense inviting destruction. To inspect, she goes up in a plane (going aloft is presented as being in a sense made free). With great joy she perceives that the village is perfectly camouflaged and as if non-existent; and she promises herself the reward of painting a camouflaged easel-picture! But the next instant she is in despair, because there is no satisfaction of the heart in nothingness.

Note that the order of the narrative here is, roughly, temporally progressive both in overt action and in her thoughts, as if in imitation of an historical event. A device of the correspondence of internal traits and external objects is used throughout for psychological exploration. An obvious symbolism broadens the situation to include moral and social issues. That is, the handling of these main literary methods refers us outside the work.

A cubist version of the same story was then written:

3. The original situation was regarded as a theme, Architect-mind vs. Camoufleur-mind, and this theme was completely expressed in *each* of a series of passages: (a) A description without verbs, mainly a pattern of contrasting colors and shapes, of the camouflaged village in its instantaneous appearance both to sense ("splashes") and to feeling ("a rage of disorder"). (b) A series of

aphorisms (as, "For too much mind the Emergency has sharp eyes.") (c) A pair of sorites, concluding in the paralogism: "The original artist is not to be entrusted with the camouflage; especially the original artist is to be entrusted with the camouflage." (d) A prose rhapsody of foreboding, embellishing the moral that what is done or believed is a mask for what is repressed. (e) An interior monologue of associations to certain details of a house. (f) An angry dialogue between Chairman and Architect. (g) Exclamations of joy and despair, the details being taken from an experience of Flight.

The material for all these ways of grasping the theme exists scattered in the previous narrative, which throughout contains description, reasoning, feeling, interior monologue. Here, however, the material is separated out and concentrated into simple effects, as against the thick complex presented previously. And since more or less the same original idea is appearing again and again the attention is centered rather on the difference of approach each time. The progressive narrative is scrapped, but in its place—and this is perhaps the most important thing—*a new literary principle of order begins to appear:* the principle of increasing complexity of the kinds of syntax, from the short phrases of the description through the triplicate propositions of the syllogisms to the proustian business of the interior monologue; and along with this complexity an increasing definiteness and intensity of statement, especially in the aphorisms and the rhapsody. But then the dialogue interrupts the progress of the complexity with simple stychomythia, and the exclamations are monosyllabic outcries; but the intensity increases to the end. Such a structure has perhaps an analogous appropriateness to the theme, but in itself it is already abstract.

4. Roughly accepting this overall order as the main design, an abstract version was then written, abstracting from the contents of the cubist passages and expanding independently. Here what was originally scattered throughout the narrative as the description of the village and the dangerous prominence of the architect's own house, appears as follows:

> This that the other neither here nor there. Some not quite, some too so, some—
>
> Nevertheless! nevertheless! a certain one in by for itself—

Little by little less and less especially by contrast with a hardly anyway—

No, here! hear!
In the offing!
Look out!
. . . told you so.

The attempt to resign her post and the revelation of her secret desires has become:

"I won't!"
"Oh yes you will."
"Why just me?"
"Especially you! who if not you?—"
Ah, so. "Well, then, I. But *I*!—"
"You (unprintable)! . . ."

And the freedom and dismay in the aeroplane is:

Oh those thisthats and neitherherenortheres, those whatnexts and hopefullymaybes!
But meantime meantime there's this
Mh mh

V. CUBISM

Regardless of the merits of any of these versions—to my taste they are all feeble—it is evident that the narrative and the cubism are richer literature than the original situation or the abstraction. In general, let me assert without proof: the richest literature is in the resolution of the tension between natural subject-matter and the signifying of it by various literary devices. (Perhaps the proposition requires no other proof than that almost the whole of literature falls in the class.) In the classical genre this resolution is such that no subject-matter as such seems to exist except as an appropriate content for the approach used, while the approach itself, the Style, calls no attention to itself whatsoever. In our little examples here the narrative leans toward the natural event, for instance in taking its sequence from the progress of the imagined event; the cubism, we saw, leans toward the verbal signifying, for instance in taking its sequence from the syntax.

With regard to abstraction, however, since we are discussing abstraction, I should like briefly to argue that a strong abstract work requires the incorporation of natural subject-matter, that is that a kind of cubism is preferable to pure abstraction.

I am aware that any such decision for or against a genre is fallacious in principle, for it reduces simply to the fact that the theorist cannot conceive of a sufficiently strong work in the genre; but naturally not, for that is just the work of the inventive artist and not the theorist. The legislative critic can confidently expect to be refuted as soon as an enterprising inventor reads his challenge. (A use might be found here for legislative criticism.) The following point, then, is made in the more modest field of "average audience comprehension."

The point is simply that the abstract parts of an overall abstract structure will be more apparent and can generate stronger forces for combination where they are presented on the scaffolding of a usual experience and can draw upon the combining-power of meanings of usual experience. (The experience must not be unusual or it would preempt the attention away from the abstract effect of the whole.)

Let me illustrate from painting: suppose the composition requires a certain shape to dominate, the shape will dominate more forcibly if we allow the introduction of the illusion of depth and place the shape in the foreground. Even further, suppose a direction of movement is required, this movement can be forcibly presented if a recognizable head is drawn staring in the direction. (I am thinking of Picasso's *Artist and Model.*)[3]

This use of representation for abstraction is the inverse of the age-old use of compositional and other abstract elements to heighten representation or to comment on it; thus a character in the background is given prominence by making him stop a receding plane.

But in these *mixed* structures, the chief expression of the whole

[3] This argument cannot be pressed, for the pure abstractionist will at once ask: "What are the associations which make the experience of a staring face directional? Then find the abstract equivalent for each of these and you can synthesize a structure at least as directional as the natural experience." A dedalian enterprise but by no means impossible.

will modify the handling of the parts of opposite type. Thus in a quasi-naturalistic narrative the logical structure of the situation is likely to be introduced piecemeal at plausible occasions of dialogue or interior monologue. (A rare case where this is not done is the inter-chapters of *War and Peace.*) And so conversely.

Of the most important contemporary approaches, social-realism and surrealism evidently tend away from abstraction. But it is interesting to notice how expressionism and the more and more recurrent symbolism often land in cubism, but for opposite reasons.

Expressionism takes its characters and situations in a conceptual form. Now if these concepts are then combined according to their scientific meanings and scientific functions, we get a result closely akin to exemplary sociology or psychology, not unlike the types of Max Weber. But this is rarely done. The combination is most often in terms of dramatic conflicts and resolutions; and the main interest then strongly shifts from the commentary on the natural situation to the handling of the dialectic; but such a dialectic, however relevant to the original situation, is always interesting in itself as a literary method. The main organizing principle, that is, is not expressionist but abstract.

In symbolism, quite the other way, the main organizing principle, namely what is symbolized, withdraws more and more from the foreground of attention; in the best cases it is not even expressible except just through the symbols (this is the difference between symbolist and ordinary allegory). Then, freed from the close control of their main object of imitation, the parts often begin to generate a strong organization from their merely formal possibilities; I am thinking, for instance, of the beautiful combination in *Ash Wednesday* of the slow cyclical progress described in the metaphor of the stairway with the syntax of "Because I do not hope" and "Although I do not hope" in the first and sixth sections.

This essay was written in December 1941, and published in 1942, in the *New Directions* Annual 7, as "Literary Abstraction and Cubism." The version reprinted here is from *Art and Social Nature.*

Literary Method and Author-Attitude

In ancient criticism the word "Manner" is applied only to the distinction between narrating the story and acting it out. In modern usage it often covers the whole topic of literary methods, such as the naturalist manner, the symbolist manner, the surrealist manner. Such questions are hardly touched on by the ancients, except in the contrast of the so-called Attic and Asiatic styles; yet if one were concerned to prove the catholicity of the ancients, I think it could be argued that their distinction of narrative and dramatic is a right introduction to the entire study of literary method. The distinction is explicitly not one of means or medium; nor is it like the distinction between comic and tragic (which is discussed under subject-matter). A possible interpretation would be that it deals with the author's approach or method in relating the subject-matter to his verbal and rhythmic means, keeping in mind his attitude toward his own role and his relation to the audience.

In any case, by the time we come to Goethe and Schiller we find that the distinction of narrative and dramatic has blossomed into a perfectly modern discussion of the different possible kinds of authorship, with different attitudes toward the subject-matter and different rapports with the audience.

Now every kind of manner, whether dramatic, symbolist, naturalist, or their combinations, has structural properties discoverable in the mere formal analysis of the works themselves, apart from either their creation or their communication. Thus, the immediate objective presentation in the dramatic manner is formally the unities of time and place; the formal property of symbolism is the existence of a system of metaphor over and above the particular uses of metaphor in the literal story. But here I want to deal not with this structural part of literary manners, but with their meanings as author-attitudes, a branch of psychology and social-psychology.

At the same time, let us not directly discuss the author's relation to the audience (the problems of communication), but precisely the author's freedom, that is his ways of being a creative author. In general in criticism, we can talk about the author's action or the structure of the work or the experience of the audience.

In talking about the author's action, it is useful (tho of course not essential) to draw upon his own concrete experiencing of it. So now I, having written many works in different manners, will tabulate briefly what seems to me to be the attitudinal meaning of my own use of five or six different manners. These remarks are drawn from my own experience as an author; it is unlikely that they apply to many other authorships, and without doubt my reading of my own behavior is often incorrect. But that there is in general a relation between attitude and manner seems to me quite certain.

I. SYMBOLISM, NATURALISM, REALISM

When in a period of acute consciousness of dissent from the political and moral values of my society (America 1941) I came to revise a little novel I had composed several years before (1935), I found, as is common enough, that it was written in a manner I could no longer master. The difficulty was twofold. The incidents, descriptions, thoughts, and characters of the story were continually and consistently overdetermined by a symbolic idea, growing in body throughout the work but at no point directly expressed. But in 1941 I was seeing things (and dismissing them) in terms of simple causes—not necessarily correct. Secondly, the earlier work consisted largely in a naturalistic presentation, accurate as I could make it, of an experienced environment—for the immediate story had not been used as a framework for a symbol, but other meanings had forced themselves into expression while I was trying to transcribe certain incidents that I remembered. But it was this naturalistic detail even more than the symbolic overtones that was impossible to me in the period of dissent: I was now too impatient to describe in detail scenes of a society which as a whole had no fascination for me.

Then I realized that the naturalism and the symbolism were parts of the same attitude, and that this attitude was itself a previous stage (certainly not the primary stage) of the social-estrangement that I later came to suffer in actual consciousness.

The formula of the symbolism was that: *it is intolerable that this scene should be merely what it seems, it must have also some other meaning*. But the other meaning was of course not apparent to me, in 1935, or I should have used it as the subject-matter of the work. Nevertheless! clear or confused, I was willing to regard the scene and the society as *my* scene and *my* society, rich in interest, still possessing the potentiality of life, worth transcribing with fidelity: this was the naturalism. It was my society and I felt uneasy in it; I felt that if I could reach toward other meanings I could resolve the uneasiness and achieve the unity of a work of art. Yet since the meanings were not to be attained it was inevitable that the subject-matter of this novella and numerous tales of the same period should incorporate hitch-hikes, canoe-trips, and other chancey travels, *in which one becomes involved yet intends to go away.* (And structurally: new beginnings and ambiguous or dual-paralogistic resolutions.)

Going further into the past of my writing (1931), I found examples of the naturalism pure, unrelieved by symbols, yet always expressing the latent estrangement by a malicious or indignant selection of the pointless or unsavory, though usually softened by youthful compassion. These were copies, of course, of the formula of High Naturalism: *To bring home the grim facts to the complacent*, as if to say, "*This* is our world, damn you."

I should now say (1945) that such youthful, unsophisticated naturalism, whose formula seems so conscious and rational, is the expression of a quite unconscious cleavage, between the innocent, frustrated effort to be happy in the big Society and the fact, in which the personality is grounded, that the Society has inhibited natural drives from the beginning and therefore one does not really want to be happy. This is then not simple *dissent* or withdrawal from the social values; it is *alienation,* socially-caused estrangement from the natural values.

The expression of simple dissent is probably nothing but a kind of Realism: the interaction of the author's sense of what is meaningful and at least the potentiality of the scene accurately described: on both parts there is a free passage of potentiality to act, the activity of authorship being one of several efficient causes. But this attitude, this confidence, I could rarely find in my early tales.

The emergence of the symbolism in the naturalism, then, may be taken as the deepening awareness of the author's alienation; but this is the same thing as the stirring of natural drives, though in a personal arena withdrawn from the big Society.

II. EXPRESSIONISTIC NATURALISM AND MIRACLE

Let us turn to the author in the full consciousness of alienation. The key to his method is his conviction that *their* world is not his world, and the forming of a literary defense against them. (At the same time he does not yet know what is *his* social world, or he would not expend himself in defenses.)

At this period (1940-42) the method that I habitually employed was a kind of expressionistic naturalism. Literary expressionism in general proceeds by abstracting from the scene concepts and ideas, and activating these as character, most often in a kind of dialectical drama. But I preferred to abstract what I took to be the true causes of events, both sociological and psychological, and to activate these in imitation of the likely interplay of causes in the world.

Then in these stories, since the emphasis is so strongly on the causes and their interplay, the acts and characters are reduced almost to X-ray pictures or schemes. But I intended them to be scientific X-rays, without my own—and certainly without their—mythology; the picture was to add up to the actual world. And if it was a somewhat dry and empty scene, so, I thought, were the lives of the people.

This was the last stage of the withdrawal that was already apparent in the innocent naturalism. But now the scene was not even admitted to be *my* scene; its living details were meaningful only to them, but I was impatient to present anything but its schematism, which I analyzed and abstracted with the more ferocity in order to put it in *its* place, and what had that to do with me? As if to say: *There* is what *they* think reality is, that error, America 1940, compelled this way and that, and *comically* compelled, by causes that in themselves have no special value (except that they are clear and beautiful). Far from having a larger, symbolic significance than those people suspect, these incidents have even less significance than they believe, and they are feeble believers. But I, thanks be to God and my ill-luck, am sufficiently withdrawn to portray those things in their proper little places in the reality in which I have my secret faith.

"Secret" faith, because in the naturalistic portrayal of the scene, no hint could be given of the author's position which therefore seemed no where to have a place. And yet the author himself knew, if not where he stood, at least that he stood somewhere: for we are describing not a self-centered ego but an active author. Therefore the tone of the schematic naturalism, which could easily have been horrible and grotesque, always turned out to be cheerful and comic. The characters were indeed rushing to their disastrous ends, but to the unsympathetic author those ends were indifferent one way or the other as against quite other (unexpressed) values; and comedy is the representation of "destruction without pain or harm." (This is the contrary of Shakesperian tragedy where the characters are likewise rushing to disaster, but since the author respects the motives and the forces at work, there is everywhere, as Bradley puts it, the sentiment of "waste.")

The schematic naturalism, impatient of detail, was the means of defense against the scene, of the author who had confidence in his private position.

The author was alienated not absolutely (it is impossible to be alienated absolutely and be a creative author), but only relative to the social institutions and mores and his own habits and fears. Against these he could place his own natural existence, proved by his activity; and also, as an author—I think I speak for every artist on this point—a familiarity with the creator spirit in whom his works have been again and again completed (for it is the completion of a work that confirms the artist). Yet the natural causes, both sociological and psychological, for instance the origin of his food or his erotic desires, which would ordinarily serve to interpret and heighten, if not explain, these vantage-points of nature and creativity—these causes were for him already trivialized, because they were the public explanations of the very life from which he was alienated.

To solve this dilemma, of being confident without a cause, I boldly adopted the device of introducing angels and other miraculous incidents to open out again the dead-ends of worthlessness into which the characters' 1940 dispositions had betrayed them. The angels speak unintelligible syllables; the incidents are causally improbable, though not necessarily artistically improbable. The themes are crime, drunkenness, gambling. This kind of plot satisfied the author that the desperate view of the scene which he was complacently demonstrating was nevertheless somehow adequate to the reality he knew intimately. *Miracle is confidence without a cause.*

So, as the estrangement of the scene became acute, the earlier symbolism was thinned and intensified into miracles.

III. ABSTRACTION, CUBISM, AND HEROIC PORTRAITS

We turn now to the attitude of such an author vis à vis what he is sure of, nature and creativity, quite apart from the blight of alienation. (A "blight," though I would not for a moment question its truth or necessity.) First let us discuss the attitude of creativity in alienation.

By an artist as opposed to a dilettante I mean, with Goethe, one concerned not with his own feelings or the effect on an audience but with the structure of the work; and by an artist as opposed to an amateur I mean one who brings projects to completion. But the repeated experience of artistry forms in the artist an habitual attitude, namely confidence in the medium and the plastic devices, whether conventional or original, that have not failed him; and invention.

Now in my own case, through the last half dozen years, I have found that since the conventional patterns of artistry—for instance the well-wrought 3-act play—are so bound up with the very subject-matter from which I have been estranged, it is in inventive play in the medium itself, more or less abstracted from the represented scene, that I have most freedom. The abstraction of literary expression is to the "means of signifying": making a plot out of acts of denotation and connotation, demonstration, exclamation, etc. Such a method of abstraction in my case, then, has been the expression of *artistic confidence under the conditions of alienation.* One can easily see genetically how the passage from method to method must lead to abstraction if (a) the art seemed more and more worth the trouble and (b) the scene seemed less and less worth the trouble.

Yet in fact I have rarely been able to generate sufficient interest in pure abstraction to energize complete works by this method. (Obviously, for to an alienated person such abstraction is maintained only with effort, it is not free play; in a sense the abstraction is a natural defense against the forces of personal and social nature that must storm to the surface when the big Society is at least effectually dismissed.) Then I resorted (1936-1943) to a kind of cubism, that is an abstract handling of a concrete subject. But what were these subjects? Portraits of ancient and classical heroes: as the madness of Saul, the pleasures of Tiberius, or the non-violence of Alcestis. We see—omitting always the pathological factors that are no doubt also active here—that just these heroes are exempt from the estrangement of the social scene; they are proved by time and enduring significance, there is no need apparently to relate them to the present concern. Further, the portraiture is static: it is a cluster of concepts, images, and symbols; far from imitating the dramatic action of conscious desire; close to the unity of dreams. Thus the author could find in these heroes the natural forces and motives that in himself and in the contemporary scene he could not find.

In general, the freedom and confidence expressed in the abstract and unconventional handling of the medium sought out such subjects as were free, in the author's mind, from the trivializing bondage he saw roundabout. But he had not (and I have not yet, in 1945) attained the freedom and power to see as such every subject whatever.

These works are affirmative in that I found myself able to present the characters and their motives without hedging, without pervasive irony and ambiguity, and without miracles. I do not mean they are optimistic; on the contrary, most of the cubist pieces tell the tragic story that such and such a motive leads to a bad end or is in itself a bad end, for instance that the music of a certain composer is the same as bouncing a ball in a little courtyard of an asylum. But the motives are the true motives of the characters and the characters are really what they are presented as, and this is far different from calling precisely this into question, as I was forced to do in the naturalistic works. But it was easier to maintain such an affirmative attitude in writing of heroes mythical or long dead. The power of Saul, for instance, "to do as his hand should find," was impossible to describe in a contemporary scene, as in *The Grand Piano,* without humor and sarcasm; and without the classical example of Tiberius, I should have been unable to represent my own little pleasures with a straight face.

IV. DRAMATIC MANNER

This little study was sketched out in 1942. Writing now in 1945 I cannot but see that such an analysis is nothing but a kind of schematic naturalism applied to my authorship itself: it is a defense against that authorship, as if to say, What has that to do with *us*? That *craft idiocy!* to the band of our natural friends. But of course we do not thereby impugn the power of the creator spirit, given to us and not made by us (certainly not made by me); these poems, such as they are, are also among our social inventions and realize our capabilities. But the author who understands this will no doubt have a different attitude and a different manner.

(But one cannot foresee the manner of works according to a previous program, for it is only the work that explores and proves the existent power of authorship.)

In writing a play in 1942, I found what it is that has always brought me back to the dramatic manner: the glorification of simple overt acts—the finite physical reality of a few actors on a little stage. The dramatic manner is *the celebration of a natural existence with which one is acquainted, without exhibition of the power of the author himself at all.*

The classical property of the dramatic manner is the unity of time and place, both for verisimilitude (formally speaking: the expressiveness of the medium in its material characteristics) and for concentration on the single passional act. For the most part the drama itself has never strayed far from the spirit of the unities. But let us consider a play in which the unities are in fact absent: where between two scenes there is a change of place and there is a discontinuity in the presented stage-time. Then the world in which the audience is absorbed is no longer the one directly presented, but is somewhere poised between the imagination of the audience and the intention of the poet. If the scenes are juxtaposed for special esthetic effects, such as contrast, we see that the stage is being manipulated extrinsically from the world of its characters: we have passed over into narration. The dramatic manner, then, properly belongs only to the single scene, and to the degree that the audience is absorbed in the scene.

Simple overt acts are serving a cup of coffee to a stranger, a fight, the play of an old man with a child, the juxtaposition of colors, the standing of a tree. To present such matter without the intrusion of the author, because it is felt as simply important in itself.

Perhaps the single scene is the extreme limit of natural, unalienated authorship *within the possibility of isolated authorship* altogether. (The little poems of introspective monologue that many of us are in the habit of writing are nothing but such single scenes.) But it must be said that the isolation of the act of authorship from other natural powers is itself, *if insisted on,* a sign of alienation: of withdrawal from natural society, of craft idiocy. The very insistence on pure authorship which vis à vis the big Society is a sign of honorary revolution and of refusal to be treasonable to nature, is in natural society a sad relic of our childhood blasted by coercion.

The man of letters, with his special gifts and the habits of a craft, is one of the band of natural friends, a poet rarely, a spokesman sometimes, not often indeed a man of letters. But just in this band of freedom we do not prejudge occasions: when the poet in the grip of a strong dream will utter it, or the dramatist decorate our common behavior, or tell us stories, or the expert exercise himself for his joy and solace, or plead for us in their courts.

V. FURTHER REMARKS (1942)

I have thus given a little lexicon of the literary methods answering my own occasions. It is personal, limited both in extent and definition. I am even surprised to notice, for instance, how such a major method as Impressionsim has not been valuable to me as a poet when it is so delightful to me as a reader. It is personal, yet inasmuch as I have not drawn on the material causes of the attitudes, socio- or psychopathological but have restricted my remarks to the formal relations between attitude and method, even this list attains a certain generality.

Stating these formal relations by no means prejudges the causal question: which is prior, the method or the attitude? though non-creative people will always think of the attitude as the cause and the method as the effect. But especially among artists we must often expect that a certain inward bent rules *both* their lives and their works, so that it is as true to say that they experience what they will write as that they write what they have experienced.

It is not by wishing, nor because it would be convenient to write in a different way, that an author can alter the attitude on which his style feeds. A man would be glad not to write what expresses his misery or the evil of the world; yet write in this way he must. But who would deny that *disgust* of a style is a powerful life-sign for an author?

Because of biographical accidents, an attitude and method are tied to certain images, themes, and scenes. (One hardly realizes how restricted he is by such associations.) To give a personal example: I seem to remember that a kind of accurate, hostile, and somewhat standoffish observation was most dominantly my conscious attitude during some seasons at the seashore during my middle adolescence. (The causes were both psychosexual and associated with a fear of drowning.) Now much to my surprise I find that the stories I have written in a naturalistic method gravitate inevitably to such seaside-resort locales and incidents, even when—as in a novel about the economic depression—there would seem to be no intrinsic connection. And contrariwise, the symbolist parts gravitate toward a childhood memory of the mountains (another vacation environment!) And I find scenes of realism referring back to an in-between period of boyish games—which I would, again, refer forward to 1945 bands of natural friends. But the result is that the associations are severely limited: discomfortable weather is always hot weather, never wintry weather or storm. And without doubt the naturalistic handling of personal relations is restricted to the suspicions and ironic insights of the age of 16. The understanding treatment of children will be imbedded in prose of one method, of adolescents in another method, of adults in another method, and of old persons in another method! And the same holds for the critical situations of life. But we can see exactly the same limitation in a master like Balzac, whose handling of virtuous young women is in a blurred Lamartine manner that might be enormously effective if done in extenso, but it is overwhelmed and made pallid by the strong naturalism and realism of the rest.

But freely handled, the great literary methods ought to be powerful world-outlooks that could find meaning anywhere!

A literary method, as the critic rather than the creator would view it, is a moral hypothesis completely general in its scope, far more general than any theme or subject-matter could hope to be. And from the point of view of the creator, it is more than an hypothesis, it has the reality of necessity.

Method is close to the heart of writing, Style. It is Style that most confirms an author in the secure consciousness of being an artist, of being able to fuse the details that press on him inwardly and outwardly into a whole work. I have mentioned various attitudes, but there is above all this one attitude, of being a free artist rather than something else. To speak by analogy, Style, could be called the method of this attitude of being an author.

Begun not long after he finished "Literary Abstraction and Cubism," this essay was not finished until 1945, to be included in *Art and Social Nature*.

Some Problems of Interpretation: Silence, and Speech as Action

I.

In interpreting a text, Professor Kristeller has recently warned us, we must not read between the lines, or we must do so very grudgingly. (Especially when, as with the pre-Socratics, there is only one line to read between.) What a man meant is what he said. As a student of literature, and even more as a poet, my bias is certainly the same. I have found that by scrupulously saving the minute details of a great text, I have learned new things, my preconceptions have been changed, I have been moved in ways that I had not expected. And as a poet, I have often been impatient when a critic has used my little hard-won book to write a lazy book of his own, without bothering to understand me at all. I sometimes wonder why a critic thinks I bother to write, if my meaning is only the commonplace banality that he reads onto my page—especially when I have explicitly pointed out that it is what I do *not* mean!

Nevertheless, the professor's wise maxim cannot stand as a general rule of interpretation, for it misunderstands the nature of language. In all critical and historical studies there is a kind of regulative principle, namely, that those people made sense understandable to us, they share our common humanity. And it must have been with them, as it is with us, that very often the meaning of a man and his situation is not expressed in speech and even less so in writing. Sometimes it is irrelevant to speak, sometimes one cannot or dare not speak. Sometimes the mere act of speaking is a lie. Sometimes speech is a systematic avoidance of meaning, and sometimes one must speak indirectly. Sometimes speech is the beginning of conveying meaning, but the essential meaning occurs in some other action than speech. All these are commonplaces of ordinary experience, and a critic, coming afterward and looking for the historical, philosophical, or poetic essence of a situation, must bear them in mind as likely possibilities. Scholars tend to suffer from a fetishism of texts. To them it is the most obvious thing in the world that the truth and reality of men are conveyed in books. But if we go back to the origins of our Western academy in the Pythagoreans or Socrates, we seem to be told that this is neither possible nor desirable. In the tradition of Lao-tse even vocal speech is suspect.

Speech is not merely a communication of ideas and descriptions from one head to another. Perhaps it is essentially so in the reports of natural philosophy and in accurate journalism; but much more primarily, and for the most part, speech is an action, a peculiar action in a series of other actions, to be explained by all the causes relevant to sequences of human actions. I think we have here one important reason for the immense complexity and the inevitable vagueness and speculativeness of humanistic and literary studies. Not only must they start with the formidable apparatus of philology, logic, and poetics, in order to *have* a text, but then they must go on to rhetoric, history, psychology, and anthropology in order to see how the "literal meaning" *is* the meaning. Scholars may not like the imprecise, but, as Aristotle says, it is the sign of an ignorant man to be more precise than the subject warrants. In our own classical times, let us remember, all such studies were considered as Rhetoric, that is, as occupying a middle position between linguistic and practical analyses.

With this much introduction, I want in this essay to point to three or four contexts in which, bearing in mind the nature of speech, it is necessary, in order to interpret a text, to go beyond the text.

II.

Often speech is an irrelevant or inappropriate action. Then, if there is a speech or text to be interpreted, this is in itself problematical. If my friend says, "Please pass the salt," I pass the salt, saying nothing. I might pedantically say, "Here is the salt"; but if I say anything more, I have missed his meaning. This is simple, but consider an only slightly more complicated situation where the misunderstanding of the essential irrelevance of speech is momentous; in my experience, it is one of the hardest neurotic symptoms to liquidate in psychotherapy. Suppose we have the two premises: "I want so-and-so" and "So-and-so is there and nothing hinders." The conclusion of this syllogism is an action, to go and take it; it is not a verbal proposition like "I could take it," "I ought to take it," "May I take it?" or anything of that sort. *Any* verbal statement in such a case is a sign of obsessional doubt, disowning responsibility, or some other neurotic maneuver. (One is reminded of the academic book reviews that exclaim, "What can Professor B. mean when he says, etc?"—when indeed the professor sits in the office across the hall from the reviewer who could knock on his door and ask him. To be sure, such an action would bring down a vast edifice of protocol in a cloud of plaster. And of course many battles of book reviews have no relation to inquiry, being written for ceremonial reasons or for spite.)

In general, many events will not normally be spoken about and a fortiori not be recorded, simply because a quite different action is relevant. This has no relation to their importance. As I have pointed out elsewhere, there is an almost total absence of plays and poems about happy marriage, for there is nothing to write. Conversely, the vast plethora of romantic literature has been correctly interpreted, as by De Rougemont, to indicate a nonacceptance of the sexual. Let me give a beautiful example of delicate understanding in this line by Johann Sebastian Bach, a powerful interpreter of texts. In his cantata setting of Nicolai's *Wachet Auf,* in the part where the Bridegroom is searching and the Bride is waiting, the duet is in serious opera style. When they find each other, the style is operetta, almost like Sir Arthur Sullivan. But when they *are* together, Bach simply repeats the chorale, and

Nicolai's words are, metaphorically, about the Pearly Gates:

Kein Aug hat je gespürt
kein Ohr hat je gehört
solche Freude, des sind wir froh
io, io!
ewig in dulci Jubilo.

The reticence refers, of course, to the ineffability of mystical experience, but it means also that in the connubial metaphor there is nothing more to say. So Bach adds nothing. Here we have a typically Christian text; but along the same line, may I suggest that, with all due respect for the keen scent of the author of *Mimesis,* his comparison of the Christian and Greek texts with respect to the pregnancy of their meaning might fail to take into account that the Greeks were in many ways psychologically and socially healthier than we. They write with a sharp foreground against an empty background because this is un-neurotic perception; a good Gestalt has an empty background undisturbed by repression. The Greeks did not need to fix in literature certain dualistic difficulties which they could still cope with in the travails of the flesh and in the secret mysteries of the community. It does not occur to Auerbach that the Christian *saying* might be problematical. But as Kafka pointed out, "*Man kann nicht Erlösung schreiben, nur leben.*"

To generalize still further, we are faced with the dilemma of the *argumentum e silentio.* The absence of a text might mean that there was no such event. But in some cases it surely means that the event was too frequent, too practical, and too important to get recorded in mere texts. Recall the maxim, "A happy people has no history." This does not mean there is monotony, but that prudent and natural activity is not a matter for records. Consider, for example, how the ceremonial art-works of some of the Polynesians are burned on the day after the festival. And let me again cite a giant of humanistic interpretation, Shakespeare. At the beginning of his Histories he shows us old John of Gaunt as the wise statesman who rebukes Richard II for his bad management, but who is by no means willing to interrupt the legitimate succession to the throne. Then John dies and we are at once plunged into seven plays of bloody civil war. If prudence had prevailed, the poet is saying, there would be no Histories.

As another example of a pregnant *argumentum e silentio,* let me offer a speculation in American history. During the first thirty years of the Republic only 5 to 10 per cent were enfranchised and as few as 2 per cent bothered to vote. But the conclusion to be drawn from this is not necessarily that the society was undemocratic. On the contrary, apart from the big merchants, planters, clerics, and lawyers, people were likely quite content, freed from the British, to carry on their social affairs in a quasi-anarchy, with unofficial, decentralized, and improvised political forms. It was in this atmosphere that important elements of our American character were developed.

III.

But there is a valid and exactly contrary use of the *argumentum e silentio.* There may be no text not because speech was irrelevant compared to some other action, but because speech itself was in the situation so powerful an action that it was forbidden or later excised. This is the case with official censorship. The libelous, whether true or not, is censored because it is an act; the pornographic is censored because it leads to likely acts; the blasphemous because it breaks a taboo in the utterance; political opinion when there is incitement to riot; *lèse majesté* is censored because certain thoughts must not exist—e.g., the deposition scene has dropped out of *Richard II* in the first two quartos. In such cases the interpreter will take the known absence of a text or the evident deletion of certain passages as very significant. But we know from overwhelming common experience that the implicit censorship of social condemnation leads to important reticence or various dodges, like esoteric writing, which then must be read as esoteric. An amusing example is the delicious periphrastic style of Thorstein Veblen which, it has been held, he concocted in order that his students might not have any simple radical proposition of the professor to report home to papa!

But the case is more disastrous when, because of absolute social taboo, we are left in the dark on vital information. To mention a case of great importance to a psychologist of art: What sexual outlet, if any, did Beethoven have? Did he at least masturbate? How did he masturbate? Any one who would say that these are irrelevant questions doesn't know what he's talking about. A scholar *must* speculate about them; and yet he knows that, given the kind of texts possibly available from that period, he cannot possibly get textual evidence. Yet he cannot modestly say, "We don't know," because there is only one Beethoven, and we must explain him one way or other. So the scholar has to resort to far-fetched psychoanalytical guesses between the lines, and face the scorn of his critics.

Habent sua fata libelli, books have their destinies. Since, as Kierkegaard urged, a book is the act of a man in a concrete situation, it is often essential to study the public fate of a book in order to understand the weight and bearing of its literal meaning. By and large, where censorship of certain ideas is strong, the ideas are taken seriously. E.g., in Czarist Russia nearly every important political and moral writer was at times in jail or in exile. Even if their books appear to be abstractly theoretical, they are implicitly heavy with concrete reference; and the interpreter must explicate this, for it is the meaning that the ideas had in fact for both author and public. On the other hand, the kind of total freedom that we have for such writings may be evidence that reasoned ideas don't much influence our institutions. Indeed, the fact seems to be with us that such ideas can first become effective when they enter the mass media, and it is at this point that they are strictly regulated in style and content. With us it could almost be said that *format* is the chief meaning to interpret. To break the format is the censorable act.

In historical studies the problems of the absence of texts have risen globally as our focus of interest has shifted away from kings, war, and intellectuals to social conditions and everyday morals. Texts are scarce because sometimes such important pervasive matters did not have to be noticed in writing, and sometimes, according to the ideology of the scribes, they were not worthy of being noticed in writing. Historians have then delved manfully for every kind of unlikely laundry list and other relic, and by reasoning, often between the lines, they have made them speak.

IV.

Next, there are those cases where a text cannot be taken literally because it is deceptive. Most simply: the text is willfully deceitful, slanted, or unfairly selective, as in outright forgeries, propaganda, or histories that are really campaign documents. From the Renaissance on, the exposure or reasonable domestication of such texts, by internal and external evidence, has been the spectacular work of interpretation, naturally sometimes overreaching itself in debunking or in the beginnings of "higher criticism," genre of Reimarus. At its best, however, this cutting of a text down to true size is a typical act of the Enlightenment. It is not reading between the lines but reading with skepticism and sophistication.

But the problem is very different when it is felt that the text is deceitful and the speaker could not help deceiving. He was self-deceiving, or betrayed by prejudice, cultural, or class bias. Or perhaps, to go to the extreme, the whole logic of his thinking and even his perception was such that he *could not* tell the truth or even make sense according to our notions. From the beginning of the nineteenth century there has been an increasing emphasis on this kind of interpretation; consider the spectrum from D.F. Strauss and Marx to Lévy-Bruhl and Freud. The texts are shown to mythologize or ideologize or rationalize, or they are prelogical altogether, really dreams. Then what else is there to do but read between the lines? In the appropriate situations, there is nothing else; but I do not think it is enough understood that this kind of interpretation is *argumentum ad hominem;* it says, "We cannot make sense of the text as it stands, either literally or by internal and external correction; but if we transform the speaker and put him in *our* realm of discourse, then we can see what he really means to say." To make a fair analogy, the interpreter treats the text as if it were psychotic.

Suppose a psychotic holds an idea that is imbedded in his system, and we try to reach him, either to understand what he really means or to tell him what we mean, perhaps to dissuade him from jumping out the window. Ordinary dialogue is fruitless. His logic may be impeccable, or his dreamy logic may seem consistent to himself. More important, there may be no sharing of perceptual evidence; he may blot out what we point to or, more likely, its *weight as evidence* may to him be entirely different. Kinds of facts that are basic and irrefutable in our experience, prove little to him; whereas some chance circumstance is to him vastly significant. When such a man is a patient, the usual recourse in institutions is to physico-chemical or, better, physiological and nonverbal interpersonal efforts to alter the man and so alter the speech. But similar problems arise outside of institutions. A child in a tantrum, a youth in love is unreachable. Whole populations suffer from endemic prejudices or emotional epidemics. In a culture a superstition may have an overwhelming social consensus and so predetermine all thought and literature, like religion in ages of faith or the present-day belief in the omnicapability of Scientific Method to deliver truth or happiness. In such cases one soon despairs of mutual understanding unless there is a change on one or both sides as to what is accepted as reality.

In my opinion, there is great humanistic power in the argument *ad hominem* if it is a two-way affair, if *both* sides risk their unexpressed presuppositions, in a dialogue not of speeches but of men speaking. Some of our best modern criticism has had just this character. As a corrective to the previous attitude that important speech and text had to be reduced to our kind of experience, there was bound to be the response that perhaps our kind of experience is inadequate. To correct Lévy-Bruhl's excessive devaluation of the logic of primitive man, Franz Boas modestly urged that primitive man's syntax and arithmetic are as reasonable as anybody's, if we take them relative to his needs, technology, and institutions. This is plain sense; but at once there follows from it, in Boas's school, that every society, including our own, must be taken as a functioning whole and interpreted in its own terms. The resulting cultural relativism has had, I think, a salutary pedagogic effect for ourselves, leading to a radical unsettling of our own presuppositions. (Of course, such a theory springs from an already unsettled culture.)

Let me give a different kind of example. Albert Schweitzer's interpretations of the New Testament depend on the thesis that those people thought they had a real experience of a new heaven and earth, making them believe things senseless to us. But perhaps they did have the experience; then it is we who are thrown off balance. A variant is the method Buber sometimes uses in *Moses*: the people experienced something so extraordinary that they were threatened with losing their wits; and the texts we have are rationalizing reaction-formations, in order to grip again to our common world. This is like Bergson's ingenious theory that the apparent species are not the forms of life but are the negative impressions of the *elan vital* in inert matter. Using a different metaphor, Karl Barth says that the Bible consists of burnt-out volcanoes from we may guess the fire that was there—the theory of his *Dogmatics* is that the fire recurs when the preacher ascends the pulpit. Barth explicitly speaks of criticism as a two-way affair: we question the Bible and the Bible questions us.

This is a new kind of theological reading. People started by reading the Bible literally in faith. When it was intolerable to plain sense or rational philosophy, they began to allegorize it. They then subjected it altogether to a rational philosophical reading, "like any other book," as Spinoza said. And now they have come out on the other side of the philosophical reading with a new kind of theological reading. To return to our analogy with the psychotic: the assumption now is that our sane criticism is not humanly sufficient; perhaps the psychotic fantasies of the sacred texts make more sense for our existence after all; they even might be "literally" true if, by grace, one could share their "wholly other" experience. We see again the power of the formula *credo quia absurdum*, and if so, the necessity and plausibility of the formula *credo ut intelligam.*

But more generally, quite apart from theology, it seems to me that the man-to-man encounter, going through the text and beyond the texts, and risking one's own logic in the interpretation, is indispensable for humanism. Especially when texts are weird, repugnant, or foolish, we must maintain the common sensibility of mankind. Experience teaches us that it is very unlikely that the other knew the truth, and it is quite certain that we don't.

V.

Most of the readings that we have just been discussing seem to commit the "genetic fallacy." They make the truth or falsity of the texts depend on their origins and backgrounds, whether the text is interpreted as an ideology, a rationalization, a function of its culture, or a reaction to a divine seizure. But I think the situation can be described more accurately as follows: These critics are talking directly not about the truth of the proposition at all, but about the existence of the speech as an act—how and why did it come to be? Compared with this, the truth, in many cases, might not be very important. The test whether or not the truth is important is this: if the origin is exposed or the background is altered, is or is not the proposition dropped? Does it continue to be affirmed or cease to be affirmed? Let me say that to anyone who has practiced psychology and has seen many a stubbornly held true rationalization of vital importance to a patient, as he thinks, simply vanish under analysis because it has become boring and of no practical use to him when he has learned its source, the logic condemning the genetic fallacy is rather trivial in moral and psychological matters. It is a fetishism of propositions. I do not mean that moral propositions are not importantly true or false, but that the importance of their truth or falsity cannot be dissociated from *how* they are held by the man: on what grounds? from what background? were they imposed on him, or self-imposed, or has he really grown into them? The very same sentence that is a platitude when said by any man is importantly true when said by Goethe.

VI.

Speech is a man's act, it expresses a truth, and it is a real thing in itself. The relations of these are problematic, often ambiguous. Any interpretation makes an assumption about the metaphysical status of its text, whether it is a man speaking, a proposition, or a kind of thing. For instance, when texts are authorities, a characteristic behavior of interpreters is to *save the texts,* as if they were themselves independent things. We know how this often leads to pious fictions of allegorical interpretation, not unlike legal fictions; but indeed the authoritative text *is* a pillar of the immutable social reality, like other laws. But consider how in some of the Zen anecdotes they seem to make exactly the opposite assumption and flout and deride the sacred Buddhist texts; I take it that this is part of the Taoist tradition in Zen, that speech cannot tell the way, for "the Way that can be told of is not an unvarying Way—it was from the Nameless that heaven and earth sprang." Since in this philosophy we want to get rid of ideas, the more authoritative the speech, the more it must be put down. Also, in the main line of Western poetics, from Aristotle down, texts are taken to be things; poems are "like animals whose end is in themselves." To be sure they are also "imitations" and have some relation of truth to a model. The entire history of Western literary criticism is taken up with this ambiguity.

Speech is sometimes interpreted primarily as an action. Let me give a beautiful illustration. When Milton in *Tetrachordon* has to choose between the two possible readings of Malachi 2:16—"Let him who hateth put away, saith the Lord" or "The Lord saith . . . that he hateth putting away"—his decision is that God, speaking through his prophet, cannot speak of Himself indirectly in the third person, but always speaks full-faced in the posture of command. Milton's method here is identical with Buber's in *I and Thou.* We have seen that in legal interpretations of texts, it is primarily the act and effect of speech, rather than its truth, that has the most weight. But also in the analysis of modern poetry, the poem is regarded first as an act or gesture, or as an act with its effect, and much less importantly as either a self-contained "animal" or as a communication of a model truth.

VII.

Let me offer an interpretation of my own to show the importance of assuming the right metaphysical status of the text. In the Book of Job the obvious crux, which various commentators wrestle with variously, is that the argument seems to have no logical validity. The poems of the end, Warhorse, Behemoth, and Leviathan, do not refute the hero's reasoned dissatisfaction with the consolations and criticisms of his three cronies. I think, however, that a more careful consideration of a few sentences in the first two chapters will show that any possible "logical" answer would be precisely irrelevant, whereas the movement from reasoning to presentation and action-speech is exquisitely relevant to the problem as posed. (Assuming that the prologue is a later level of the text, I take it to be an ancient, and correct, interpretation of the meaning of the text.)

What do we know about Job? He is a man prosperous and righteous. But his righteousness is peculiar; it is portrayed for us in one detail 1:4-5: that when his sons have feasted, he cleans up after them and offers purifying prayers, because "*It may be* that my sons have sinned and cursed God in their hearts. *Thus did Job continually.*" We are told no more, but it is enough, for this kind of doubt, projection, and perseveration are unmistakably revealing. This is an obsessional character, as we would say, one who wards off, by repeated rituals that prove his own purity, a sin that he readily projects upon others. By this means he constructs himself an invulnerable righteousness, forgetting that he is a creature in the world. Satan accurately describes him by saying, "Hast not thou made a hedge about him?"—so long as he is prosperous, he will never be touched by life. Further, the peculiar detail of the boils is typical for obsessional cleanliness. Finally, the only other thing that we know about him is his wife's remark: "Dost thou still retain thine integrity?" (2:9). I take it that this is the angry sarcasm of a bereaved and despairing woman who has lived long with a self-righteous, invulnerable, and abnormally unfeelingful man. We do not read, for instance, that Job weeps at the death of his sons; he merely performs the ritual acts. Contrast, e.g., 2 Samuel 18:33, David "went up to the chamber over the gate, and wept."

The middle of the story follows inevitably. Job's tone is alternately complaining, resentful, self-cursing, resigned. At no point does he lose control of himself or the situation, in either bawling or hot anger. His anger is irritation, the counterattack against the consolers and critics who attack his invulnerable position. In principle, rational argument cannot reach him, for in principle he has constructed himself perfectly in the right. It is summarized by saying, 32:1, "he was righteous in his own eyes." Therefore the feeling of all the characters, and of the readers, becomes impatience. The three cease to reply to him.

It is this ceasing from the obsessional duel in which he has trapped them that allows some primary feeling to occur. It appears in the wrath and enthusiasm of Elihu, who is defined emphatically as a *young* man and who says, "Behold, my belly is as wine which hath no vent; it is ready to burst like new bottles." (32:19.) Elihu's tone makes possible the denouement. He is angry but he does not reprove Job, which would only throw him back on his defenses. Rather he invites him forth with his warm enthusiasm, and he offers him the bait of a mighty identification.

"There are questions," said Franz Kafka, "which we could never get over if we were not delivered from them by the operation of nature." Just such a question is what to do with the stubborn obsessional character of a Job. It can be touched only by an action. And so the story climaxes. God confronts him "out of the whirlwind." (William Smith, giving the Biblical uses of this term, says, "They convey the notion of a wind that sweeps away every object it encounters, and the objects so swept away are tossed and agitated.") God does nothing but present Himself, and He has no argument but the encounter itself: "Here am I, and who are you?" It is therefore at this juncture that the text, preluded by the livelier tone of Elihu, changes in metaphysical character and becomes the spine-tingling poem. The poem is both a vivid *thing* and an action on the reader. To my sensibility, the power of the poem makes credible the incident of the Whirlwind. In the story, in turn, Job is not persuaded by a reason but moved by a fact, and so repents.

The one point I would here make is that the powerful poetry of the climax of Job is conclusive just because it is poetry, a kind of presentation and action; whereas, given the character of Job, any continuation of argument in a lower-pitched language would come to no conclusion. Job is changed because he is moved. As it is set up, he is done poetic justice by having a great fact to identify with; in comparison with which, his own stubborn self-righteousness, heroic though it was, was a small thing. Therefore the work has a happy ending.

Interpretation of this text, then, must also flexibly change in its assumption of the nature of the speech. The interpretation of the argument must test the logic of the argument; interpretation of the poem must prove the excellence of the poem; and the interpretation of the whole must be a kind of philosophy of language that can unify both reasoning and feeling, truth and act.

We are here touching on one of the most puzzling, never finally resoluble, problems of the human condition, the relation of knowledge and ethics. There is no doubt that the thinking of prophets, scientists, and artists has been powerfully normative for behavior. Nevertheless it is a fair challenge to ask how any proposition about reality can possibly be normative; how can we get from "is" to "ought"? Modern logicians tend to deny the possibility and to hold that ethical sentences are, ultimately, not propositions but commands or expressions of feeling. There is a pathos in this positivism, for these philosophers are dedicated to natural science, yet their logic makes it unthinkable to develop a naturalistic ethics. Then the search for truth and the searchers for truth are at the moral mercy of any kind of venality, fanaticism, bullying, or caprice.

But the case is less desperate if, as we have been urging, there is always a complex relationship between act and truth, between speaker and speech. Logical validity depends on what we take sentences to be, how much is to be included in the meaning of the sentence. For instance, the statements of scientists are behaviors of a character of men, and that character has very often been, we know historically, normative in the most crucial matters, hostile to superstition, humble and loving toward nature, and frank to publish for the consensus of all observers. Whether or not we can logically ground ethical sentences depends on how complexly and humanly we take our primitive propositions, how much of the speaker and his behavior we want to include in their meaning. Further, it is certainly false that feelings and emotions have no cognitive value; they are structures of the relation of organism and environment, and they give *motivating information* (how else would the animal survive?) And even more, by the working up of feelings and emotions into articulate literary speech—which is a storehouse of perceptions and memories, nicely discriminating and structured from beginning to end, and, not least, embodying the social wisdom of the vernacular—we are given ethical premises grounded in the nature of things. Indeed, if we consider the human sciences, we may say that the concrete "complex words" of stories, plays, and eloquence are more adequate observations and hypotheses of reality than any formulae and samplings of psychologists and sociologists; but besides, they are exemplary and moving. In brief, students of poetry, history, philosophy, and natural philosophy, do not *in fact* find the gap so unbridgeable between "what is the case?" and "what ought we to do?"

First published in *Utopian Essays and Practical Proposals* (1962).

On a Poem of Catullus

Iam ver egelidos refert tepores,
iam caeli furor aequinoctialis
iucundis Zephyri silescit auris.
Linquantur Phrygii, Catulle, campi
Nicaeaeque ager uber aestuosae:
ad claras Asiae volemus urbes.
Iam mens praetrepidans avet vagari,
iam laeti studio pedes vigescunt.
O dulces comitum valete coetus,
longe quos simul a domo profectos
diversae varie viae reportant.

[*Carmen* xlvi (text of Merrill, but reading *varie* for *variae*)]

(Now spring brings back ice-free warm weather,/now the rage of the equinoctial sky / is quiet in the pleasant breezes of the west wind. / You must leave, Catullus, the fields of Phrygia / and the rich land of steaming Nicaea: / let's fly to the famous cities of Asia. / Now my fore-trembling mind wants to wander, / now my joyful feet grow strong and eager. / O farewell sweet intercourse of comrades, / who set out at the same time from home far-off, / whom different roads variously carry back.)

In these verses of Catullus there is nothing problematical in the relation of what he is telling about—spring, departure, prospect, farewell—and the feelingful modifications of the rhythm and the sequence of the narrator's involvement in the situation. There is *something* to be excited about, and he speaks *excitedly,* and *he* is excited; this is direct feelingful speech. But in many lyrical poems this is by no means the case; often there is no (direct) relation between what is told about and the mounting excitement conveyed, so it is profitable to make a distinction between the direct and what I shall call the "vehicular" expression of feeling.

An exclamation directly expresses feeling; but any word may be said in an exclamatory tone (e.g., a name called in a tone of anguish). If the poem turns not on the particular words but on their intonation, the words are vehicles. So further certain properties of grammar and syllogism are feelingful: there is agitated speech, confused speech, leaps of thought; all such require sentences to be feelingfully modified, and these sentences may directly imply the feeling or may be vehicles by which the feeling is conveyed. For instance, in a novel, conversation about the weather may express amorous embarrassment because conversation of another kind is expected. Contrariwise, when in *Philoctetes* the embarrassed Neoptolemus falls silent, the silence is directly feelingful, since his dilemma leaves him nothing to say; but, if he showed his embarrassment by turning to a tangential subject, the subject talked about would be a "vehicle," but the tangent would be the direct expression. Very different aesthetic effects result from the more or less use of vehicles and their distribution among more or less striking parts. Ring Lardner and T.S. Eliot, to instance two modern writers, achieve a kind of contemplative satire by the feelingful modification of trivialities; and Henry James relies heavily on feelingful tangential avoidances. (These are mixed-ethical vehicular effects.) "Understatement," again, with its peculiar effect, is just the other side of the medal; what is told about evokes feeling, but the rhythm and involvement are neutral.

The speech of Catullus is unusually direct. (Sappho, Li Po, and Tu Fu come to mind as the only obvious comparisons; perhaps Wordsworth when he is writing about his childhood.) More typical lyrical poetry seems to me to have the following structure: The narrator is telling about something that is conventionally, symbolically, or otherwise indirectly moving; this subject matter forms a pattern with the verse, the imagery, the rhetoric, and this pattern may be very beautiful, but it has no motion of feeling or involvement of the narrator; nevertheless, feeling, involvement, and motion of thinking occur, using the pattern of the subject matter as a vehicle; and perhaps, toward the close, a more direct subject matter emerges that may or may not be akin to the apparent subject matter of the poem. Readers who happen to share the same character defenses against direct speech as the poet do not perceive that the subject matter is a vehicle, and they think they are moved by what the poem is "about." Critics, on the other hand, tend often to say that the poetic quality, the lyrical feeling, has nothing to do with the subject matter.

Let us return to Catullus' poem and see if we can find what gives this poet his peculiar power. It is his attitude or, what is nearly the same, his style. The style pervades the verses from beginning to end—it is always immediately experienced—but it is habitual; it does not have the motion of the particular incident and feeling; and, indeed, it is the same as in dozens of other poems, with different feelings. We do not much look, in Catullus' book, for great single poems, but we hear everywhere a single voice. Yet the power and charm of this voice are just that, again and again, it allows for the direct expression of different feelings; it is not a "style" apart from the feelingful occasions, yet they gain importance because they are given in the style of Catullus.

The attitude is at the same time both completely direct and intimate and yet elegant and curious (Alexandrian); elegant but rarely sought out, for it is always easy. We have already noticed this attitude in the conversational yet quite formal handling of the lilting meter. Notice, too, the narrator's assumption that all the biography necessary for the action and feeling is known or obvious; there is a naïveté and self-centeredness, yet the "I" appears from the environment and merges into a thought of his friends with modesty and courtesy. The sentences are short and easy to conceive, yet the accurate meteorology and geography of the first five lines are completely Alexandrian. "Praetrepidans" is a little odd, just as the rich "ad claras Asiae volemus urbes" is a little campy, and the alliterations call a little attention to themselves, and "profectos-reportant" is a little neat; yet the over-all motion is so direct, and the subject is so matter-of-fact, that everything seems unaffected.

It is an educated and high-born style that yet (or with luck, therefore) remains free-born and happy, with plenty of youth, friends, sex, and self-esteem.

In its earliest version, this essay was part of Goodman's Ph.D dissertation, "The Formal Analysis of Poems." This book finally became, after major rewriting in 1954, *The Structure of Literature,* from which the present version is taken.

Wordsworth's Poems

To make some kind of sense of the everyday, just to live on a little. My way of being in the world is writing something, to remain with my only world when, as is usual, she doesn't come across for me; or if by exception she does come across, I accept also that event by celebrating it in verses. Last year I suffered an event too hard to bear, but I coped with that also by repeating many times, in verses, the one grim fact. But it would be impossible to live on by versifying if we did not have a tradition of it.

From my teens I hit on three poets who coped in this way with both their everyday and their extreme chances, and who have served me as supportive proofs and models. Catullus, whose little book I learned by heart at City College, has been my model of saying with well-born frankness the sadly comic vicissitudes of my own arrested adolescence, but he died much younger. Tu Fu, the T'ang poet whom I studied in the translation of Florence Ayscough, said the everyday of exile, grieving and complaining, but fortified by the beauty that is nevertheless in the nature of things. There is a joy we writers get in formulating just how it is, however it is. When we are saying it, we do not notice that we are unhappy, so perhaps we are happy; and I sometimes wonder how other people manage who do not have this recourse. But especially the poems of Wordsworth have served me; they are in my English tongue; not very different from how I have it myself, an educated speech deliberately cut back toward the colloquial.

Wordsworth was tireless in making do, or staying in there pitching anyway. Distracted by timid inhibitions and fatigue itself, he remained fairly sane and pretty good by continually saying into being some meaning or other. Maybe this is not a high achievement, but it stirs my sympathy and admiration. Critics judge that he was humorless, and it seems so. His work has a solemn seriousness, like an animal's face, so lacking in irony or tragedy that, for an intellect of his scope and depth, there seems to be some human screw missing. But instead, he lets himself wander into fugues of fantasy, often to the edge of being dreamy, and surely there is a kind of mischief in being so odd with a dead pan. It is British. Yet he is never grotesque like Dickens, for he had a good childhood, and he does not mock himself like Lewis Carroll, who had to satirize him, for he was not despairing about his life.

Poets who cope with everyday vicissitudes by saying them do not tend to produce fully formed, self-standing "poems." We have neither the luxury to be detached craftsmen nor the divine grace to lose ourselves completely in great imitations. Rather, it is each one's persistent attitude that is his poem; the whole book is a more objective poem than any of the poems. Even so, in the helter-skelter of English poetry since 1800, Wordsworth's "Resolution and Independence" is still the most classic performance, with the sobriety and controlled terror—and deadpan strangeness—of Sophocles. It cannot be accidental that its theme is Staying In There Pitching. It was precisely the virtue that moved Wordsworth to bitter grief of himself and to celebration of an old leech-gatherer as if he were a victorious athlete of Pindar.

I still cannot read it through without breaking down and sobbing. (I have just again put it to the test.) "I thought of Chatterton, the marvellous boy," is the verse that begins to get to me. "We Poets in our youth begin in gladness," he wrote in 1802, "but thereof come in the end despondency and madness"; but he had a better recourse than he feared, and it served him out. "Such seemed this Man, not all alive nor dead, not all asleep—in his extreme old age . . . a flash of mild surprise broke from the sable orbs of his yet-vivid eyes." " 'Once I could meet with them on every side,' " says the old man, " 'but they have dwindled long by slow decay; yet still I persevere, and find them where I may.' "

Let me insist. It is not in his majesty or astounding moments, though they are frequent, that he is Wordsworth for me, but in his pervasive saying his kind of speech as a way of being in the world. What is always emphasized, of course—and it is important—is his simplification of vocabulary, and the connection of this with the speech of unsophisticated people and the expression of feeling. But even more effective, though hardly mentioned, is his exquisite syntax. In my opinion Wordsworth is the most knowledgeable grammarian among the English poets, except maybe Milton. Syntax—tense, mood, voice, agreement, sentence structure—is the immediate expression of disposition and character; it is the way of seeing, grasping, giving. Wordsworth's so-called "theory of perception," indeed, is identical with his syntax and sequence of exposition. (I will illustrate this briefly in a moment.) But I do not mean that the kind of perceiving determines the syntax, or vice versa; rather, for these poets of mine saying is the *same* as finishing experiencing, closure of experiencing. Goethe put it wryly when he explained that he did not write from his experience, for instance his love affairs, but that he tended—unconsciously—to experience what he would come to write.

Consider "There Was a Boy." Mainly, the poem is a description in past tense of a boy hallooing in a valley. But toward the end of the descriptive part there occurs (my emphasis):

> Then, sometimes, in that silence, while he hung
> Listening, a gentle shock of mild surprise
> *Has carried* far into his heart the voice
> Of mountain torrents . . .

The present perfect here is grossly ungrammatical, even shocking, as if it were a misprint. Nevertheless, that tense is the fact—of how one hears in the silence, the non-anxious surprise of insight, the fixing of permanent character by childhood play, making poetry by spontaneous recollection; and because it is these facts the erroneous present perfect tense is crashingly right. Almost immediately there follow the lines:

> This boy was taken from his mates, and died
> In childhood, ere he was full twelve years old.

Those past tenses return like a blow in the pit of the stomach. Ay! "Pre-eminent in beauty is the vale"—we are now making do in the terrible dispassionate present—"where he was born and bred . . . there a long half-hour together I have stood mute—looking at the grave in which he lies!" In which he *lies! Has* carried! *This* boy! I have stood.

Or notice the tenses in the divinely *faux naif* sonnet "With Ships the Sea Was Sprinkled Far and Nigh." The octave is again a description in past tense, of the harbor and of one vessel. Then the sestet,

> This Ship was naught to me, nor I to her,
> Yet I pursued her with a Lover's look;
> This Ship to all the rest did I prefer:
> When will she turn, and whither? She will brook
> No tarrying; where She comes the winds must stir:
> On went She, and due north her journey took.

That's a mighty brave and tearfully looking past tense in "went." The capital letters are here just right, though Wordsworth is usually too free with them. Those who charge this kind of poetry with committing the pathetic fallacy, projecting human feelings upon nature, do not know what experience is and that the best speech is saying just how it is. Both things: oneself is part of how it is, and also Thou art That.

It is interesting to contrast the two anthology poems, "The Solitary Reaper" and "I Wandered Lonely as a Cloud." In "The Reaper," the description is in the present tense, then Wordsworth suddenly shifts to a peculiar kind of past, qualified as lingering: "Whate'er the theme, the Maiden sang as if her song could have no ending . . . I listened . . . long after it was heard no more." Yet in the daffodil poem he tells a seemingly similar experience in the opposite way, going from past to present: "And then my heart with pleasure fills, and dances with the daffodils." How is it with him? Is it because the strain of the maiden is melancholy, but the dance of the daffodils is sprightly? I mean, phenomenologically, that he cannot *now,* while actively making a damned good poem, be *with* the sad song, he must alienate it, but he can be with the gay dance. In any case, there are few poets—Rilke is one that comes to mind—with whom it is plausible to raise such a question.

The Wordsworthian "moment" of experience is easy (in our times) to define. It is what Freud called fore-feeling, inattention, and the return of the repressed. One is attracted by something interesting; one is slightly distracted either by one's mood or the circumstances; the full meaning of the object, and of how one is, is revealed. "Revealed" means behaving in a new way, doing something in the "environment"—for instance, reforming one's relation with others by new poetic saying, and then there abides the poem. Freud puts it: "The art-work solves an inner problem." But notice that the psychologist uses terms like "repressed" and "inner," whereas the poet does not need to make metaphysical assumptions about outer and inner. Anyway, from where the poet breathes, how would he judge?

With Wordsworth, it is his way of saying that has influenced me, consoled or made me cry—they come to the same thing. It is not what he says about. His subject matter has gaps: he avoids what is sexual, what is political, and even much of what is humanly noble, e.g., in high civilization. Yet in concluding this little essay, I want to assert that, in my opinion, his idea of pedagogy is true and primary: it *is* the beauty of the world and simple human affections that develop great-souled and disinterested adults. A few years ago a professor of astronomy at Yale explained to me that his students were superb mathematicians, they had mastered the subject; they would fly to the moon—but they would never be astronomers, because, he said, "They don't love the stars." How to produce disinterested and magnanimous people, whether scientists or artists or physicians or statesmen? But I have not heard that the Office of Education, or the National Science Foundation in its curriculum improvements, or the Congress when it votes billions for schooling, cares about these things at all.

First published in the *New York Times Book Review* (January 12, 1969).

Reflections on Literature as a Minor Art

I.

I am setting down the following melancholy reflections not with any hope of a remedy, but because the matter is important and nobody else seems to be saying it.

In many ways literature has, in this century, become a minor art, more important than pottery or weaving, perhaps less important than block-printing or other graphics. Firstly, it is no longer an art of either the mass-audience or an elite audience. Cinema and radio-television, journalistic photography and series of illustrations, and persistently architecture and a kind of music: these are arts of the great public in a way that books, even best-sellers, have ceased to be. For the elite, the policy-making, audience there is no particular art as such; in its artistic taste and needs this group does not distinguish itself from the rest of the people. (To be sure, rich people collect *objects* of paintings and sculpture and thereby support artists, but these artists do not produce their works for the collectors any more than poets write for them.)

To the extent that in metropolitan centers the stage is still a popular art, it is not a literary stage, the emphasis being rather on the stars, the spectacle and music, and the production.

The diminution of letters is especially evident to those of us who write very seriously, who try for the classical literary functions of subtile ideas and accurate distinctions, ingenious and cogent reasoning, distilled learning, poetic expression. These functions are not easily or often adapted to the major modern media, to cinema, photography, or television, for in the adaptation they are blurred, blunted, curtailed, and lost. We are not then deceived, like other writers, by the illusion of finding ourselves in the swim; we cannot be made use of; we practice a minor art and occupy a minor place. The comparison to pottery and weaving is apt, for what we are doing is analogous to individual handicraft, no doubt rare and beautiful, compared to the major media of the present which tend to be produced by teams with a standard technique, not unlike machine-production.

These are, I suppose, the first decades in the western tradition that letters have not been a major art. It is a situation so peculiar that it is not noticed. Now the shift to other media is not necessarily a cultural misfortune. It happens that, on the whole, cinema and television, etc. have so far produced pathetically inferior works that cannot pretend to compare with the masterpieces of book and stage over 2500 years; but it is not inconceivable that the new media will get hold of themselves (I do not say "mature" since, in cinema at least, the works of a generation ago were much more promising than those today). Naturally, for men of letters our new status is personally unfortunate. We were trained in a tradition where letters had a quite different ambition and scope; our adolescent fantasies of becoming major artists are doomed to be fantasies; and ironically, just because we are too good for the current scene—for we draw on a tradition better than the current scene, but that tradition is irrelevant—we find it hard to adjust to the realities. Also, when, as often, we are called on to teach our English and our Literature, we find ourselves like curators in a museum; the average student (like the average editor and publisher) no longer reads English like a native. This is lonely-making. But as Trotsky said, "History fells the dead wood and the chips fly off."

II.

A second way in which literature has diminished is that it is no longer the source of ideas important for social policy and moral behavior. Such ideas as now get influentially abroad—I am not often impressed by their wisdom or brilliance—originate among economists, social scientists, administrators and businessmen, and technologists. Now this lapse of letters from a major position is not a new thing. When Shelley spoke of poets as "unacknowledged legislators," he should have meant not merely that they were unofficial but also, by his time, unaccepted. By the 19th century, compared to the preceding 500 years, although men of letters still had respectable positions in the homes and palaces of the policy-making elite, they certainly had ceased to function as important first sources of ideas that would eventually shape practice. The exceptions stand out and illustrate my point: the social-revolutionary ideas of the Russian writers that brought nearly every major Russian man of letters to jail or exile, or the moral ideas of the European and American writers that at once awakened the censorship. These writers were thinking up ideas not for the makers of policy, but against the makers of policy.

(In general, through the ages we can estimate the importance of letters as sources of policy by the negative test of the censorship of letters. Where books are heavily censored, books are important for social policy and moral behavior; and throughout the high middle ages and in modern times there was always a heavy censorship. But through the 19th century, except in Russia, this decreased, and in our own days it is trivial. Of course in America it is not from the government that we would expect the important censorship of ideas or expression, but from those who control the capital-means of communication, the owners of radio stations, publishers, theatrical producers. Let me then suggest the following possibility: since what these persons do diffuse is not important, policy-making literature, if there exists any important literature at all, it must be in what they refuse to diffuse, what they censor. It is possible that that exists. Note that in our times the question of the *quantity* of diffusion of ideas is essential. Since there is little legal censorship, it is possible for nearly any idea to get itself printed; but our country is swamped with printed matter—more than twenty books a day are printed in large editions and literally tons of newsprint and magazines—and there is no difficulty in muffling any idea at all by refusing to spread it widely. Indeed, we have the interesting paradox of precisely the overworking of printing-presses being a possible cause of the reduction of literature to a minor art.)

So far as the subtile, learned, reasoned, and persuasive treatment of ideas is a function of letters, our present shift to other major media, and literature becoming a minor art, *is* socially unfortunate. Cinematic and pictorial arts do not treat ideas adequately; that is a verbal business, it is specifically literary. Moving pictures can powerfully determine norms of behavior and style of life. The picture-coverage of an event in an illustrated magazine can powerfully direct what people feel about it. But subtile and learned explanation, the application of history and experience, the play of thought and hypothesis, the effort toward the truth under the surface that does not leap to the eye, everything Matthew Arnold meant by "criticism of life," these things are not skillfully accomplished without letters and training in letters and a high expectation from letters. In the earlier and hotter days of thought, Socrates complained that a book was a poor thing compared to a man because you couldn't question it and reason with it; he would have taken a dim view of audio-visual education.

III.

In one important respect, however, literature cannot become a minor art, for it is the art of language. In every generation, the art of letters renovates and codifies the style of speech, assimilating what has sprung up new, inventing new things itself. This is far-reaching, for the style of speech is our interpersonal attitudes, which are largely patterns of rhetoric and syntax; and also the style of speech is a good part of our philosophy of life, for a point of view proves itself viable and gets abroad by being able to tell a real story in a new way. (So the plastic arts, drawing and painting and sculpture, cannot become minor arts for they demonstrate perception, how people can see and are to see; and so a people's music is its kind of feelings.)

Speech is not going to stop changing, and so men of letters, marking down the speech, relating it to character, and developing the characters, are always indispensable. And the strong and subtile writers are fulfilling this function as always. But the mass of speakers are faced with the dilemma: on one horn they must get their style from the writers; on the other they have ceased to follow writing, or expose themselves to it, as major artistic experience. The result is that the ever-new speech is not strongly characterized and explored into its poetry and ideas and assimilated with a great humane tradition; people get their speech, in low-grade letters, as a caricature and a stereotype, with the conformism and thin conversation that we hear.

This essay was written for *Dissent* (Summer 1958), not long before Goodman began the writing of *Growing Up Absurd.*

Let me praise rapid speech
that says how a thing is
in my dear English tongue
that I learned from a child;
forty years and more
carefully I have copied
the meters of my breathing
and pruned out words not mine.

II

DRAMATIC ART AND THEATRE

The Drama of Awareness

I.

An important distinction between the noh-play and our western drama is that the former imitates a State, of the soul or of nature, and the latter an Action. The movement of drama is the working out of will, character in a situation coming to an act, and one act leading to another; the movement of noh is rather enlightenment, a coming to awareness (on the part of the audience and of the character, the *waki*), and a corresponding change from an apparent to a true state (on the part of the dancer). This effect of initiation into a true awareness of something, that dawns on one, so to speak, is not unknown to European lyric poetry—I am thinking especially of such poems of Wordsworth as "I Wandered Lonely as a Cloud" or "The Solitary Reaper"—and Ezra Pound has called a noh-play a "long imagist poem." But the Japanese have invented a technique for producing this effect in a play; and it is this single aspect of noh I have tried to borrow from, and not the music, which I have never heard, nor the harmonious ensemble of dance and mask, which I have never seen. It is the adoption of this technique that has made me call my own poems noh-plays. And in what follows of this brief essay, I shall try to develop the relation between the technique and the effect achieved.

II.

In the first place, noh is a dance. The turning-point in the performance is the subtilely prepared transformation of the disguised dancer (the *shite*), from being just one actor in the dialogue, into his real state as the dominant spirit of the noh; and this state is expressed in a solo dance, which is the climax of the play. Now a dance is of course a motion and can best imitate movements, as in *Yuki* the dancer imitates a flurry of snow or in *Ebira* the fury of a battle. Yet always, in noh, there is a certain changeless or static quality to this choric imitation, not as if it were leading to anything, as a story does, but as if it had attained a certain pause of perfection, of self-realization—the dancing warrior will never win or lose this battle, but will fight on forever. The dance is preceded by cautionary words, to set the mind at rest—"be calm, observe," "pay close attention while I dance for you," as, in Seami's *Ebira,* to refer again to this wonderful play, Kagesuye, the *shite,* impassioned by the recollection of ancient battles, suddenly declares: "Even in such confusion, let us quietly look on for a time—" and the Chorus replies: "Yes, in confusion like this, let us calm for a time our spirits and look on."[1] And the dancer dances the idea that has him in its grip . . . This expression of a state of the soul in a dance recalls the well-known sentence of Parmenides: As at each time the much-bent limb is composed, so is the mind of man.[2] Yet note, it is not even the dance that expresses the state, but the Posture of a dance, its "composure."

III.

That it is a state, and not an action, of the soul that is expressed, can again be illustrated by the fact that noh is a ghost-play—the dancer is most often a ghost or an immortal nature-spirit. The assumption is that by his death each person arrives at the unchanging meaning to which all his life has merely tended—just as the Inferno is peopled with the symbols of fulfilled desire. The Buddhist ghost haunts the earth, working out his ruling

[1] Translated by Mme. Suzuki, in *Nogaku*.

[2] Quoted by Aristotle, *Metaphysics* (III, 6).

passion—"I plundered men of their treasure, that was my work in the world, and now I must go on; it is sorry work for a spirit," cries the ghost of Kumasaka.[3] Or in *Ukai* (which is a kind of *Rime of the Ancient Mariner*):

GHOST OF THE CORMORANT-FISHER
The night is passing, it is fishing time,
I must rehearse the sin that binds me.
PRIEST
I have read in the tales of Hell
how sin-laden the souls of the dead
have toiled at bitter tasks;
How strange, before my eyes
to see the penance done![4]

"The ghosts . . . have been given over into the prison of their own Selfhood; their passions and memories have made their cage; they have no escape in life or death."[5] . . . Or a gain, it is some local genius that is the spirit of the Noh—as in *Oimatsu* or *Aridoshi*—or the spirit of some natural phenomenon, like the Fay in *Hagoromo* who dances "the dance-tune that makes turn the towers of the moon . . . I will dance it here and leave it as an heirloom to the sorrowful men of the world."[6] The relation of all this to Zen Buddhism with its Karma doctrine on the one hand, and to the nature-spiritism of Shinto on the other, is clear enough. In adapting the form, I have tried to procure a similar effect through the machinery of Platonism, the platonic ideas that appear to the fascinated spectator and seize hold of his mind—

I need not explain that there are eternal forms:
it is an ancient doctrine.
By love and abstraction are they known,
a process of two steps.

IV.

But just as there are these conventions, of dance and ghost, for

3 Translated by Fenollosa and Pound, in *Noh or Accomplishment*.
4 Translated by Waley.
5 "The Ghost plays of Japan," an interpretive essay by L.A. Beck, in *Japan* (June 1925).
6 Translated by Waley.

representing the state of realization of the *shite,* there is likewise a conventional technique of initiation, whereby the *waki* is brought to the moment of awareness. In the words of one writer, referring to the travel-song of the *waki* that occurs at the beginning: "A travel-song is intoned and gives a series of dissolving views that serve to awaken the imagination in preparation for the spirit of the Noh, which is presented subtly and indirectly, never directly, to the appreciation of the audience."[7] Or as Waley says, "Noh does not make a frontal attack on the emotions. It creeps at the subject warily." This initiation takes the form of premonitions, of dreams, of the evoking of a twilight and mysterious atmosphere. Local associations and the retelling of old legends work on the mind to render it receptive. Symbolic objects, as the iris in *Kakitsubata,* induce a state of vision; and as the psychologists know, a condition of fear and exhaustion does likewise, as during the storms of *Yuki* or *Aridoshi.* The recitation of prayers and the performance of rites also have a potent hypnotic effect; thus in *Atsumori*—

PRIEST

How strange! All this while I have never stopped beating my gong and performing the rites of the Law. I cannot for a moment have dozed, yet I thought that Atsumori was standing before me. Surely it was a dream!

ATSUMORI

Why need it be a dream?

(How many speeches of the *waki* begin with the words "How strange!" or "What a curious thing!") If there are any prayers or relevant poems about the locale, says Seami,[8] they "should be introduced at the end of the third part of the development"—that is to say, right before the climax, or transformation of the *shite.* . . . The psychological effect of all this, to sum it up, is "concentration" or "distraction"; and the end is to cast the *waki* into a trance. Or to awaken him from one—depending on the point of view! For to the pious Buddhist, and to many philosophers, it is just in such "distraction" from the conventional world that one gets to the intrinsic being of things; as it is said—

Life is a lying dream, he only wakes
who casts the World aside.[9]

[7] F.A. Lombard, in *An Outline History of the Japanese Drama.*
[8] Quoted by Waley in his Introduction to the second edition.
[9] The opening couplet of *Atsumori.*

V.

Now to act all this out on the stage, noh makes use of three and only three, speaking roles, the *waki,* the *shite,* and the *chorus;* for these are respectively the one to be initiated, the object of awareness, and the initiator or interpreter. And since the action falls naturally into two parts—before and after the transformation—both the *waki* and the *shite* appear in two states; but the *chorus,* who in his function of interpreter serves to relate the two parts and therefore transcends them both, necessarily preserves his identity throughout. . . . Another way of interpreting the three-characters is as follows: the *waki* represents the audience, the *shite* represents the Idea of the play, and the *chorus* represents the poet. There is a saying of Seami's, quoted by Waley: "To understand the noh, abstract from the audience and look at the play; abstract from the play and look at the dancer; abstract from the dancer and look at his idea; abstract from the idea, and you will understand the noh." What is the abstraction from the idea? Obviously it is the activity of the idea, or the poetic power; that is, it is *noh* itself—"talent" or "accomplishment."

VI.

What the *shite* is, is already clear enough; he is the Dancer, whom the play is about, and every word is artistically meaningless that does not allude directly to him. At first the allusion is veiled, because we do not know who the *shite* is, there is a certain double-entendre; later everything becomes luminous. The *shite* has often been compared to the protagonist of Greek drama (and the *waki* to the deuteragonist), but this is wrongly done; for the *shite* does not act, he is revealed. Rather, the *shite* is the concrete principle in the mind of the poet, that creates—in that it is the fascination of this idea that produces the poetic activity at all; and that selects—in that everything is ordered to him. As has been said, the *shite* appears in two states, before his transformation (or in the world) and transfigured. In the first state, in the Japanese plays, he occupies some commonplace situation of life: he is a reaper, or a band of reapers, or a fisherman, or often an old man. Yet there is something peculiar about this old man, some distinguishing characteristic; he possesses a wonderful flute on which he plays a sad tune, or he refuses to depart from a certain plum-tree in blossom.

Likewise, there is something striking about his speech; his opening remarks do not seem exactly to fit a person of his apparent condition. Thus the way is prepared for the transformation into the second state (accompanied by a change of costume) and for the Dance representative of his idea.

VII.

But to my mind, the most remarkable of the personages of noh is the *waki,* or subordinate character; the invention of this type (a type brought to perfection by Seami), the wandering monk, impressionable, inquisitive, full of common sense, somewhat timid —is the triumph of the whole transition. He is the type of ordinary tourist, with no heroic personality of his own, and thus can be transported by any personality whatever; in this way he is like the audience, which also has an infinite potentiality to be formed. At the same time, the *waki* is a monk, therefore more pious—or superstitious—than the usual man, and more willing to believe in wonderful signs; and likewise he is a traveler, out to be impressed. In these ways too he resembles the theatre-going public. He starts out on his travels with an original "mental set," as the phrase is—he wants to visit a certain distant shrine; why should he not see what is to be seen, before he becomes old and blind?—it is no wonder then that he wanders into an enchanted forest, or suddenly alongside the road meets the ghost of an ancient hero. This wandering monk is our representative on the pine-tree stage, the innocent public on whom the amazing truth slowly dawns. . . . To the *waki* belong the action and passion of the play; it is he to whom the events make a difference, not to the *shite,* who is a ghost and forever the same. The *waki* appears on the scene in a trusting mood, undergoes a powerful experience, and like the wedding guest in *The Ancient Mariner,* is not the same after as before.

VIII.

The third role is the *chorus,* and I confess that here, both in interpretation and practice, I have introduced a meaning beyond what the classic Japanese plays imply. I regard the ubiquitous chorus as the element connecting the parts (in a type of play where one action does not lead to another); this is perhaps why the chorus is made to sit to one side, almost offstage. "The Chorus," describes Lombard in his Outline History, "sits at one side and chants when the nature of the dance makes it difficult for the *shite* to deliver his own part. Occasionally, also, like the chorus of the Greek drama, it serves as a direct interpreter of the action." At the same time, though sometimes descending into the play, the chorus is not a person, but a perfectly generalized function: "il ne represente jamais un groupe de personnages determines, comme dans la tragédie grecque."[10] A perfectly generalized interpreter—seizing hold of this idea, I have made the chorus represent the mind of the poet himself. The chorus is the person on the stage who has consciousness of everything that is going on; he can think together the prior and posterior states of the dancer, and he can perceive the *waki* going into a trance—which the *waki* himself, of course, cannot perceive any more than one can watch himself falling asleep. The chorus, like the poet himself, is at once within and outside the play; he is within in that he too falls under the fascination of the dancer (that is why the poet is led to write the poem); he is outside in that he can judge and interpret, and compare this dance to other dances. A striking function of the chorus in noh is to chant as a substitute for one of the actors—and this separation of the action from its corresponding speech creates an amazing effect of intimacy: the chorus is set up as a confidant between the actors and the audience, to win the audience to closer communion;[11] and whose role is this more properly than the poet's? Likewise the chorus is the informant and confidant of the *waki;* he answers all questions, and by his answers helps instill the mood of the noh. Thus I have sometimes presented him as a guide or an inhabitant of the countryside.

[10] Peri, in the Introduction to *Cinq No.*
[11] Cf. Jean Baelen, "Le No Japonais," *Revue de Littérature Comparée,* (July 1932), 485.

This essay on the Noh drama was the preface to Goodman's own plays in imitation of Noh, *Stop-Light*, in 1941. The present text follows a reprinted version, undated.

Notes on a Remark of Seami

I.

"If there is a celebrated place or ancient monument in the neighborhood, [mention of it] is inserted with the best effect somewhere near the end of the third part of the Development." (Seami Motokiyo, *ap.* Waley.)

Seami is prescribing the construction of a Noh play. The Development or middle section he has divided into three parts, of which the last is to be heightened by animated dance motions or "simple chant," and it will lead into the ending, the climactic dance and full lyric song in which the Noh spirit reveals itself undisguised—that is, in gorgeous costume—to our awareness. The action of Noh as a whole is a progressive seeking, explaining, hinting at, adumbrating such a revelation. By the end of the Development, the preliminaries have been animated to the emotionally warm esthetic surface of dance and chant; and the climax is the present dancing-out of the thing that is made aware. Lêt us then ask: Why is the celebrated place in the neighborhood brought in just at the end of the Development, as if it is *this* that precipitates the climax?

It is because pointing to the place or monument in the neighborhood arouses belief. It is the evidence that what might be, what has been presented as a meaningful and interesting possibility, is indeed a fact and compels the assent of our senses. (It is the real reference that changes emotional excitement into full emotion, for an emotion, as I shall try to show, is a kind of cognition.)

As if a poet said, "I have been telling you a story of the olden times, exploring its allusions, explaining its moral, collecting the associated ideas and images. But this story is true, it is history." By true he means that it exists in some way in your environment too—you live with it. Go there and you too will see the very cherry grove whence he took the sprig and put it in his hat before the battle; or the churchyard where they buried the Boy who used to whistle in the valley; or the cliff overlooking the Hudson where the general stood peering hopelessly through his spyglass.

There are other ways, and stronger ways, than pointing to an historical marker, by which a poet compels us to take his fiction as not merely an entertaining fiction, but as important to us, as making a difference, as something we must henceforth put up with because it is real. (And I suddenly remember that terrifying anecdote about Goethe bursting into tears when Beethoven was improvising; the composer leapt up and shouted at him, "Admit that it's important!"—that is, that it *means* something.) There are other ways than the historical marker; nevertheless, it is a great ease and comfort to a poet to be able, just before his climax, to astound us with this particular trump card of factual demonstration, because he can then, at the very moment he is performing his risky and socially dubious deed of giving us the strange, feel the security of a common home from which he cannot be excluded. He has a Public Occasion, as if he were to say, "The occasion for my poem is our one and only world; you cannot deny me the right."

II.

Seami's prescription for the right use of the historical place is natural; it is a correct reading of, and reconstruction of, the process of comprehension and awareness. Let me illustrate this by briefly analyzing this single aspect of one of our own occasional poems, Emerson's *Concord Hymn.*

Emerson begins:

> By the rude bridge that arched the flood,
>   Their flag to April's breeze unfurled,
> Here once the embattled farmers stood
>   And fired the shot heard round the world.

We know it is a dedicatory occasion and that the poet and his audience are at the very scene, yet he begins as if he is telling them a story, for there is no bridge. "Here" then is ambiguous; it might, but faintly, refer to the present place; more strongly it means simply, "and it happened to be in that place that they took their stand." A particular and undistinguished place, an astonishingly loud report.

> The foe long since in silence slept;
>   Alike the conquerer silent sleeps;
> And Time the ruined bridge has swept
>   Down the dark stream which seaward creeps.

The use of the definite past in the first of these lines gives one a curious wrench. It is as if he is *merely* telling us an old story, that has no relation to any present. And the present-tense "sleeps" in the next line is in its strongest sense even more estranged, for it is the eternal present. At the same time it is a present tense, and the poet will use it as a transition. Eternity makes us think of Time, and the next verb is "has swept," a past indefinite that therefore has reference to our present. Even so, it is such a reference as proves that the whole affair is dead and gone: "You see, there is no bridge any longer, and as for the stream, all streams flow on forever to the sea."

But no—

> On this green bank, by this soft stream,
>   We set today a votive stone;
> That memory may their deed redeem,
>   When, like our sires, our sons are gone.

It was *here* (where *we* are), in *this* place. Here is the factual demonstration of the history. The reciter must quietly emphasize the "this" (the first of them; I think it is more delicate and musical to let the second emphasis fall on "soft"). What he means to show is not that streams flow forever to the sea and are therefore "dark," but that we are now standing looking at the very stream, and therefore it is "soft." We are dedicating the marker. (Let me say that the third and fourth lines of the stanza are, to my taste, academic and pretty frigid, although good enough for the rhetorical occasion—they do not ruin the poem. They introduce a solemnity different in tone from the simplicity of the rest; the rhythm too doggerelizes. The word "memory" is excellent, but the thought ought, I think, to be more like the following: "How strange, *I* suddenly remember something; I mean, I *really* remember it, as I look at this place.")

Spirit! that made those heroes dare
  To die, and leave their children free,
Bid Time and Nature gently spare
  The shaft we raise to them and thee.

We must certainly punctuate "Spirit!" with an exclamation point, as a sudden recognition and apostrophe. The direct address to something that has suddenly revealed itself. And this revelation has been precipitated by the moment of presentness, by the feeling that this is the very place, by pointing to the votive marker. (One can imagine the same climax treated dramatically: the Noh warrior himself appears.) The appearance of this Spirit is apt and thrilling, but such an ideal creature could quickly freeze us. Emerson, however, admirably restrains him to the same theme of time and change as the rest of the poem. The hymn is touchingly brief. And certainly the modest wish of the last two lines rings truer than the grander boast of the ending of the third stanza. The thought that a memorial, *any* memorial, is always also dedicated to Time and Nature, is good. And I personally do not find anything objectionable in the indicated sociable goings-on among the Ideals of the Transcendentalist pantheon.

III.

Again, let me illustrate Seami's remark by a point from the psychology of the emotions. The case is that an emotion is not merely a state of the organism but is an awareness of a relation between the state of the organism and something in the environment.

This can be shown experimentally in psychotherapy, when the problem is to bring a man to feel emotions that he has ceased to be able to feel. By body concentration and muscular exercises to loosen tension, it is possible to remobilize the particular combinations of body behavior that embody the emotion: e.g., for anger, tightening and loosening the jaw, grinding the teeth, clenching the fists, gasping with the upper chest, and so forth. All this will rouse a kind of restless excitation: a feeling of the inhibited anger. But if to this proprioception is added perception or memory (but ultimately present perception) of something in the environment that one can be angry *with,* at once the emotion flares in full force and clarity, with flushed or white face, ringing or dark voice, and menace about to act. (Conversely, of course, it does not matter how emotional the "real" situation is; a man will not feel unless he accepts the corresponding behavior of his organism.)

A moment's reflection will show that there must be such immediate and urgent awareness of one's relation to the world. For an animal in a difficult field must know immediately and truly what the relations of the field are, and must act. Therefore, as Aristotle pointed out long ago, to explain an emotion we must give its material cause (the body state), its formal cause (the relation to the object in the field), and its purpose (as action). For instance, longing is the heightening of appetite confronted with a distant object, in order to overcome distance or other obstacles; grief is the breaking of the tension of loss or lack in accepting the absence of the object, in order to withdraw and recuperate; anger is the destroying of an obstacle to appetite; spite is an attack on an unavoidable overpowering enemy in order not altogether to capitulate.

That is, "the emotions are means of cognition. Far from being obstacles to thought, they are unique deliveries of the state of the organism/environment field and have no substitute; they are the way we become aware of the appropriateness of our concerns: the way the world is for us. As cognitions they are fallible, but are corrigible not by putting them out of court but by trying out whether they can develop into the more settled feelings accompanying deliberate orientation—e.g., to proceed from the enthusiasm of discovery to conviction, or lust to love." (*Gestalt Therapy,* by F.S. Perls, R. Hefferline, and P. Goodman, vol. II, xii, 6.)

IV.

The historical place helps to induce belief, to make the emotion flower. This is what Seami is saying, and it is very well as a prescription for reconstructing the world, in poetics; or for removing hindrances, in psychotherapy. But more philosophically considered, all this is quite upside down. The historical place or other existing thing is not something that can be simply added on to an art-work or an excitement; for the existing is certainly something prior to the other devices and structures of experience which are, indeed, only aspects of the existing. There is no art without the real, and there is no excitement without the real. To have Occasional Poetry, they must give you an occasion. Take this very instance of the historical place that is our theme. Salomon Reinach showed that when there is a myth of origin of some sacred place or sacred stone ("here he leapt into heaven leaving behind this footprint"), we must assume that the place or stone was sacred from a more remote antiquity than the myth; it was sacred and one did not know why—so that the same shrine serves many a creed. The myth is invented later as a confabulation to explain or otherwise domesticate the unknown and probably maleficent power latent in the thing that is present.

Perhaps it is best to speak as follows: Quite apart from any local taboos, or from the fact that a meteorite unaccountably fell from heaven and frightened everybody, or that some grove or fountain seems to have a peculiar investment of mana, we must say that any existent thing that confronts us, any historical place where we know we are, anything that is present, has power. It has the power by which a possibility has broken the barrier into being a fact; the pouring, inexhaustible power by which a present thing maintains itself as a present thing. If we ask what is this power, it is incomprehensible, for, as Kant said, any explanation will again establish only a possibility and will never show the difference between the imaginary Hundred Dollars and the real Hundred Dollars. But fortunately, it is *just* in this case that we do not come to ask, for the present is given with perfect evidence, shaping us with its power. And one of its beautiful properties is to be an inexhaustible reservoir of explanations.

The audience, however, happens not to be confronting its present. The poet, by his language and construction, turns them toward it; and then we are aware of the existent place and feel ("remember") its power.

As we are, the present does always seem to be dangerous and taboo, and we hedge it with avoidances and superstitious explainings-away. Doing so, we indeed make it impractical and therefore dangerous. It is the role of poetry and other humane philosophy to eradicate our superstitions and make us stop avoiding, skirting, shutting our eyes. To open our eyes. And then we see our celebrated place and ancient monument patiently burning up in the day and not consumed.

First printed in *Kenyon Review* (Fall 1958). The text here is from *Utopian Essays*.

Occasional Poetry

I love neighborhood ceremonies and I went with pleasure to the laying of the cornerstone of the John Lovejoy Elliott Houses around the block. But the third-rate band of the Sanitation Department (the unofficial ranking of occasions is 1. Police band, 2. Fire band, 3. Sanitation band) played perfunctorily; Mayor O'Dwyer came late, left in haste, and his few remarks were ill-concealed time-serving; there was no poetry and no new score like Beethoven's *Dedication of the House.* So that, as is usual with intellectual artists with sociable interests, I had to occupy my spirit with satirical observations: O'Dwyer's offhand gesture of greeting to the crowd after shaking hands with the top-hats on the platform, an over-familiar gesture that would have been insulting if one could not sense in it habitual fear and (I think) a little shame; or the fact that the cornerstone is put into the completed building like a false tooth, it is no foundation-stone nor is it "the capital of the pillar." Most important, of course, assaying the rather ugly houses themselves, the object of it all, concerning whose architectural plans and social policies I had already had far too many melancholy thoughts.

Now Goethe held, truly, that Occasional Poetry is the highest kind: the use-music that serves coronations and weddings, mourning, rites and feasts, anniversaries, and the giving of prizes to culture-heroes. The poetry not only decorates these events but heightens them. It proves their importance by interpreting it universally; it formalizes the passions and interests involved; it endures to memorialize a great moment. All art is the wilful immortality of the artist (Rank): but this art has the great advantage for the artist that he releases that part of his deep energy that is shared and approved by all; his art-guilt is lessened, his art-joy is redoubled. Further, he directly gives, and is paid for, just the service at which he is excellent in the general mutual aid. So the social group is advantaged, the artist speaks with a more confident voice, there is no difficulty of communication because it is just from the shared unconscious that the images jangle forth.

The precondition for this gracious kind of poetry, however, is that there be in fact a community of sentiment deep enough for creativity and yet near enough to the surface and fitting enough to the ordinary mores to sing on a public occasion. Occasional poetry is a sign that the customary behavior is reasonably related to the spontaneous life. I think that this relation can be objectively studied in the social occasions themselves. Because the Elliott Houses are so little humane—and this can be shown from the plans and policies—it was inevitable that the ceremony would be either colorless or falsely flashy (I return to the alternative below). We have then the kind of vicious circles that is familiar to radicals: an occasional poet can strengthen the sense of community if the sense of community is strong. But as Morris Cohen used to say, a circle is not vicious if it is big enough, because then there is plenty of room to maneuver and live on a little.

At present there is no occasional art. This does not prevent there being art and even socially important art, for the artist still draws on his deep energy and touches depths in others—but in a more combative and private way, not heightening the public functions. Now quite apart from the loss of personal satisfaction and happiness, I think we artists suffer a great technical loss in being deprived of the immediate social scene and functions. A loss in brilliance of color, communicable gayety and grief, immediate topical liveliness, everything that goes by the name of Showmanship. For example, compare a pompous court piece of Handel with a piece by Stravinsky that is equally loud and fast, or the eloquent sorrow of a Bach church-piece with I don't know what. I should agree that surface showmanship is not of the essence of art, but it is what makes for shared enthusiasm, the tingling of the spine, and the flush of glory. What I am saying is simply that immediate communicability does not depend on triviality of idea or treatment but on the fact that the common depths of artist and audience have an easy relation to the same ordinary scene and function.

What has become of showmanship? for it is instinctual (exhibition) and cannot disappear. A vast part of this beautiful energy has been cornered by advertising and ballyhoo. For example, supposing the laying of the Elliott cornerstone took place in the election year, then the ceremony would have been not colorless but flashy. It still would not have been occasional art, because the project would still have been inhumane and irrelevant to the common depths of the performing Mayor and his cynical public; but it would have been more expensive and might have been more exciting, especially because of the willed shared interest in the imitation election.

I am not a friend of advertising, but as a friend of art I must say that there is more inventive showmanship, in layout, calligraphy, musical setting, and almost in diction and syntax, dedicated to these stupid commodities, than poets dare to muster for the truths of the heart. These ads are our occasional poems, as the purchase and sale is our public occasion. It was interesting to see that even the last war (especially the last war) could not evoke anything so neat and shiny as the singing-commercial for Cresta Blanca Wine—a product, I hasten to add, that I do not buy, for I belong to that numerous wing of "free consumer's choice" that, by revulsion, avoids every brand that it has heard on the air.

Then the wonderful Occasional Poetry, that Goethe called the highest kind, has fallen apart into the following melancholy specialties: 1. honest art, without social pleasure for the creator or the audience, and often difficult to communicate; 2. inventive showmanship, largely cornered by advertisers and experts in public relations; 3. perfunctory Gebrauchsmusik, played by the Department of Sanitation.

This essay first appeared as one of Goodman's irregular columns on "The Social Format," written for *Politics* (March-April 1947).

The Chance for Popular Culture

For a decade now the critics have told us about the unfortunate state of popular culture, the culture of the mass-media. Previously this culture was attacked by the acute for particular political and moral tendencies, commercialism, aesthetic ineptitude. The difference in the later, usually socio-psychological, analyses is that the culture is now told off *en bloc*, as a hopeless state of mind, a general character-symptom of the social disease; the culture is inauthentic, superficial, falsely professional, coordinated, etc.; there is no point in singling out for attack details or trends or individual works. The critics are of course merely explicating in theory the long-time attitude and practice of most of the best artists of the twentieth century; indeed the artistic attitude of rejection and withdrawal goes so far back that its earlier rebellious insults are now, in reproductions, a great part of popular culture.

Much, even most of this recent criticism is correct. But the critics do not sufficiently feel, I think, what a bleak and lonely prospect they envisage. To put it bluntly, if the critics were more frequently creative artists they would not so blithely observe, and annotate, the disappearance of a popular audience for good work; they would suffer anguish and shrink inward, as most artists have done, or fight back for our audience, as I hope we all shall do. The coldness of the critic toward this calamitous loss is itself a phenomenon of the superficial culture they assail; perhaps it is just this that is needed to sting the creative man to revulsion, to make liars of these wiseacres.

In the following remarks I am myself, as a poet, looking for a way out. First, to see the situation as it is, I summarize the gist of the usual, correct criticism of popular culture; but by looking at the case a little more simply than is usual, I think I can view it more charitably (more hopefully for myself). It is a maxim of our psychology that every symptom of disease is a sign of vitality.

I.

There is more art—more art-works and more experience of them—in America at present than at any time or place in history. By "art" I mean simply the communication of feeling through images, stories, tones, and rhythms: the evoking and displacing and projecting of dormant desires by means of some representation. Half the population sees a two-hour drama every week; the radio nightly presents long hours of vaudeville to millions; records beat out music everywhere; there is no measuring the floods of printed matter, merchandising pictures, cartoons, that have, whatever else, an artistic purpose.

Now this sheer quantity itself is the first thing to explain. But the explanation seems to me to be obvious: people are excessively hungry for feeling, for stimulation of torpid routine, for entertainment in boredom, for cathartic release of dammed-up emotional tensions, etc. The life the Americans lead allows little opportunity for initiative, personal expression, in work or politics; there is not enough love or passion anywhere; creative moments are rare, But they are still feeling animals; their tensions accumulate; and they turn to the arts for an outlet. (I say they are "excessively" hungry for feeling because feelings alone cannot satisfy the lack of creative life, still less can the feelings released by even the noblest art.)

They are a passive audience; they do not strongly or overtly react, nor do they artistically participate themselves. There is, of course, no point in overtly reacting to a movie-screen or radio; but it is the audience passivity that has made these canned arts become so important. They dance to music but do not make it; they hardly sing; and less and less frequently do they participate in religious or other ceremonials. Contrast, for instance, the musical spirit of a dancing party with a live pianist, where sooner or later people gather round and sing, with that of a dance where the music is supplied by a radio or phonograph. There is, again, less and less place in the mode of economic production for the expression of artistic feeling, craftsmanship. It is possible to conceive of a society equally rich in art-works where the art is active, for instance in the society described by William Morris in *News from Nowhere*; but our America is drowned in passive art.

And this passive reaction is superficial—this is why it is perpetually sought for again. It does not unleash, like the tragic or comic theater of old, a violent purgation of the deepest crises and thwartings, death, lust, scorn. These things are not purged every morning and night. Rather, *the American popular arts provide a continual petty draining off of the tensions nearest the surface.* Their working can be fairly compared to chewing gum as a means of satisfying an oral yearning for mother love and sustenance.

The social role of this gum-chewing is not obscure: it is to make possible an easier adjustment to the air-conditioned world by quieting the nerves. The very conveniences and comforts of the American standard of living, the quarantining of suffering, and the lack of physical danger, are an emotional disadvantage, because they prevent the occurrence of real objects of effort, anxiety, and passion. The arts give imaginary objects. (The war, again, gives a real object.)

Lastly, works of popular art have the following form: they present an important emotional situation, of love, danger, adventure, in a framework where everything else is as usual. The detailed routine of life, the posture and speech-habits of the actor (and the audience), the norms of morality, the time-table of work, these things are not deranged by the plot; they are not newly assessed, criticized, X-rayed, devastated by the passional situation. Therefore the aesthetic experience remains superficial; the passional story releases a surface tenseness, but there is no change in character, habit, or action. One does not sink into these works or return to them, for what is there to sink into or return to? and therefore again there must be more and more. (In the popular music the form is that the outer limbs are moved, even violently agitated, but no visceral sentiment or tenderness of the breast is touched.)[1] By definition art of such form can have no style, for style is the penetration of every least detail by character and feeling. Somehow the popular arts have won the reputation of having a "slick," professional style; but this is false, because the least scrutiny or attempt to feel the meaning with one's body or experience makes one see that the works are put together with preposterous improbability. It is a Sophocles or a Shakespeare who is professional and workmanlike; in comparison with the style of *The New Yorker,* Dreiser is slick and neat.

II.

In this ambience of too much art, what faces the good artist, the artist who draws on a deep dream and alters his character, the artist who means it, who has style, who, that is, experiences a world starred with his truth? His outlook is bad. (I do not mean, of course, so far as his creation is concerned—for this, at least in the limits of a discussion like this one, is simply mysterious—but so far as his action and happiness as a social animal are concerned.)

To begin with, he sees his productions swamped and drowned in the mighty flood of art-works; how can his win much notice? Among all this printed matter, how to win attention for what could be called a book? Also, quite apart from economic deprivation, which is likely not so appalling to a person who is daily justified in his work, he cannot fail to see that the stupid and preposterous are rewarded, and unless he is rarely philosophical this makes him bitter and envious and, by reaction, foolishly boastful.

[1] An important part of the popular culture is the large audience of concerts and records of Beethoven and Mozart. Let me say, angrily, that this is a cheap and safe emotion. What would those masters say of programs made up, as ours are, of works not written last week, of works whose passion has been absorbed and made safe by a century of habit?

But then, more important, he sees that the elementary passionate themes and the popular idiom have been preempted and debased by the multitudes of art-works, not to speak of advertising and journalism. Simple stories are "corny" and the language of the heart is devaluated. So in recent history we see that the good artists have turned to subjects and methods not immediately and directly communicable to average audiences. (I do not mean "private" subjects and language, for it will prove in a generation or so that just these works were the communicable and important ones of our day; certainly I mean "personal" subjects and language, but these belong to all good work of whatever kind or period.)

Let me hasten to say that if serious artists have avoided corn and directness, we are justified, for we work by an inner necessity.—In my own case, because of the chances of my life and the twists of my character, I most often find it so hard just to say what I mean and what presses uppermost, that I have no energy left to bother also about whether you understand it or it is immediately important to you.

III.

Well, all this is fairly familiar. This is the mass-culture analyzed by the critics and this is the plight of the honest artist. Everybody is blameless all around and we are all wretched.

The situation is outrageous and intolerable! I do not choose to endure it any longer. Why should we have robbed from us our elementary passionate themes? And why should we not dare to speak our dear English tongue? And what! are we never to get the heartenment and glow of pleasure that comes from our words being greeted by a roar of laughter, hushed attention, and gleaming tears?—but these greet only what is elementary and direct. The animal proof of the demonstration in the theater or the buzz that follows hard on publication. In this animal warmth it is possible to go on, next time, to what is more daring.

The question is this: how can the artist express himself, have style; and yet communicate to most people the elementary "corny" situation in a popular way? The answer is easy, easy in theory. No!

it is easy in fact, easy to do. (If we do not in fact do it it is because of a moral defect.) What is necessary is to love the popular audience, a few members of the audience; to *want* to entertain them and to move them. Then the work is both the expression of deep feeling and is aimed to communicate directly to the few and the most.—If then the work *fails* to communicate, the situation is distressing and terrible, but it is not a cold distress.

When I tell a story to my child, I express my best feeling and use my best language, yet I carefully follow her comprehension, interest, and excitement (she is an active audience); there is no incompatibility because I am here concerned, in love. But I do not in fact feel the same toward the corner grocer—I speak of him as the type of person with whom one has daily dealings, friendly but defensive, this is the average audience (of course there is no average audience). Now if I tried, this moment, to entertain and move him, I should likely begin talking down to him and I should certainly bore him; but this is neither my fault nor his; it is simply that my relation to him is not concern, love—nor hot hate, which would serve almost as well. Therefore my subject and words would be not mine, but a presumptuous guess at his.

That one feels concern or not is a fact; but it is this fact—however caused—that determines whether or not one can be a popular artist, have style, and also be greeted by an audience; it is not considerations of debased language, corny themes, corrupted audiences.

Presumably there was a time when the artist turned to his audience as a matter of course, on a basis of love, respect, and fear, as one tried to please and show off to parents or wooed a notoriously fickle beloved. Concern existed as a matter of course, how strange that seems! just as the words communicated by convention. What is the case now of myself as an artist? I seen no grounds for an intelligent man to respect the American public in its mania; yet thinking about it, I do not really take their mania seriously, *nor do I think they do* (if I'm wrong I'll get rapped for it); and this mania aside, I respect my brothers and sisters pretty well. What I find lacking in me is the desire to please; I want their love without giving myself to the wooing. Aha! it is the *fear* that is too strong. I do not love the audience because I am afraid of the corner grocer! Fear of rejection? fear of blows? fear of contact?

IV.

"The audience is corrupt." This statement must mean two things: that the audience is so accustomed to the stereotyped use of language that it cannot hear the ring of urgent presentness, and that the audience is so fearful of any feeling that might work a change that it freezes against giving in to unsafeguarded experience. Both these things are true of the popular audience. Yet if we state them thus, we see at once that the audience cannot be much corrupted. An art-hungry public is not unfeeling; in fact the Americans are too vulnerable because of their passivity (and ignorance), so that small novelties effect crazes and fads. When a man, or an audience, freezes against the deepening of feeling, the threat of its working a change, the problem is a simple one: to find at just what point the freezing occurs and to sensitize that point. Surely the artist can recognize that point, *he* is not insensitive there, otherwise how is he an artist? And as to the language of communication: ultimately it is the English language of childhood and of occasional adult passion; the musical rhythms are those of walking and skipping, for those who still walk somewhat and used to skip.

Suppose a delegation of the taxi-drivers came and asked me to write a vaudeville to entertain the taxi-drivers. This would not be difficult; one could always, at least, have recourse to pornography. If one felt concern for this audience, the work would be beautiful and releasing (the pornographic raised to beauty and understanding). Suppose a couple of sensitive and intelligent gentlemen on the radio directly and feelingly expressed their convictions, without making it nice? Would not the effect be electric?

V.

There is an obstacle in these pleasing fantasies. Between the artist and the public stand those who control the mass-media, the publishers, impresarios, etc.

It is important to remember that from time immemorial an essential characteristic of the great art-media (architecture excepted) is to be cheap: paper, mud, rock, tinkling, humming, talk, agitating the limbs. It is on these poor nothings that great spirits have lavished endless labor toward their immortality. The media of communication served as means, not as obstacles. But now suddenly, because of our peculiar social arrangements, a feature of the mass-media is expense; and expense is controlled by, let us say, "social policy."

Thus, if I want to move a million people, I must also persuade the editor of *The Saturday Evening Post* to let me. It is not a question of moving him aesthetically, as one member of the audience, but of stirring him to *practical approval* of the way he has been moved. This persuasion I could never accomplish. As an audience, he is a human-being; but as a controller of capital-means he is an intermediary something, not a human-being at all. For instance, he maintains a policy, and I don't give a damn for his policy. As a responsible agent he looks into my credentials, but I trust my poetic act has no credentials. As a business-man he has an empirical notion of what will appeal to many readers; but by now this empirical test is meaningless, for the readers get nothing else in the mass-media except what he gives them, so perforce they like what they get. But what they get and take demonstrably does not *move* them, make any difference to them, for we see that with so much art we have the society we have. In fact he does not know what will deeply move people, nor do I; but he can never know, whereas I might find out by inventing it. How to get by this fellow? He, like any member of the audience, is afraid to be moved; but because of his role he holds on to himself very tight, much tighter than they. No doubt he is afraid to have the audience be moved (this is called "the storm of angry letters" and "cancellations of subscriptions." Is it the case that magazines have foundered in such storms?) He seems to me to have a certain lack of daring; there is no reason why a profitable institution should be daring, but at least let us not talk about "what the public wants."

In the whole dilemma of popular culture, this difficulty of proprietary control of the media by the tribe of intermediary bureaucrats is, I think, the only fixed reality. The natural problems, of themes and language and taste, solve themselves by natural means. If the audience and artist are brought in contact, concern must follow, and following concern a deepening of communication. To the extent that editors, impresarios, etc., are human beings, they too are a part of nature; but most often one has to do with them as dummies of public policy and profits.

So we come, finally, to a hackneyed political issue. And frankly, as an unreconstructed anarchist, I still must consider the solution of this issue easy, easy in theory, easy in practice; if we do not apply it, it is for moral reasons, sluggishness, timidity, getting involved in what is not one's business, etc. The way to get rid of dummy intermediaries is by direct action. Concretely, in the present context of popular art (I am always fertile in little expedients): let actors get themselves a cellar and act and forget about the critical notices; let writers scrape together a few dollars and print off a big broadside of newsprint and give it away to all likely comers on 8th Street; forget about Hollywood movies—they don't exist—and how surprising it is to find one can make a movie for a couple of hundred dollars and show it off in a loft. I don't want to lay stress on such particular expedients; but it is ridiculous to gripe about vast socio-psychological labyrinths when what is lacking is elementary enterprise and belief.

You see, I myself am waiting for my friends to open a little night-club where the talents that we know galore can enliven us, instead of our frequenting idiotic places that bore us; and where I myself, setting myself exactly to this task, with concern and love (and a little hot hate), can move an audience to the belly and be greeted by a roar of laughter, hushed attention, a storm of anger, gleaming tears.

"What's this? he speaks of popular culture, mass-media, the state of society, and he ends up pleading for a little night-club where he and his friends and their hangers-on can display themselves!" Listen, here is my concern: I want to be happy; I am an artist, I'm bound to it, and I am fighting for happiness in the ways an artist can. If you, audience or artist, take care of yourselves, the intermediary somethings will get less take at their box-offices, and we'll have a popular culture.

First published in *Poetry* (June 1949).

The Shape of the Screen and the Darkness of the Theatre

In a controversy some ten years ago on the best shape for the cinema screen—the occasion was the abortive introduction of the Grandeur screen—Sergei Eisenstein contended for the Square as against the Flat Oblong (5:3, 8:5, etc.) His interest was to give the director more latitude for "vertical compositions." In practice, as it turned out, he lost the argument, for although a few theatres have square screens, all film-frames remain oblong. Partly to explain this outcome, so far as it can be done on merely psychological and esthetic grounds, I should like to discuss the Screen-shape in a more fundamental context than was at that time proposed.[1]

To begin with, let me add a few notes to the old discussion. Eisenstein summed up the arguments for the oblong under three heads, which he then refuted: theatre-structure, physiology, and esthetics.

1. The overhung balcony requires a screen lower than the square in order not to interfere with the line of sight of the rear seats; but the new theatres, argued Eisenstein, could dispense with

[1]Quite apart from this entire discussion, I should say that a sufficient explanation for the oblong shape for average use is the physiological one that the *field of vision* is broader than it is high, so that the flat oblong presents a larger easily visible area than the square.

such balconies (which were indeed invented for audition without amplification, for reasons of rent, etc.) But other architectural considerations must also be kept in mind, namely the pitch of the seats to insure a good direct line of vision, and the avoidance of obstruction from the heads in front.

2. More crucial are the physiological arguments: that the field of stationary vision is broader than it is high and that the moving eyes cover a wider angle horizontally than vertically. It seems to me that these are refuted too cavalierly by the great Russian when he says that the head itself can be moved; for it is all very well to look up and down at a painting, but for the ninety-minute-long attention to a movie, every cause of strain or effort must be absolutely minimized before any other consideration. 3. Thirdly, the esthetic arguments are twofold: that the majority of paintings are oblongs, and that the oblong (e.g. the golden rectangle) is demanded by dynamic symmetry. Let us pass over the discussion of dynamic symmetry. As to the other point, first he denies the statistics, then goes on to say that it was not the influence of painting that made the screen oblong, but of the stage-opening. But cinema must cease to copy the stage (this was of course just at the commencement of the calamitous retrogression of the talkies). Whereas the stage must be an oblong because human action spreads out horizontally, since men don't fly, the cinema, he argues, is not restricted to action in this sense. These points are capital and certainly true; but the question must still be asked whether there is not a basic affinity between the stage and most cinema as spectacle as well as action. The entire question of how the screen is and is not like the stage-opening, and again, the relation of the screen-frame to a picture frame, is just what I want to go into more fundamentally.

I. THE ILLUSION OF THE TOTAL FIELD

Reverting to the physiological fact of the field of vision: since this field is a kind of broad ellipse flattened at the top and bottom, the question must first arise why the screen, or again the picture-frame or the stage-opening, is not elliptical rather than square or oblong.

Now of course the scene, whether in cinema, drama, or painting does not fill the whole field of vision, but only the center of attention. The scene is not identical with our spatial reality, but is an object *in* the space, which also contains the walls, other spectators, etc.; and there is no doubt that the restriction of the audience to psychological participation in the scene rather than overt participation, and to a kind of psychological participation rather than the total psychological participation of dreams, depends on the persistent sense of this spatial discontinuity.

At the same time the scene is not a *mere* object in our vision, as a man or a chair might be an object, for the scene is (in most cases) an *imitation of the whole visible field.* If this were not so, we could not project ourselves into its world without asking ourselves, What other objects are there *alongside* the scene? and such a question would be destructive of dramatic illusion and the self-containedness of the spectacle. That is, *the illusion, the self-containedness of the spectacle, and the discontinuity of the scene-reality with the physical reality are mutually involved;* and an artist bent on *avoiding* one of these, must also do something about the others.

The original ellipse of the physical total field to be imitated, therefore, must always bear some influence on the shape of the screen or frame. The *degree* of this influence, however, will be great where the real space and the action of the actors in it is a major object of imitation—the case in most landscapes or in presenting the world of the drama; but the degree will be less where more particular *body* is a major object, as in the portrait of a man or in the recitation of a soliloquy. There are thus three cases: On the one extreme, where total and even overt participation of the audience is required, as in the "audience-participation theatre," the ellipse broadens out to become identical with the physical space; there is no frame or proscenium. On the other extreme, where the attention is to be centered on a particular object in itself, the ellipse is irrelevant. In the middle, where the illusion of a world is required, there is a frame and it is elliptical.

But why the flat oblong then (as nearer than the square to the ellipse) rather than the ellipse itself?

In the second place, granting that in a given case the illusion of the total field is the effect aimed at, nevertheless the visible arts in general exploit *interesting objects as their most immediate presen-*

tation. These are for the most part men, animals, trees, buildings, all seen with relation to the horizon and the foreground, that is in a system of verticals and horizontals. A composition whose members have no rectilinear relations—e.g. a group of shapes by Miro—at once seems to be in the vacant sky or in the depths of the sea; and such a picture often seems more "real," to hang together better, in an irregular oval frame. But to the degree that the horizon-line and its system of perspective belongs to the objects of interest, and these objects are the immediate presentation, the scene as a whole will come under a rectilinear influence; the frame correspondingly—for in the end the function of the frame is to confirm the spatial system of the scene—will be square, vertical oblong (as in the portrait of a man standing), or flat oblong.

If we would then require the *combined* effects of illusion of the total field and immediate presentation of terrestrial objects, perhaps the flat oblong is the most serviceable simple shape. Given a single problem, a peculiarly appropriate shape is always most expressive, for instance a little upright oval for a miniature of a face; but the movie-screen, we must remember, is the common-denominator of an indefinite number of usual problems. For a very special effect we may work *within* the common-denominator, for instance mask the screen to isolate a figure or iris down to a detail.

II. THE SQUARE AND SYNTHETIC MONTAGE

When I speak of the "illusion of the total field," I do not mean that the scene-space must be illusory in the sense of reproducing the very same spatial properties of the physical space. For instance the scene may have different laws of perspective, as in many Chinese paintings, or be the space appropriate to phantastic space-time juxtapositions quite different from the world we are used to seeing. And in all painting, in abstract painting especially, the illusory space tends to become two-dimensional and none other than the space of the canvas itself.

Nevertheless, all these *scenic* arts, which begin from the real space and either reproduce it relatively unmodified (the case where the frame is like a window), or distort it to create effects of unreality (as in *Caligari* or the paintings of Chirico), or abstract it to the two-dimensional conditions of the canvas—all these are to be distinguished from those arts which from the outset disregard the existence of a persistent space and *construct* objects and designs without determining their space at all. Léger's *Ballet Mécanique* is of this sort and the so-called non-objective paintings like Kandinsky's (as opposed to abstract paintings). And to understand Eisenstein, I think it is in this direction that we must look.

Consider the following series of effects in cinema: Scenes of cinema often achieve the pictorial, e.g., much of Murnau's *Sunrise* is Dutch landscape or chiaroscuro interior, and the poses in Dovzhenko's films are certainly portraits. In such cases the screenshape is not unlike the corresponding picture-frame, and it has the pictorial function of bounding the determined space, guiding the eye back into the composition, and completing the static whole. (By "static" here I do not exclude motion across the scene but only the movement of cutting from scene to scene.) Such active preoccupation with a single shot as a completed whole, however, tends to destroy the temporal flow of the *sequence* of scenes, and is therefore eschewed in most cinema, for instance in any ordinary story-telling film. Here the screen-shape is looked *thru* rather than looked *at*; it offers the means for looking out, so to speak, at the world behind; that is, it acts purely as a window. But now supposing no illusion of the total world is desired at all: then the screen-shape may simply be disregarded as a part of the spectacle, and the composition may be formed of objects succeeding each other as if in an indeterminate space or even in no space. This effect, most obvious in the light-play films, sometimes moves so far from the conditions of ordinary vision as to be analogous to music, cf. the efforts of Scriabin. But if the presentation is not to be mere play of lights, but objects determined by an horizon, then the Square shape might be just the most suitable space, for, as Eisenstein insists, it allows the greatest quantity of expansion in the relevant directions; as a rectangle, it supports the design of each shot of objects; as *not* an ellipse or flat oblong, it neutralizes the sense of an actual visible space. Now any one who has admired the marvelous synthetic montage of this director, which is not the turning of a scene before the camera (illusion of the actual total field), nor yet the posing of a static composition (picture-frame), but a unity of cutting and synthesizing a sequence of images of objects by means of their psychological and philosophical associations, will easily understand why Eisenstein asks for the Square. *The square is the convenient screen for synthetic montage.*

The square neutralizes not only the illusion of the actual visible world, but also the sense of visible spectacle altogether, for it does not play to the visual potentialities of the spectator, but retracts from the largest area that he could conveniently rest his eyes in. This leaves the way open to the *non-visual* play of attention, unconscious, visceral, and theoretic, that Eisenstein so much delights in exploiting. He does not speak to the sight. It is then in this double sense, first as getting away from the limitations of physical visible reality and secondly from the sentiment of spectacle altogether, that Eisenstein says the cinema must not copy the stage. But expressionist staging tries at the same freedom—let me mention the expressionist dictum that "vertical motion is more interesting than horizontal," so that actors somewhat "fly" after all.

We now ask, however, How are the *sequences,* whether of pictorial images, synthetic montages, or dramatic episodes, organized into the ninety-minute-long film? In answering this, we shall again have to return to the relation of the screen and the stage-opening in a more fundamental way. But let me first indicate another possibility.

The *ideal* for Eisenstein would no doubt be that the whole should be one vast synthetic montage of parts of synthetic montage. This result is even somewhat achieved in *Old and New,* where the overall changes of tone and rhythm are a direct expression of the general theme, while the narrative is reduced almost to a story-framework for the montage. But certainly for the most part in Eisenstein, Pudovkin, Trauberg, or any of the others, the organization of the sequences of montage is not itself montage but either narrative or drama. As such, it draws again on the illusion of a whole visible world. Do not misunderstand me: the narrative and drama may themselves be symbolic and not the chief expression, which may be an idea; but the point is that this idea is not presented directly by the montage, but indirectly thru the narrative and drama, with their sense of a self-contained illusory world.

III. SOME KINDS OF STAGE

Let us now broaden our scope from the screen or stage-opening itself to the more inclusive whole of the scene-opening in the theatre, with its conditions of light or darkness, silence or music, and other spectators. My contention is that the flat oblong screen and the ordinary dark cinema-theatre are conditions for the same kind of illusion. But I can analyze this out better first in terms of some kinds of stage.

The argument against the peep-hole or absent-fourth-wall stage has generally been wrongly proposed as an absolute rejection, but the correct formulation should be: The peep-hole has an expression incompatible with the theme or attitude that we now wish to express; or again, the peep-hole produces a psychological state in the audience that makes impossible such and such a communication; or again, putting it formally, such and such a stage and theatre-conditions are good for such and such a plot or probable sequence.

Consider some properties of the peep-hole theatre. The house-lights are dimmed, the audience is silent. Not only are the stage-lights always brighter, but they belong to an independent system of lighting and they illumine an independent space. The stage-space is made distinct from the audience-space in other ways also: is raised above it, framed in a proscenium, etc. Further, the sense of an absent fourth wall gives the stage-incidents an independent time and causality, for the stage-events can no wise act on or be reacted on by the physical audience. But since the dimly-lit and silent audience has no life of its own, its entire activity must consist in mental projection into the stage-world. There, of course, it has the liveliest interests, interests which are indeed intimately personal to each member of the audience; but these interests assert themselves and are gratified under the conditions of phantastic projection. In short, we might say the following: (1) The peep-hole stage expresses an illusion of the total visual field. (2) It keeps the audience all eyes. (3) The probability of the plot on such a stage seems to be given entirely thru the actors, who are self-subsistent and on their own, for there is no other continuous reality. (4) The scenery must also add up to a self-subsistent reality, tho of course it need not be realistic; but bare stage-boards will not do. (5) The audience-interest is given under the psychological conditions of projection, as in day-dreams.

Now contrast such a stage with a daylight performance (of, say, a masque) on a lawn or in an amphitheatre. Here there is a continuity between the visible audience and the stage and actors; and this might express, depending on the ethical tone of the plot and the occasion, the sense that the actors are amateurish neighbors, subject to running comment; or that they are heroic surrogates of the audience, perhaps in a religious act like the mass; or that the play is a mere spectacle or pageant, an interesting object *alongside* the other sights in the total field of vision. The unity of the whole, we must then say, is partly given by the audience's sense of its relation to the play. (I do not mean this to be a description of the Greek theatre, where the Chorus *both* unified and divided the play and the public.)

Consider, again, the Elizabethan stage with much of its action on the apron—I am speaking more of the stage of Marlowe than of Shakespeare, and more of the chronicle-plays than of the tragedies. Suppose on this stage the poet violates the unities of space and time at will, brings forth his speakers on the apron or on the inner-stage as suits his purpose, etc. Such a stage makes more indirect the illusion of a presented world, it introduces effects of narration into the drama. (At the same time there is still the illusion of a world, tho with indefinite geography and perspective.) Psychologically, there is a more direct communication between the poet and the audience; the unity is partly in the poet's interventions and juxtapositions, whether for rhetorical or lyrical effect, or reportage, or to tell a story. Here elaborate asides to the audience and topical jokes do not seem out of place. It is interesting to observe how the conventions of the Living Newspaper, like vaudeville before it, have tried to adapt the architecture of the peep-hole stage to the direct communication of the Elizabethan platform.

The expressionists, as I have mentioned, sometimes neutralize the sense of an (imitated) physical world entirely. The revolving stage, the spiral stairs that rise from the flat on which men ordinarily converse, the timeless masks and costumes—these all speak in terms of theory or inner perceptions; there is still a self-contained visual pattern and therefore the imitation of a total field, but the pattern is more abstract and indeed tends to spread out to include the architecture of the theatre itself, which is preferably styled according to the same canons.

Quite another effect, again, is that of the audience-participation theatre, for here not only are the play and the public physically and psychologically continuous, but—in the ideal case—the overt reactions of the audience ought to alter the events of the play. Strictly speaking, this is not a "theatre" at all. Here we enter the realms of political meetings, religious revivals, and parlor conversations; and have come a long way from the hush, the three knocks, and the footlights lit, before the curtain rises.

I have introduced these few remarks only to demonstrate that the flat oblong of the peep-hole stage is by no means due merely to the fact that human-beings do not fly, but especially to the fact that its peculiar properties, which are not the properties of the Stage in general, strongly call for imitation of the total field and illusion of the physical space.

IV. THE DARKNESS OF THE THEATRE

The movie-theatre is darkest of all. The movie audience consists preeminently of *individuals in isolation.* And the *discontinuity* between the audience-space and the space of the scenes is of course absolute. If the effect of the brightly lit stage is a controlled phantasy, the flickering lights of the screen working on the ninety-minute attention unrelieved by intermissions produce what is nearer hypnosis (where it is not perfect sleep). Certainly, especially in a small theatre, the stage is warmer and more intimate in appeal than the screen, so long as the phantasy is more nearly like what we are used to or consciously desire; the actors are flesh, the shadows are only shadows. But let the cinematic attention become fascinated, as it does as the minutes flow by, and these huge shadows press in closer to the mind at this deeper level than the sight of real flesh can penetrate. The disjoined and composite space created by cutting from scene to scene is more like the space of dreams than the quiet stage can hope to imitate.

These circumstances explain easily enough why cinema has devoted itself almost exclusively to the excitement of ordinarily repressed feelings and even unconscious connections; and why, tho clearly visible and therefore more patently absurd than literary phantasies, its world of desire is not immediately rejected. Adding the mass-production and the enormous audience, we have the principle of selection of these feelings, and we understand the usual plot, the star-system, the surrealist interiors, etc. Indeed, the real difficulty is to see why the movies have not more directly imitated the actual technique and contents of dreams—consider, e.g., the extraordinary compulsion of *Le Sang d'un Poète,* where this is done. But the reason for this abstention may well be audience fear and modesty, which are even stronger than audience desire. To put this another way: the *public* moving picture that the audience talks about after the performance, or reads about before it in the reviews, is not the same as the actual experience of the solitary spectator; but this actual experience is hinted at in the advertising.

How far this tepid bath is from the intellectual synthetic montage of Eisenstein! His constructions are passionate and rich with dream-symbolism to be sure, but like other artists he gives these in effortful stabs to a *disturbing* depth, at which the audience cannot rest.

It would be further still from a "film of political participation," whatever such a thing might be. (Does it not seem to be impossible in principle?)

The hypnotic absorption, again, was immensely aided by the continuous and not independently interesting musical accompaniment of the old films. This music neutralized the audience noises, lulled the muscle-jitters, and restricted the only possible field of sensuous interest to the eyes. Its continuity provided just the matrix needed for the scene-space, to keep it one despite the often kaleidoscopic cutting; when the music stopped, the mechanism at once became apparent.

The fact that both the peep-hole stage and the movie-screen imitate the total world in conditions of phantasy is a chief cause, it seems to me, of the remarkable phenomenon of audience-interest in the personalities of the actors themselves, a phenomenon not apparent with respect to other arts and spectacles, even musical performances or oratory. The conception of "Hollywood" is of course pat for this argument: here is a distant and paradisal world inhabited completely by the beings of the world of phantasy, but come to "life." And the machinery of Hollywood publicity is designed precisely to controlling that life so as not to jar with the properties of the other world.

Let me make still another sociological observation, a point of the highest importance, but almost completely disregarded by the critics of stage and screen. I have mentioned the "drama of political participation." Now certainly the most determined essays in both stage and cinema have been made towards direct rhetorical appeal, for ends both high and low. By "direct rhetorical appeal" I mean both the rousing of feeling and the presentation of arguments, especially by dramatic example, for or against something with the end of producing appropriate overt action of the part of the audience. But first: is it the fact that the excitement roused in the theatrical condition of phantasy can bridge the discontinuity and survive in the public world? might not the *contrary* be partly true: that the energy attached to such theatrical symbols is thereby fixed at that level, permanently submerged beneath the political level? (This is the old story of the women who exhaust their unction of benevolence in the esthetic splendor and sexuality of religious ceremonials.) Secondly: is it likely that the desired reactions, whether of horror or enthusiasm, when fixed in the phantastic world, reappear in the public world with the same positive or negative value? Perhaps with even the opposite value! as a child frightened by a gangster film or by images of the horrors of war may retain, when he "awakes," the sentiment of a forbidden thrill. Certainly the American public, presented with the usual images of filmic luxury (still, in 1941, in the style of the Paris Exposition of 1925), does not react with either emulation or resentment, but rather with a dreamy delight in these *ideals,* which exist in the mental world somewhere near the ideals of honor and divinity. What then? Am I arguing that these arts can not or ought not to aim at rhetorical ends? Certainly not; but that from such rhetorical calculations we must not omit a dimension which may turn out to be absolutely vital. A necessary safeguard is the analysis of the expressive medium.

V. CONCLUSION

To sum up: I have tried to distinguish between artistic imitations of the seen world as a whole, discontinuous from the self-conscious spectator, and seeming to exhaust the field of vision, and those other imitations which are merely part of the total field and preserve a certain continuity between the object and the spectator. I have touched on a few differences of the two types in plot and psychological appeal. I have argued that the flat oblong of the screen was not taken over from the stage merely by an historical influence, but that there is a common cause in the medium of expression of both. And I have tried partly to explain—the chief explanation, I would maintain, is physiological—the almost universal success of the flat oblong by the somewhat simplist formula that it is a compromise between the imitation of the total field of vision and the rectilinearity with which we compose the terrestrial objects within the frame.

Again, what then? The conclusion of this line of argument is by no means that cinema can not or ought not aim at effects of synthetic construction, or participation, or anything except spatial illusion—God forbid that a critic should argue for the status quo, and what a status quo! Rather, that such non-illusory effects require the invention of new technical resources and manners of handling, the work of creative directors. We have seen, for instance, how Eisenstein's Square is one such invention, more far-reaching in its expression than one might have thought, intimately related to the achievement of a non-illusory effect. An invention along another line is Herr Gropius' "Space Theatre," a plan to project films simultaneously on several different screens. The exact expressiveness of such a medium would have to be discovered by exploration, but it seems to me—on the analogy especially of the Grandeur screen—that at least an effect of pageantry could be directly achieved by this means, for the several spaces would destroy the illusion of the unique illusory space, restore the relation of the spectator to the spectacle as spectacle, and give the spectacle great magnitude. Another technique for overcoming illusion—but one which seems to me to sink even *deeper* into illusion—is the employment of news-reels or news-reel atmosphere in documentaries. Another, thrice-familiar, technique is the direct address to the audience by a huge close-up of a face—but almost always this particular sequence in the film merely clashes with everything that has gone before; let me give no examples.

This essay was written for the series of columns Goodman wrote on cinema in the *Partisan Review* (March-April 1942). The series was terminated after Goodman and the editors clashed on the issue of the war and pacifism. The version reprinted here was included in *Art and Social Nature* (which the *Partisan* vilified when it came out).

Censorship and Pornography on the Stage

I.

"The use of art is to delight and instruct." This doctrine, prevalent from the Renaissance through the Eighteenth Century, was often interpreted to mean sugar-coating a Moral to make it easier to swallow. Or more loftily, as the politically fateful Italian doctrine that only Eloquence is instructive, for a truth is empty, otiose, and therefore false if it does not come home to you. Beauty catches our interest, we become involved, and so we learn.

Often, however, the interpretation gave the contrary emphasis: that art *moves* the audience *by* instructing it, for only reality and truth are important and finally interesting; mere fancy does not make for intense experience. This is the more classical interpretation, going back to Horace: the play must have verisimilitude, he says, otherwise *incredulus odi*, I don't believe it and I despise it. And so back to Aristotle, who begins the *Poetics* with the philosopher's remark that men are avid to learn and recognize, and this is the matrix of the imitative arts.

On one interpretation or the other, the theme is still with us. It reappears, for instance, in the proposition of psychotherapy that self-knowledge is ineffectual without concrete memory and affect; with them it is insightful, integrative. Or the theme is discussed in terms of the nature of language. The semanticists seem to hold that language is primarily report and abstraction—"The map of a territory"—and to this poetry adds feeling and persuasion; it sugarcoats the pill. Other linguists, more realistically, take speech to be primarily personal and interpersonal action, acting-out, acting-on; communication is only a small part of the process; then poetry, whose aim is to move us, is more simply speech than journalism or other mere communication. A poem is the re-inventing of a primitive complex word, like the long and songful jaw-breakers of Jespersen's savages. So Artaud urges that the stage is not meant to convey psychological truths, but to act "violently" on the audience. (And I think this was what Matthew Arnold was trying to say about Poetry and Science—that the right aim of speech is behavior—except that he did not clearly understand that scientific speech itself is hypothesis-and-verification, a form of action, not of reporting.)

Now let us explore our theme in the area of censorship and pornography, for it is useful to test ideas where they make a difference and cause trouble. (I use "pornography" in the following discussion to mean speech arousing ordinarily inhibited feelings, primarily lust, though we could speak also of a pornography of destructiveness, drunkenness, etc.)

II.

At the Marble Arch in Hyde Park London, crowds gather and listen to popular orators venting their grievances and longings on every topic under the sun, freedom for Nigeria, a subscription for arms for the IRA, correct behavior in marriage, the nearest way to Salvation. Like Bernard Shaw, the orators test their powers of repartee against a mighty insolent audience. This is a British institution, it is strictly legal. I was watching this scene with delight last spring when suddenly one of the guardian bobbies dove into the crowd and hauled a fellow out and lectured him. Assuming the privilege of a foreigner, I asked the cop what the trouble was. "He came within twenty-four inches of the speaker!" was the reply.

Here we have the beautiful British compromise: a man can say anything, he mustn't do anything; a man can listen to anything, but he mustn't be roused to do anything. By freedom of speech is meant freedom to talk *about*; speech is not saying-as-an-action. (In the House of Commons itself, the Government and Opposition benches are separated by a space traditionally equal to more than two swords can reach.) The limitations on the freedom make the distinction quite clear. If because of heated circumstances there would be incitement to riot, the freedom would be curtailed. Pornography is forbidden because it is the nature of detailed sexual reporting that it leads to physiological reactions and likely acts. Blasphemy and obscenity are forbidden because they are acts as such, for they break a taboo in their very utterance, as well as presumably undamming what is held in repression by the taboo. Also there are certain topics, e.g., the subject of *Lolita,* where merely to treat them at all in some official way as by publication, whether pornographically or not—though *Lolita* also happens to be pornographic—is tantamount to sanctioning their existence in the universe, which is out of the question. (Here we have the final magical use of speech: to name the Name creates the thing.)

Let me hasten to say that, within its limits, the British freedom of speech is beyond praise. Even in Eire, where the censorship is ludicrously stringent, the *Irish Times* will print correspondence offending the dominant mores that the *New York Times* would politely have no space for. The result is that in the British press there get going excellent and deeply informative controversies, where our press allows at most one or two notices of the subject. And so the House of Commons will debate the abolition of the entire penal system, or of the laws against narcotics or homosexuality, in a way unthinkable in America. And—how strange!—the most informed debate seems to lead to better law and less social violence.

III.

But the arts are action-speech and not merely speech-about. They instruct in order to move, if only at first to move feelings. They have always been considered as the strongest influence in forming character, in education and determining attitudes. So they are liable to censorship, where sociological reports are not. And of the literary arts, it is the stage that has always been the most heavily censored. The reasons for this are instructive for our theme. First, the theatre gives more material stimulation than the book: the offensive thing is not only spoken, it is acted out in the flesh. (The shadows of cinema, also heavily censored, are both more and less stimulating: more because they are direct fantasies, close to day-dreams; but less because they are therefore more simply masturbatory, less socially troublesome, private safety-valves.) Secondly, and more important, the actor on the stage is a representative figure for the audience, and he has already dared and broken the taboo: if my model here can do it, then I can and even ought to. Actors are intensely conscious of this responsibility, and it is often with the greatest difficulty that one can find a professional actor to play certain roles, for he must protect his reputation, as if he could not distinguish between himself in the play and in society. But most important of all, I think, is that the stage plays to a public audience not isolated readers; the audience shares the risk, the excitement, and the guilt, and it responds with the mutual permissiveness and seduction of mass-psychology that easily displaces the super-ego. In the dark cinema-theatre, by contrast, one is in complicity with his immediate neighbor only: if, for instance, an obscenity is uttered on the screen, one is privately embarrassed and maybe exchanges a joke with one's neighbor; but if it comes from the stage, there is a public shock, a tenseness in the community.

In the very notion of theatre there is a peculiar tension, a kind of ambivalence. The fundamental theatrical relation is that A watches B and is moved by watching him, but he must not get up and do something on his own. (A scene is said to "play" if the spectator's excitement is greater by watching than if he merely reads it or thinks it. An actor is said to "project" when he is able to keep them watching him.) We are here drawing psychologically on survivals of very early experience: perhaps on what the Freudians call the primal scene, the child seeing the parents' sexual intercourse; but certainly and basically on the child curious about, and imitating, any behavior of his grown-ups, his heroes. In general, and even in the theatre of naturalism, the actors are "bigger than life-size."

Now the goal of the theatrical excitement may be simply abreacting, living out again, a traumatic episode in the better conditions of grown-up life, secure with one's fellows in the theatre. Then the tension can be resolved within the theatre itself, in the outbreak of grief and fear. This was, of course, the specialty of the Greek tragedy, whose audience shrieked and wailed, no doubt very like an Irish wake. This seems harmless enough, but I guess that even this intra-theatrical excitement would be liable to censorship on our stage; it would be called disturbing the peace or creating a public nuisance.

But the stage is even more liable to censorship when the theatrical tension wants to act out outside the theatre, in the community. Consider the stage of Ibsen and the naturalists that stripped away the fourth wall and made men see inside their houses. Here the urge to act out is not fundamentally to act out the apparent plot on the stage, but rather the essential action of this theatrical convention itself, namely to strip away the mask from our political, religious, and moral hypocrisy: to bring the facts of life into the open. Naturally this revolutionary action of the playwrights was heavily censored; but by and large their revolution succeeded, and censorship of this kind has subsided.

A different social threat arises with the Theatre of participation, genre of the Weimar Republic, where the plot does not end on the stage but breaks the barrier between stage and audience—and therefore spills out into the community outside the theatre. Apart from a few petty attempts in the thirties, this genre has not been tried on our stage, and is inconceivable in our society except in a revolutionary situation. (I suppose our closest approximation would be jazz-sessions that lead to various overt behaviors of the audience, but these occur among marginal groups and tend to be controlled not so much by police censorship as by police raids.) Yet the principle of such a rebellious theatre, breaking its bounds, is an ancient one: a new year's or saturnalian ritual, to forgive debts, free the slaves, and deal the cards anew.

All comedy, finally, is in principle heady and limitless, it cannot keep its bounds. It is pornographic and leads to the overt acting out of the audience; but not so much, again, because of the positive stimulation of any presented scene, but because of the comic form itself; comedy reduces the ordinary world to senselessness and there is an explosion of the underlying drives of lubricity and malice. But of course these drives are also represented in the scenes, the discomfiture of hypocrites, misers, prudes, and the aged, and the triumph of witty knaves and bawdy youth.

When the theatre exists in its greatness, as part of an integral community, there is no problem raised by any of these situations; naturally art not only moves the audience but moves it to action. Great theatre is a seasonal ritual, to enhance the bond of religion, to encourage rebelliousness, to lead to sex and procreation. No doubt also magically to influence the Cosmos. When there is no integral community, however, there is raised the problem of censorship, for the ritual of theatre is too dangerous for such society as there is.

(Here again we must admire the legal genius of the British. They have much alleviated the tension of stage and censorship by the institution of private theatre clubs. These are legal fictions, for the only difference from the licensed theatre is that one buys a membership instead of a ticket. But being "private," the Clubs are exempt from public interference, for a man's home is his castle. The Club is a remarkable hybrid, a *private community,* a characteristic British schizophrenia.)

IV.

Let us turn to our present situation in New York. There is little official censorship; yet I doubt that any one would say that we have an integral community. The explanation of the lax censorship is twofold: the censorable plays do not get through the middlemen to production, and censorable plays do not tend to get written in the first place.

Our rich and intensely organizational society has defenses in depth to ward off anything live and dangerous. This can occur quite crudely. For instance, in very recent years there was a sensational American play produced in Dublin and closed; the actors fought it out in the courts and finally won, but of course they had lost their investment. Now in New York the same play was objected to, but after the opening it was promptly tailored to meet the objections and save the investment, and nothing further said. Usually, however, the offensive is prevented far earlier. A television producer will not use a lively script because the "storm of angry letters" (about 20) might make the sponsor withdraw his support. This can go to the lengths that the owner of the real estate will insist on passing on the proposed play; for instance, one very great such owner refused to rent an uptown theater to an advance-guard group because the WPA had once given his theatre a lasting black-eye by putting on a lovely, and successful, showing of that "crazy" play *Murder in the Cathedral.* And even off Broadway, where less money is involved, the Fire Department tends to become strangely sensitive to violations when a play has appeared that offends the parish church. Last but not least, our system of information is such that the critics of the New York press exercise an almost veto power, so that it is pointless to produce what those not very daring nor learned gentlemen will choose not to notice. Thus, very little gets so far as to warrant official censorship. This has the peculiar disadvantage that the new cannot force an open battle, if only in the courts. Meantime the so-called popular culture, broadcast in its thousands and millions, swamps the intellect and feeling of the Americans.

Yet we must also say that the censorship is lax because both artists and public are failing in the ritual. The artists do not stir up what is dormant nor initiate what is unheard of; the public does not demand it, but pays its money for trivial fare. Nobody means business, so there is nothing to censor. The stage has become "mere entertainment": the attempt to delight an audience without being either true enough or new enough to instruct it—for instruction involves both truth and novelty. Such "delight" is not very moving. But contrariwise, new truth is passionately moving, disturbing, exhilarating.

In general, where censorship is strict, we will find that passions and ideas are serious business. In the middle ages, even abstract propositions were censored. Under the Tudor autocracy, such a play as *Richard II* was censored because of the deposition scene. Under the Russian autocracy of the 19th century, nearly any writer you might name was in exile, jail, or hiding, for thinking as such was dangerous to the regime. In Western Europe and America during the 19th century, there was a stringent censorship to protect bourgeois morals.

At present, *are* there censorable plays which do not get to the point of censorship because of society's defenses-in-depth? Naturally, apart from the work of myself and my friends—which may not be worth producing for other reasons—I have no way of knowing. My guess is that the defenses-in-depth exist within the artists, too, so, by and large, the plays do not get written. First, there is the simple reflex: if a play will not be noticed so as to get audiences, there is no use in producing it; if there's no use in producing it, there's no use writing it; and if there's no use writing it, you *can't* write it, and you don't warm to it. (Presumably all this would be remedied by changing the middle-man, by lowering costs, and by using other methods of public information than the New York critics.)

Secondly, in our American democracy, we all suffer from a gentleman's-agreement that is theatrically disastrous. Consider the fact that our President cannot frame an English sentence, that his career as head of a great university was dismally hilarious, and his wife is a lush apt to engender embarrassing moments. *Dwight Eisenhower at Columbia* is a title to arouse Aristophanes, and in the 18th century Ike would have been richly mauled. But our satirists on the stage and TV avoid the subject, even though it would be legal. Therefore there is no great comedy, for if you dare not mock the pink elephant looming in the foreground, you can't mock anything. Instead, our satirical comedy consists of isolated gags that do not add up to a big explosion.

(But satire is an essential of democracy. In our democracy there is no personal risk for the leaders—they either get the job or they don't, and they won't starve. How can we expect them to be men? Instead, they are front figures for other interests. At the other extreme, in the USSR as in Tudor England, a man risks his head when he risks his opinion, and this is politically disastrous, for it prevents the continuity of the opposition. Surely we can hit on a mean, where a man is protected in his right to stand for what he stands for, and yet takes the risks of his personal engagement.)

Let me here mention a tiny item of censorship that seems to me to be peculiarly American. Last year the little town of Hicksville banned the showing of four ancient one-reel comedies of Chaplin, made around 1915, because his present known communist leanings would rouse community resentment. The case is remarkable, it is censorship of the person, of his having existed, rather than of the work. When the Irish archbishop effectually banned Joyce in Dublin last spring, it was for the morals. When the Russians silenced Pasternak, it was for the thoughts and attitudes. But we ban the person. This is indeed the America of the Organization Man, who must not be a man at all.

But perhaps the most important inner clog to the creation of works that go beyond accepted ideas and mere entertainment, and would therefore be liable to censorship, is a kind of artistic despair. In many of its ways, our society is so radically absurd and yet so physically huge and deeply entrenched, that an artist despairs of the power of reasonable words or the inspiration of the spirit to effect any change. Most oppressive, of course, is the atmosphere of war and the bombs that we have breathed now for half a century. This poison is intolerable, absolutely meaningless in any humane terms, and getting worse. Nevertheless, I do not recall in recent years a single play (and hardly a novel) that tries to cope with anything so monstrous. Is not this absence remarkable? If I may speak as an artist myself: let me say that some of us seem internally to have quite simply given up on these people, their insane war, their governments and foolish laws, and inane standards of living: all that is not worth addressing, it is not interesting. We therefore pose and probe our problems in more modest ways, and on themes, that seem to *us* alive. Maybe we are wise to behave so; certainly we shall not be censored, for avoidance is not censorable. But the situation is frightening: just as the young men who should be socially ambitious are delinquent and stick with their gangs, so the artists are delinquent; and for the same reason.

V.

Let me conclude with a word about pornography on the stage at present.

As facts or ideas, the expression of what is sexually and morally unconventional is fairly untrammeled, and increasingly and healthily so. Thanks to the trevails of Flaubert, Ibsen, Zola, Wedekind, Joyce, and our Dreiser and O'Neill, the problems of adolescent sexuality, of illegitimate children, of homosexuality, and adultery can now be fairly frankly treated. Even the use of matter-of-fact language and words of one syllable is no longer out of the question, although such words as "fuck" or "cunt" that an author might use to preserve the Anglo-Saxon texture of his speech and affirm the corresponding blunt attitude still do present a difficulty for performers confronting their audience, as if they were breaking a mild taboo.

When we come to moving the audience's feelings, however, the situation is less satisfactory. Even in our burlesques, there is little of the springtime ritual. There is nowhere a simple acceptance of the bawdy and pornographic as a legitimate aim of theatre.

Instead, our "serious" stage devotes itself to representing neurotic masturbation-fantasies (genre of Tennessee Williams). I say neurotic because the plays, unlike proper masturbation-fantasies which are frankly pornographic and lead to heightened excitement, tend rather to proceed in guilt and end in self-punishment; they are sado-masochistic. This ensures their popularity, for they express the sexual troubles of our unhappy generations; people feel that they are "understood," though in fact nothing is understood. In the end the plays do not come off; they are certainly not censorable.

The "comic" stage presents stimulating entertainment—let us take a hit French revue, *La Plume de Ma Tante,* as typical; this consists in repeating a Peeping Tom sketch in a variety of forms; that is, imitating on the stage what the audience is doing in their seats. There is no confrontation of stage and audience, no theatrical tension, because A is not watching B doing anything imitable; but there is the sharing of an erotic subject-matter. *La Plume de Ma Tante* has, however, one sketch that has theatrical life and comments on all the others. In this, "Classical Ballet," the Prince (mimed by Pierre Olaf) throws open his cloak in order to dance and discovers in his tights a genital basket just a wee bit more prominent than that usually displayed by the boys of the ballet. He becomes self-conscious and then, for five delicious minutes, mimes the acute embarrassment of a man who feels that his crotch is being stared at: haughty dignity, nonchalance, studied unconcern, wild suspiciousness, anger, panic, withdrawal. The scene is excellent because it hilariously emphasizes the truth, the actual situation of the actor of that kind and the audience he confronts; it moves us by instructing us. In the ancient comedy, of course, such embarrassment would not end in withdrawal but by breaking through into exhibition, and the mime would produce us a phallus as big as a bologna sausage.

The artist sets before us, and we attend to, what is lifelike, true, recognizable, like ourselves. But all this is set in motion again, in play in the medium, with freedom and imagination, and according to the laws of poetic justice. Then we are moved: what is out there becomes actual to us here and now, sensory and alive.

If, however, the true and recognizable is what is usually kept out of mind or behavior; or what is crucially important to us in a time of decision; or what touches our bodies; or what is new and surprising—then our notion of artistic excitement is likely passionately to break the bounds of just watching. And then there is the problem of censorship.

This essay was presented as a lecture in the Living Theatre series, "Creative Theatre: Lectures in the Form of Inquiry," on April 4, 1959. It has never been printed. Goodman and the Living Theatre were close all through the Fifties, and Julian Beck and Judith Malina produced several of his plays.

Obsessed by Theatre

I.

Artaud's little book on the theatre is by a man in love and banking everything on his love. He wills this love to give a meaning to life and he wills by this love to counterattack in the society where he is desperate. What he says is often wrong-headed and he often contradicts himself, but he also sees and says important truths with bright simplicity. "I will do what I have dreamed or I will do nothing"—naturally, this comes to doing very little; yet since his death the passion of his dream has moved and conquered theatre people. "He was the only one of our time who understood the nature and greatness of theatre," they say of this confused little book (I am quoting Julian Beck). Now if here for a few paragraphs I try to distinguish the true and false voices of this explosion, it is not to diminish the idol of the theatre people; his passion is more important than sound sense; but it is to help simplify their discussions, in order that that passion can be more effectual.

Everywhere Artaud betrays the attitudes and prejudices of a puritan, self-depriving and with a nausea for ordinary food. I should guess that he clung precariously to his sanity by warding off fantasies of cannibalism and other things he thought depraved. When the theatre broke through this shell and provided him a real excitement, he inevitably thought of it as totally destructive and hellish; it had raped him. The theatre, he says, is "the exteriorization of a depth of latent cruelty by means of which all the perverse possibilities of the mind are localized."

He is wearing blinders. He does not seem to conceive of the more ordinary neurotic or simply unhappy man to whom the magic of the work of art is its impossible perfection, its promise of paradise. And for the happy there is no art: "Where simplicity and order reign, there can be no theatre."

So he famously derives the theatre from the last stages of the Plague, when "the dregs of the population, immunized by their frenzied greed, pillage the riches they know will serve no purpose or profit. At that moment the theatre is born, i.e., an immediate gratuitousness provoking acts without use or profit." He goes on to quote St. Augustine's horror of the theatre's poison. And he ends with a rhapsody on Ford's *Whore,* whose content seems to him to be the plague itself. All this is brilliantly told, with good oral savagery; it may be only a partial view of theatre, but it is a hot one that could give birth to fine works.

II.

Alas! as he thinks it, he becomes frightened of his love, and he beings to reiterate a tediously moralistic theory of illusion and catharsis, false in itself and in direct contradiction to the best things he has to say elsewhere. The action, he reiterates, is only on the stage, it is "virtual" not actual, it develops an illusory world like alchemy; its aim is to "drain abscesses collectively." He seems to think that this symbolic action is the primitive theatre magic, but the very point of the primitive magic is that it is not virtual, it makes the grass grow and the sun come back; the primitive is not afraid of the forces he unleashes.

Artaud's theory of draining the abscesses seems to look like the Greek view of catharsis, but there is a crucial difference: for when it had purged the passions the Greek play restored its audience to a pretty good community, further strengthened by the religious rite that the play also was, that sowed the corn with the dismembered limbs. But Artaud's play would purge the audience of such vital vices as they have and let them down into the very world from which there is no escape but the asylum. Just so, Artaud is beguiled by the wonderful combination in the Balinese theatre of objective and accurate complexity with trance and indeed witchcraft; but he astonishingly does not see that this is possible because it rises in and still rests in the village, its everyday way of life, and its gamelan. Artaud makes the fantastic remark that the Balinese dances "victoriously demonstrate the absolute preponderance of the *metteur en scene*"—there is a delusion of grandeur indeed!

Artaud betrays little humor, but his view of comedy brings him to the same dilemma, the fear of total destruction. Comedy, he says, is "the essential liberation, the destruction of all reality in the mind." No, *not* all. Comedy deflates the sense precisely so that the underlying lubricity and malice may bubble to the surface. Artaud always thinks the bottom will drop out and that through the theatre one is "confronted with the absolute." But it is not the absolute but always a risky next moment that is very real.

But let us start again on a positive tack, and see where Artaud is strong. Artaud is great when he insists that theatre, like any art, is an action in the sense of a physical cause; it is not a mirroring or portrayal that can be absorbed by the spectator and interpreted according to his own predilections. It is not a fantasy. He rightly compares it to psychoanalysis: "I propose to bring back into theatre the elementary magical idea, taken up by psychoanalysis, which consists in effecting the patient's cure by *making* him assume the apparent and exterior attitudes." Let me say this my own way: the moment of communication we are after is not that in which a structure of symbols passes from the system in one head to the system in another, when people "understand one another" and "learn something." The semanticists, the language-reformers, the mathematicians of feedback do not give us what we are after; the interesting moment is when one is physiologically touched and one's system is deranged and must reform to cope with the surprise. This Artaud wants to say and does say.

III.

It is in the context of theatre as effectual action that Artaud comes to his celebrated assault on literary plays, his refusal to use text to direct from. It is not that he means to attack speech as such, for he understands perfectly that speech is a physical action, it has intonation, it is continuous with outcries and natural signals. He wants, he says beautifully, "to manipulate speech like a solid object, one which overturns and disturbs things, in the air first of all." And his remarks on breathing in the essay on Affective Athleticism are solid gold; for the breathing of anger or some other affect has far more theatrical value than the verbalizing or confabulation about it, which can certainly profitably be diminished.

But there is an aspect of the action of speech that he quite neglects and that makes his attack far too sweeping. Words have inter-personal effect, they get under the skin, and not only by their tone but especially by their syntax and style: the mood, voice and person of sentences, the coordination and subordination of clauses. The personalities of men are largely their speech habits, and in the drama of personalities the thing-language that Artaud is after is not sufficient; we need text, but a text not of ideas and thoughts, but of syntactical relations. Artaud polemically condemns Racine as literary, but he surely knew that Racine's theatre did not depend on the content of those speeches, but on the clash of personalities in them, and especially on the *coup de théâtre* of the sudden entrances and the carefully prepared big scenes. *Coup de théâtre* is theatre as action. If the old slow preparation makes us impatient, the fault may be ours.

Artaud neglects these obvious things because he has, I am afraid, one basically wrong idea: he says that the art of theatre aims at utilizing a space and the things in the space; and therefore he makes quite absolute claims for the *mise en scène.* But this is too general; for the theatre-relation is that some one looks at and is affected by, not a space with things and sounds, but persons behaving in their places. Theatre is actors acting on us. So the chief thing is neither interpreting the text nor the *mise en scène,* but the blocking-and-timing (conceived as one space-time solid): it is the directedness of the points of view, the confrontation of personalities, the on-going process of the plot. Artaud was misled, perhaps by his experience of cinema, where the one who makes the montage, the so-called "editor," is paramount, for what we experience is the flow of pictures. But for the blocking-and-timing of theatre we need, as is traditional, the collaboration of three: the actor, the director, and the dramatic poet.

Goodman's review of his friend M.C. Richards' translation of Antonin Artaud's *The Theatre and Its Double* is especially interesting in the light of his and Artaud's sometimes overlapping, sometimes antithetical influences on the Living Theatre. It first appeared in *The Nation* (November 29, 1958).

New Theatre and the Unions

I want to discuss a mistaken policy of certain theatre craft-unions, and suggest a remedy. The matter has an importance in itself, because in recent years there has been a growth in the new theatre "off Broadway" that may, if it is encouraged, come to some real living theatre. The union policy has been a discouragement—almost as bad as the unavailability of real-estate—and it has been attacked with the usual jeering debater's points by the tribe unsympathetic to unionism as such. But especially I want to discuss this question because it is, *in parvo,* a remarkably apt case of what is becoming the chief problem of our contemporary culture: how to live and breathe creatively in a society whose technology and organizations unavoidably make for conformity.

Without mentioning names, let me tell the story concretely in a case where I happen to know the facts. Here is a company devoted to new theatre that has now for nearly ten years kept at work under arduous conditions, in larger or smaller quarters as it could get or build them by their own and their friends' voluntary labor. The nucleus of the company is a group of theatre-people, actors, musicians, dancers, and writers—some of them of great reputation—who have all of them, for from ten to fifty years, given themselves, often financially unrewarded, to the development of our modern art. They are a constellation comparable, for example, to the fine group that cooperated as the Provincetown Players. Nobody would question that they are devoted to the growth of theatre and not to making money; they try to make enough to sustain themselves.

Now in casting their productions, they want to employ Equity actors. Many of those who voluntarily built the place they now occupy are Equity actors, and naturally, having laid the bricks, they want to act. By and large, professional actors belong to Equity and most of the best actors are professional, so you want to cast them. Now the situation among actors is as follows: (1) About 95% are chronically unemployed. (2) Actors have a kind of hunger, a need, to act. (3) Understanding this, Equity permits its members to work, in certain circumstances, for as little as $40 a week, regarding this figure, I guess, as pretty near the decent subsistence-minimum that a person must have, no matter what his enthusiasm or other satisfaction in the work. When, then, this company sends out a casting-call in the professional journals, there are hundreds of responses from actors eager for any part, hoping to advance their careers by appearing and getting notices, and many of them glad to work in a cultured non-commercial atmosphere on intrinsically more interesting material, where they can learn something. That is, small non-commercial theatres of high standards, and trained professional actors, are mutually useful to one another; and Equity recognizes this obvious fact.

The professional theatre, however, is organized also on the principle that Equity players may not act in a non-union play, a play whose staff is not union. In my opinion this principle is a correct one (for reasons I shall briefly mention in a moment). But unfortunately it works out as follows: When the director of the company goes to the various craft and staff-unions to get a counter-signature to allow Equity players to play, he is told that he must employ 1 union stage-hand at $137 a week, 1 union press-agent at $145, 1 union scene-designer at $40 per day (for at least 3 days); and whenever there is to be a little live music, there must be union musicians at similar figures. All this amounts to a financial burden out of all proportion to the company's other expenses, and to the profits they expect or even hope for; it is quite unfeasible. (The theatre has less than 175 seats; some are kept at $1, so students can come; figure it out.) In the case here, the burden happens to be particularly galling because the director himself is a gifted and well-known scenic-designer; like all other artistic groups, they prefer to couch their press-releases and other public relations in their own style; the work done by stage-hands is what almost everybody connected with a little theatre is skilled at and does with pleasure; and everywhere in integral theatre there is a need for live music, it can never be omitted, and canned music is deathly.

The unions are inflexible in their demands; the company cannot fulfill them. In this impasse there is at once generated enormous heat and idiotic remarks. "If you don't have the money, stay out of the theatre!" says a distinguished functionary of one of the unions; "you're a painter," he says to the director, "why don't you stick to pictures?" On the other side, the Equity actors connected with the company are in a rage and about to tear up their cards. Those who are politically hep point out that organized labor has fallen into the hands of racketeers. And the paranoid demonstrate that there is a conspiracy among the unions, the critics, and the owners of theatre real-estate, to prevent anything new and better from happening.

NECESSITY OF THE UNIONS

Let me insist that the principle of total theatre unionism, including Equity, seems to me to be correct. This is simply because of the nature of the theatre arts and crafts. Our city abounds in people of artistic talent, eager to exercise their separate talents. By disposition such people are free-lances; and the state of serious art in our society is such that, until they make a lot of money, free artists have little status or security and cannot easily maintain their rights and dignity. As a group, then, they are peculiarly subject to be taken advantage of and exploited by producers who can give them any work at all; and when taken advantage of, they act effectually as scabs and lower the standards of honest employment.

That is, it is precisely the intrinsic virtues of the talented, their hunger to work and their solitariness, that make them socially weak and liable to lower social standards. Poor gifted musicians, painters, poets, dancers, and actors are severally weak indeed; by insisting, even inflexibly and intransigently, on their union, one can give them collectively some strength.

What then? The principle of unionism lays an unbearable burden on any new non-commercial company; it works to the disadvantage of Equity actors; and yet the principle itself is a necessary one. Nevertheless, dispassionately considered, the solution of this dilemma is easy. Briefly, if we carefully consider the nature of theatre, we shall see that new theatre in general *cannot* make money and must overcome great obstacles in order to exist; and yet eventually it must in turn become immensely popular and make a lot of money, becoming the exciting novelty in commercial theatre. The process has two steps, and mindful of their own interests the unions must have a dual attitude: positively to foster the new and non-commercial, and to protect their standards in the commercial; and there ought to be a definite rule to mark the passage from the first stage of the process to the second. There is no doubt that it is a vague or clear understanding of this that, in part, had led Equity to its own more flexible policy.

THE NATURE OF NEW THEATRE

Reflect a moment on the following commonplace observations:

(1) The theatre is a fine art for an immediate present public; and it is also a collaboration of many skills. Therefore, theatre requires a large social effort, setting many people in motion, and a certain amount of social capital. (Not necessarily a large capital, compared, say, with architecture, where the very medium is expensive; but an even larger social effort than architecture.)

(2) Radically new theatre, like any new art, cannot expect a mass-popular response, for it presents what is unfamiliar and is even actively resisted as meaningless, perverse, or dangerous. The sign of successful new theatre is that the audience is torn between

fascination and the impulse to walk out in disgust. The anxiety of new theatre is greater than with other new art because theatre demands a response in public, and its medium is exceptionally close to the animal and social behavior of life. The same anxiety, by the way, is felt even more by the players than by public, as any one who has rehearsed new theatre with conventional actors can testify. Therefore, it is *only* from small intensely personally involved groups, and a small public of the life-minded, that we can expect new theatre to emerge.

(3) But conversely, once a new theatrical advance has been made, it is likely to become immensely popular, for it is shared excitement. A new advance in some other art need not become popular in this way, for, although humanly important, it may be specialist and learned; but theatre art is common and simple.

(4) So-called "little theatre" groups, making a great social effort and overcoming great obstacles, from real-estate to interpersonal relations, and with little income to ease the path, are driven by an artistic fatality into the daring and the radically new. They are not dilettantes or amateurs; their aim is to achieve at least the excitement of the big professional entertainment—otherwise, why bother; yet their means are limited. Therefore they explore new ways of handling limited means, to get as much meaning as if they had extensive means; this creates startling effects. Or alternately they make daring simplifications, and this creates startling effects.

Let me sum up these familiar propositions in a formula: The task of new theatre is to find out and invent what must be unpopular and yet will soon be immensely popular; it is in this thorny task that it makes a great social effort against many obstacles. Naturally people are not too attracted by this prospect. Like most of the "off-Broadway" theatre at present, people prefer the easier task of performing modern classics (the new theatre of one or two generations ago); of importing European successes that are exotically safe; or of giving museum-like revivals, more properly the function of university players and dedicated amateurs. All that is off-Broadway and fairly non-commercial, but it is not new theatre. (I do not mean, by the way, that the company I am discussing is a pure model of new theatre, but it is one of the best of a bad lot, and nothing is perfect here below.)

A PROPOSAL TO THE UNIONS

Bearing all this in mind, would not the wise, the statesmanlike, attitude of the unions be for them to say something like this: "New theatre! go to it and we hope you succeed. For if you do, there will be a new kind of immensely popular and paying theatre; and if you don't, there will be only a dying theatre. The policy of Equity, distinguishing a commercial and a non-commercial theatre, is a sound one; but we, of course, are in a different situation from the actors: for our carpenters, electricians, press-agents, musicians, and so forth, there is no psychological necessity to perform in theatres; unemployed in the theatre, they could get other jobs; and we see no reason, therefore, to lower their standards in any way. But as for the actors, directors, and creative artists of scene, word, movement and music, who need the theatre-public to exercise their talents, we shall not stand in their way. On the other hand, as soon as you free artists begin to get into the money, then the situation is entirely different, and we have a right to take our place in the enterprise and exact our fair shares. We have the right because all wealth is social wealth, produced by society as a whole, and it must be apportioned according to the rules that society has come to at the present time, to achieve which we in labor have fought and suffered much. Therefore we shall, by some reasonable rule of thumb, set a figure, perhaps an income-figure, perhaps a profit-ratio, at which we think your free art has entered the cash-nexus, a dividing line, at which the excitingly unpopular is beginning to be the immensely popular; and when any of your enterprises crosses that line, it must be total union. We reserve the right to examine your qualifications and check your books, and so you affiliate with us as your friends and pay a nominal dues."

This, I submit, is the wise, the statesmanlike, attitude that loses nothing for the unions, and that encourages the growth of theatre. It can set a definite rule that fits the real nature of the case, unlike the present abstract "policy" or alternative non-policy of making "exceptions"; of sometimes being intransigent and sometimes shutting the eyes; of acting *de facto* as powerful critics and censors far beyond their competence. Instead, it gives the theatre-crafts a noble and protective role in the growth of the culture of the people.

A NEW RESPONSIBILITY

I said at the outset that this small question contains a great question; without further ado, let me generalize. The case is with us in America that, by and large, vast organizations, of state, capital, production, labor, communications, education, urbanism, etc., etc. have pre-empted the means of life. This is currently inevitable and doubtless in many ways desirable, though not so unquestionably desirable as most people think. (When *everything* is done according to a certain pattern, it is hard to imagine how some other pattern could work at all.) At the same time, it is resulting in a conformity that is by now inane and boring and will soon be dangerous, for nothing revitalizing can occur in an organizational plan and when something occurs outside the plan, it may not have space to grow. All this has become a familiar complaint.

I want to suggest simply that with their power, these organizations have acquired a new, strange, and troublesome responsibility: to limit the exercise of their power more intelligently than they are accustomed to, to stand out of the way in order that there can be a future also for themselves.

Dissent first published this literary/political piece in the fall of 1959; it was later included in the appendix to *Growing Up Absurd*.

A New Deal for the Arts

I.

The recent closing of the Living Theatre in New York for default on rent and taxes reminds us strongly of the plight of such enterprises in our society. It is hard to be decently poor and to venture in a style uniquely one's own. To Europeans this was our most famous advance-guard company, and at home it was at least the most notorious. Yet simple calculation shows that it was unviable both economically and artistically. The maximum number of seats an off-Broadway theater may have, if it is to be allowed to pay the "Equity minimum" subsistence wage-scale, is 299; because of the unavailability of real estate in New York City, the Living Theatre seated about 170. Its weekly budget was $2000, of which half went for the subsistence salaries. Thus, the theater would have had to sell out nearly every night at four dollars a ticket to meet the budget and get enough ahead to mount a new production. (A new production costs eight to ten thousand dollars.)

The ticket price was out of line for an advance-guard theatre. The directors' original intention had been to keep half the seats at one dollar—for students, poor artists, beatniks. Worse, the pressure to have pretty immediate "successes" inevitably undermined the artistic intention, which was to provide new-theatre experiences and present the best available new plays, in order to enliven the torpid mass audience and form a new audience. Since the indifference or disapproval of the incompetent New York reviewers was guaranteed, one had to rely on word of mouth; but this takes months, one could not wait. Hence the temptation was strong to be sensational, or to play voguish modern classics like Brecht—which prevented the formation of a loyal new audience. If by chance there was an eventual selling notice for a play, like the *New Yorker*'s rave for Jack Gelber's *The Connection* or *Life*'s spread for Kenneth H. Brown's *The Brig* (ironically, the theatre went bankrupt when it had one of its modest hits), the audience would consist of tourists and mink coats or week-end Yalees. Worst of all, in order to cash in, it was necessary to keep repeating the successful play long beyond the interest of the directors or performers, and this undermined the original aim, which had been to do repertory. By and large, indeed, the most interesting evenings at the Living Theatre were Mondays, when off-Broadway is dark and the stage was used for irregular perfomances or readings.

The Living Theatre had a non-profit classification and sought foundation support. But somehow, though a couple of the great foundations have rather generously supported several dozen little theatres, no money was forthcoming for this liveliest one. It was rumored that the Living Theatre's connection with the Worldwide General Strike for Peace put the foundations off; Julian Beck and Judith Malina (Mrs. Beck), the directors, were in and out of jail on this issue and civil rights; also the theatre itself was a resort of known pacifists, potheads, poets, and other punks. A representative of a great foundation complained to me that the Living Theatre was not financially scrupulous; he was apparently surprised that it would pay its actors before its bills, or that artists would write bouncing checks to save the opening of a play that they had prepared for six weeks. Or maybe the lack of foundation support was just "Mathematical," as Kafka said of the mischances of this world.[1]

Needless to say, many have proposed the usual liberal solution

[1] Since this was written, the Living Theatre has been able to reopen in a new location—thanks to the proprietor of the Midway Theatre, who has donated the premises rent-free for the rest of the season.

for such problems: paste the problem on the wall and throw government money at it. Since the arts, like the poor, are worthy and neglected, there must be an Arts Council in Washington and a direct government subsidy. But I doubt that the Congress of the United States would be a more sophisticated or catholic patron than the foundations; we can hardly expect it—under the patriotic fire of Walter Winchell or Senator Eastland—to support potheads, Communists, pacifists, homosexuals, or "nigger-lovers." At best, officially sponsored theatre would be sanitary, uplifting, or mass-entertaining; it could not be corrosive, political, or intimately vulgar and popular. Artistically, official support of *new* theatre would in all probability be positively damaging. Especially under an administration with a certain moneyed cultivation like that of Governor Rockefeller in New York or that of the late President in Washington, the tendency is to support glamorous show-cases like Lincoln Center or the proposed National Arts Center, that create in the public mind the illusion that this kind of thing, with its Big Names, is the norm of living art. Every such enterprise makes it all the harder for the genuine, the modest, the outlandish, to live and breathe. (The case of the WPA theatre of the 30's was different—and I shall return to it.)

In my opinion, there *is* an important role for direct government subsidy of theatre, namely to underwrite standard classical repertory, of drama and opera, say up to 1940, a generation ago. This is simply part of the education of the young and is no different from supporting museums or schools. Such repertory provides good training for directors and performers, it gives interim employment, it can do little damage to new art, and indeed, by raising the general level of the audience, it indirectly and powerfully helps new art.

II.

How, then, can our society support necessary new ventures like the Living Theatre? Let me make a proposal springing from an analysis of the structure of our contemporary institutions. The essence of our modern problem, as I see it, is that the growth of mass communications, the centralized decision-making in the big media, their heavy capitalization, their concentration by continual mergers, the inflated costs for overhead, public relations, and highly organized labor, and the vast common-denominator audiences sought and created for the efficient and profitable use of such investments—these things pre-empt the field and make it impossible for small, new, or dissenting enterprises to get a start and a fair hearing. Even more important, the big mass media interlock in their financing and echo one another in content and style; with one tale to tell, they swamp and outblare, and they effectually set definite limits to what can "normally" be thought, said, and felt.

It is hardly necessary to demonstrate all this, but I will just mention the usual headings. (1) "News" is what is selected as newsworthy by a few men in a few news-services; three almost identical broadcasting networks abstract from the same; and then it is abridged for the *Junior Scholastic.* Even for this news only 60 towns in America have competing newspapers (in 1900 there were 600). (2) The publishing houses merge and their editorial choices are increasingly determined by tie-ins with book-clubs, serialization in national magazines, Hollywood, paperback reprints. (3) The Standard of Living, how to live decently, is what is shown in the ads in a few mass-circulation magazines and identically in the TV commercials; and movie-sets of respectable life come from the same factories. (4) The "important" in entertainment is what is slickly produced, elaborately promoted, and reviewed by the right dozen papers and national magazines. (5) Political thought is the platforms of two major parties that agree on crucial issues like the cold war and the expanding economy, and the Congress decides to abrogate equal time for the broadcasting of minority opinions. (6) Public-service communications, e.g., educational TV, are tightly geared to the Establishment universities and the middle-of-the-road school boards.

Now some of this has real advantages, and anyway the whole complex represents one inevitable use of the technology and the national economy. Yet this whole complex is gravely problematical, so problematical, indeed, that it faces us with a constitutional crisis. For in such an atmosphere of uniform thought and feeling, and potential brainwashing, it is impossible to carry on a free, rather than a mass, democracy. The attempt to regulate the media by government agencies, like the FCC, does not work; and the outcry of censorship, though entirely hypocritical, is correct in principle. (As the case is, however, the broadcasters themselves censor: they blacklist and they wipe out controversial tapes, even though they have exclusive licenses to the channels.) It has been proposed that the government itself be used to counteract the debasing media—for instance by establishing a TV channel like the BBC or by publishing an official edition of classical American literature. This is wise if it refers to transmitting authoritative information and standard fare, but it is entirely irrelevant to the problem of helping the controversial and the new, for of course the government is part of the consensus that makes it hard for the controversial to gain an entry.

Therefore, to meet this constitutional and cultural crisis, let us look for a new principle in the structure of the danger itself, and let us suggest that *it is the responsibility of the mass media themselves to support, freed from their own direction, a countervailing force of independent and dissenting media of all kinds.* Since it is mainly the size of the common-denominator audience that constitutes the peril, conceive of a graduated tax on the audience size—of the broadcasting stations and networks, big newspapers and chains, national magazines, Hollywood, the publishing combinations—*to create a fund earmarked exclusively for the support of countervailing small media:* local newspapers, little theatres and magazines, unaffiliated broadcasters. The tax would be collected by local, state, or federal government as relevant; we shall discuss the administration of the fund below. The constitutional virtue of this proposal is that it provides for the danger—of brainwashing—to generate its own antidote. Moreover, it is altogether in the spirit of the American principle of built-in checks and balances, applied to technical and economic conditions where free competition cannot work, where, indeed, there is semi-monopolistic private government paralleling or interlocked with public government.

As an immediate simple application of the principle to cases like the Living Theatre, consider the following: Instead of repealing, as seems to be intended, the war-time excise tax on theatre and movie-tickets, earmark it for a fund to support little theatre and experimental movies. This would in effect mean that the mass and commercial media, which provide almost all of the take, would be supporting the local, the off-beat, and the dissenting. I propose this immediate remedy because obviously it is easier and less painful to shift the use of an existing tax than to levy a new tax. But of course for the general application to the media—TV, press, advertising, and publishing—the rate (10 per cent per ticket) is vastly out of line. The aim of the proposed tax is *not* punitive or sumptuary or emergency, but simply to provide a steady modest revenue. We are concerned with audiences numbering often in the millions; an audience of 100,000 would surely be exempt. (Incidentally, there is now before the House of Commons a graduated tax on the advertising of the big broadcasting networks, but this seems to be partly punitive.)

III.

To whom should support be given? I am strongly opposed to having Arts Councils or boards of experts as selectors. With the best will in the world, such experts are cliquish. Many of the best artists—as it turns out—are lacking in the character and techniques to win prestigious attention; they do not attend the right parties. Much that is excellent is overlooked or misunderstood; it sometimes wins its way unaided and is then crowned with help when it no longer needs any. The thorny problem is to choose professionally—by definition, amateurs do not need "support"—and yet as randomly as the spirit bloweth.

I have discussed the matter with Mr. and Mrs. Beck of the Living Theatre and we agree that the following methods are tolerable: (1) A popular principle: to divide the country into regions and give aid to any group that can get a certain number of thousand petitions for itself. (2) A professional principle: to support any group that can win a certain number of dozen peers as sponsors—namely directors, playwrights, professors of literature or the humanities, critics, film-makers, etc. These need not like what the group does, but must be willing to testify that the enterprise is worthwhile and should be helped to exist. (3) Naturally, any group that does exist in the present conditions has proved its right to exist, and should be supported if necessary. (4) Also, the old policy of the WPA theatre has much to recommend it: this was essentially to support everybody unemployed in the field; when there were enough to form a group of any kind in a locality, the group was underwritten and the individuals employed.

Support by the fund should be very modest, of no interest to people in show business; and it should be tailored just to help a worthwhile group get a hearing and either try to win its way commercially or fulfill a non-profit artistic function. Consider an interesting case: Recently there was a little group at the Judson Memorial Church (rent free) that passed a hat for the scenery, lights, and ads; in my opinion, this group provided the best evenings of theatre in New York City in the past two years. It seems to me extremely important for the dignity of such artists that they be paid Equity minimum instead of nothing; and of course, without such pay no such group can persist. Or another kind of case: the fund might underwrite a quarterly circulation of 10,000 copies for a little magazine for, say, three years, by which time it ought to have won its own audience or go out of business. Another case (to show how little money is involved): WBAI in New York City, certainly one of the best radio stations in the country, operates for $38 an hour (its salaries are low; most of its programming is volunteer). It has no ads. More than 60 per cent of its $250,000 budget comes from its 12,000 subscribers, at $12 each. Yet the station might lapse because of the difficulty of getting gifts for the remainder. In this case, a subsidy of as little as $5 an hour would put everyone at ease.

Obviously, the fund must entail no responsibility either by or to the government. That is, it could subsidize activities politically extremist in any direction, morally questionable, or aesthetically outrageous, subject only to ordinary law.[2]

[2] The chief Congressional champion of aid to the arts is Rep. John Lindsay (R., N.Y.), and he too is earnestly insisting that a "Federal grant-in-aid program operated by a government-appointed panel should not dictate cultural tastes in America." I am quoting from his speech in the House of April 4, 1963. But affectionate as I am toward Rep. Lindsay, his proposal is a poor one, namely, that the goverment match funds with individual and foundation gifts above a certain minimum: "this would compel the organization to prove itself with the public before

IV.

Allow me a philosophical refection on the political principle that I am here using.

The justified suspicion of growing governmental power and the efforts to curtail it, usually leave the field open to the operation of private powers that are almost as formidable and yet are less subject to popular check. The exercise and not very tender mercy of private powers are in turn met by the regulatory agencies and welfare policies of public power. Sometimes these public and private powers glower at each other and clinch, and then there is no social movement at all. At other times there are unholy combinations between them, like the military-industrial, government-universities, urban renewal-real estate promoter, politics-Madison Avenue complexes, that pre-empt the field, expand unchecked, ride roughshod, and exclude any independent, thrifty, or honest enterprise. Certainly, to avoid these dilemmas, we must encourage a different concept and practice of countervailing force. In important ways, public and private power do not usefully countervail each other when both are centralized and powerful, for the independent, the new, the dissenting are destroyed by both.

In a viable constitution, every excess of power should structurally generate its own antidote. That is, power entails a responsibility to counteract the dangers it creates—though proper exercise of the power should not thereby be impeded. In my opinion, resort to this kind of built-in countervalence is often far more direct and safer than relying on the intervention of the governmental juggernaut, whose bureaucracy, politicking, and policing are sometimes worse than the disease (if one is a "conservative") or are at best

---

receiving government aid." If Mr. Lindsay thinks that rich individuals or foundations represent the public, or the artistic public, he does not know the facts of life. He moves too much in the right circles. "As a safeguard," he says, "a ceiling—say, 3 percent of the total appropriation—should be set on the amount for any single organization. This would prevent a single group from capturing the whole Federal kitty." (But it would mean that 35 prestigious groups *would* capture it.) Lindsay entirely misses the point of how to support poverty-stricken authentic art. But at least he is trying. The problem is not perfectly soluble. For instance, there are probably some kinds of art which must *not* be helped, in order to remain themselves.

necessary evils (if one is a "liberal"). The proposal of a fund provided by the mass media to support independent media and prevent brainwashing is an example of built-in countervalence. (I think the same line of reasoning could be usefully pursued in another case: to make those who profit by automation more directly responsible to provide or educate for other employment or useful leisure.)

First published in *Commentary* (January 1964).

Art of the Theatre

I.

It's a play when some do and others watch. What you needn't watch—for instance, what you can read—is not part of a play, and too much of it kills a play. But if it needs more than watching, like answering back or coming to the rescue, putting it in a play kills *it*.

Artaud, on the contrary, wants the play to come out and do something *to* the watchers, like a blow or like psychotherapy. But I'd rather have the watchers moved by what *they* are doing—watching—I guess I'm not confident enough in myself to wish to act on other people, no less to do it. I want accomplices.

Many in the audience are therefore not moved by what I show, for they *want* to be acted on and manipulated. (I like it too, within limits.) They don't want to be accomplices, or at least they don't want to be *my* accomplices.

Some playwrights seem to want to persuade the audience to something, but this is trivial. (Artaud's violence is not trivial.) What is interesting or true does not persuade, it moves us from within ourselves like a loved thing, **κινεὶ ὣς ἐρούμενον.**

But the common notion is that theatre is illusion, that what is on the stage is not real and the audience must believe that it is real. Myself, I never experience this illusion, though I observe that many people do. What is on the stage is real, it is what is watched. If it tries to deceive, it is flimsy. Generally speaking, the more illusory it is, the less interesting to watch.

For instance, I don't like to watch actors, but I am enchanted by watching people act. Actors can't act, only people can act. And when the chips are down and you ask these actors to act out an animal scream, or to let go and tremble, or not to act but just to walk across, they can't imitate anything real or do anything real, for they *are* only actors, theatre-dummies.

It is said that Quintero had to cut the crucial middle scene from *The Balcony* because the actors couldn't stop being "professional."

II.

Art moves and teaches—I agree with the neoclassical formula. But art does not move in order to teach, like sugar-coating a pill or seducing. To be moved, watching, *is* to be taught. "Thou art That."

Indeed, with some of us it works the other way: you can move me *if* you teach me. New true sentences open me up to feeling, but feeling never taught me much. (I suppose this is the definition of an intellectual.)

When I make my characters say sentences that I believe to be true, my purpose is not to convince or persuade anybody to anything. It is just that, for me, true sentences have a solid ring, a neat surface, a reliable dynamic, a definite rest. I like their esthetic surface.

I never make a character say something that I know better or could refute, although often I do not *agree* with what he is saying. My characters are at least as shrewd as I am. Otherwise I'd brief them before putting them in the play! But some playwrights run a character through a whole play in order to have him find out what the author knew in the beginning. Why bother?

III.

To my taste, the most interesting thing to watch is the everyday, just as it is.

Diaghilev used to say, "Astonish us," but I have no feeling to do this. Anyway, only an impresario would think of it. My experience is that artists find it hard enough just to make sense.

Again, many people like to watch virtuosity, skill beyond adequacy, but I prefer to see amateurs making do, and I am most moved—alas, rarely (I think of Nazimova and Merce Cunningham)—by masterly adequacy. Just as, in love and friendship, I most love the one who *comes across.*

Again, there is something finely theatrical in "camping," exaggerating and decorating something real, as Shakespere usually does and Genet always does; but this too puts me off. I am too puritanical either to like entertainment or to entertain.

When possible, I avoid metaphor, though metaphor may be, as Aristotle says, the essence of poetry. (I don't think it is.) The symbolic I positively detest. Almost always I say it pretty literally as I mean it.

Naturally, it is not always possible to put the real thing on a little stage without artificial helps. But I prefer the audience to *see* the wires by which she is flying. After all, she can't really fly except with wires.

The first plays I ever made were children spinning tops while others play box-ball; a man marking on the wall, inning by inning, the score of a game; a bagpiper, in his outlandish dress, rounding a bend in the park. The pieces were perhaps like what they now call "happenings." But the "happenings" I have seen seem to aim to be eccentric or to shock, whereas I collected ordinary things.

It's not clear to me why I should want to repeat on the stage what the audience can't help but see on the street. Yet why not, if it's pleasant? But I disapprove of retelling remediable evils, which we ought to cope with on the street rather than celebrate on the stage.

IV.

Here are examples from the plays in this volume. In *Jonah*, the people sit and have a cup of coffee. (Incidentally they talk and advance the plot, but I don't really care about that.) In *The Young*

Disciple, a man is showing a boy how to make a fire with a burning glass, and the tinder ignites with a poof; that's all the scene is supposed to mean. The logic lesson in *Faustina* is similar. Evidently I think that teaching and learning are immensely worth watching, and more important than what is taught or learnt.

The bit of psychotherapy in *Faustina,* when the Emperor plays tiger and the Gladiator realizes that he turns the sword—such a moment is fascinating to me in the clinic or on the stage. And it's good, though pretty unbearable, to watch somebody tremble uncontrolledly, as the young man does in *The Young Disciple.* When he has quieted he can say the poem.

My typical scene of theatre is in the short story "A Ceremonial," where they drop a curtain and disclose a "quiet tree with its heart-shaped leaves and a few cream-colored blossoms in the sunlight."

> This tree, at first, excited only wonder, almost disappointment; until it became apparent, just by looking at it, that the utmost tiny leaves and petals were expressive, organs, of the invisible roots. Such as it was, this tree in seclusion had come to its present being, behind a fence. Here it was, this linden tree, when the maroon curtain dropped.

In the story I let this continue for "three or four minutes," which would be vastly too long on the stage.

V.

No costumes!—unless it is just the costume, or wearing the costume, that is the deed, the thing to watch. The gorgeous robe of the dancer in the fourth part of a Noh play is itself the *coup de théâtre*; just as in Racine the expected character herself appears and Nero says, "*Dieux!*"

Above all, the stage-set must not sit there, distracting attention to itself for half an hour and an hour. Either let it unobtrusively withdraw or make it function, adjust to the action. Julian Beck of The Living Theatre understands this. He learned it, I think, from Cocteau and the Chinese property man; but not from Piscator, whose sets whirl so much that you can't see anything else—they devour you like a German director.

But there is the problem of a curtain, no curtain, the rise and fall of the curtain; of separate spaces of actors and audience, or bridging those spaces; and turning on and off the houselights or the stagelights—all these things are intrinsic in the essence of a play, some people doing and other people watching. They must *never* be taken for granted and treated conventionally.

In principle, a different kind of play requires entirely remodeling the theatre architecture. The palace front, the apron, the proscenium, the round are different kinds of *plot*.

At present the Pirandellian lack-of-a-curtain, that indicates the ambiguity between what is real and what is appearance, has become an indiscriminate fad. It was inevitable. Advance-guard theatres, that indeed have a little more community reality than the audience, turn on the audience and say, "*You* are living in an illusion!" and so they omit the curtain.

But the curtain has nothing to do with illusion, but with watching. "Look! this is worth watching. Now don't look, go home."

When, at the end of *The Young Disciple,* the bawling boy falls and half tears down the curtain, I guess I mean to say that I do not find the state of things acceptable (finished), but that you are to go home anyway.

At the end of *Faustina,* however, the actress steps through the absent fourth wall into your space, no longer an actress, and then I don't know what would occur. In fact, the lady was an actress and refused to step out of the play, so the production fell to pieces. Well, that too is something that occurs.

VI.

Acting is worth watching. Simply, that a person gestures and speaks according to some preconceived notion or formula, obedient to the unseen.

It is curious. If I notice such obedient, pre-planned, alienated behavior going on in a factory or army or where one person has fallen under another's influence, I find it abominable and I work to free the slaves. If I see a person repeating a neurotic compulsion or behaving in a rehearsed way rather than spontaneously, I am depressed. Yet if it is a parade, a dance routine or acting, either on stage or off, there is an intimation of something divine, as the folk in the Bible keep re-enacting God's plan.

My plays—*Jonah, Cain and Abel, The Family of Abraham*—are full of such ritualism; most likely this is why I retell Bible stories. In Noh plays the climax is nothing but a repetition of a past event. This is why I imitate them, and also because they finally become speechless.

Just so I find chorál speaking astounding and I write it in whenever I get the chance. All speaking the same words! Yet when this very thing happens in politics or schooling, I am contemptuous.

When it's possible, I fall into regular meters—but I don't like to subject my characters to *my* rhythms, they must come to the meter themselves. It's madly exciting when in classical plays the half-verses of the angry actors unerringly fill out the trimeters. It is because they have rebelliously broken the trimeters that we know that they are angry and that *we* feel angry.

Alas! the fact that I find this kind of ritual repetition so fascinating must indicate some important characteristic of myself, probably psychotic. But it is a psychosis so regressed that there is no cure for it, in fallen man. Perhaps it is what it is to be an artist.

If the obedient ritual is man-imposed or compulsory, we must resist at all costs. If it is free and playful, it is divine and thrilling, and for it we sacrifice our happiness in this world.

VII.

At present they are downgrading speech on the stage, and this is justified to the extent that speech is "about" something rather than *is*. For whatever is on the stage must primarily be a presence, a force, an act. (Though, of course, discursive speech is a useful auxiliary to what is going on, like any other stage property.)

But speech *is* a presence, a force, an act. It is outcries and music; quarreling and persuasion; the characteristically human acts of reciting and narrating. Especially with poets it is hard to say what is the thing and what is "about" the thing. They seem to make a love poem in order to seduce, and then we find that they have fallen in love only to make the poem!

Miming is being exaggerated today. It diminishes force and presence to make people communicate like the deaf and dumb. But miming is powerful where people are *indeed* speechless—with rage, embarrassment, astonishment, deep peace.

I myself have been most concerned to study the relation of the specific act, speaking, with the other kinds of acts. The reader will find that the crucial theatrical problem in *Faustina* is: when can characters speak and when is it absurd or sick for them to speak? My coup, I think, is to make it plausible for the Gladiator to speak rationally even when he is helpless and about to have his throat cut. In *The Return from Moriah*, when Isaac is totally bawling because mama died, he also turns it off as one switches off a light, and asks interestedly, "Is this what people do?"

To my taste, it is a weakness in Shakespere that his people blab away *in extremis,* granting that it is sometimes splendid babbling. One is almost reminded of the hilarious scene in *Medea* when, within, she is killing the screaming children and the Chorus outside keeps chattering, "Oh dear, something is amiss."

The best and, I think, complete study is in Noh: the narrative explanatory speech, the song as you go, the quarrel and persuasion speech, the gradual lyrical meters and expressive speech, incoherence, silence; reflectiveness and the return to our ordinary condition, including speech. Obviously it is this model that I am continually consulting in the dances in *The Young Disciple* and *Faustina* and in all my plays that have dances, and most of my plays have dances.

VIII.

I make plays in a long tradtion of men making plays. In my opinion, even if there were no such tradition, we would make plays. For instance, I see that at one year old my little daughter puts on shows for us to watch. But certainly I make my kind of plays because of Racine, Irish vaudeville, morality plays and Noh plays.

My disposition as a poet is not to innovate unless I have to.

Simply, if Calderon, Goethe or Synge has hit on a style or scene that, with renovation, fits me, I like to wear the hand-me-down. It's economical—it's a way to organize a lot of experience—for nobody can organize big chunks of experience from scratch. There is an accumulative history of poetry just as of science. Those who are not learned, or scorn learning, merely borrow right and left in confusion.

On the other hand, if I need something unconventional for something new, I improvise it with a good conscience and no thought whatever of being unconventional.

No doubt I have a style of my own. Any poet who works a lot and with integrity will inevitably gradually accumulate his own vocabulary; modify to his purposes the devices that work for him; and even begin to streamline his own early manner. But I have very little awareness of what my style is, and critics have not bothered to tell me.

Frankly, I am at sea when they talk about "modern" or "contemporary." The authors who move me *all* seem to me to be contemporaries—they speak to me directly—though most of them are unfortunately dead. I fancy, too, that some of them approve of me.

But it is not with impunity that I write in the Western tradition as if it were alive. (It probably isn't, but I don't have any other.) For instance, during the thick of the Civil Rights struggle, a little group revived my *Hagar and Ishmael* at a church; but the critic of the *Village Voice* complained about their mounting such a musty old story.

Naturally, as a playwright slighted by the public, I make many spiteful and lonely remarks. But I would be less than candid if I did not say that when I am actually making a play or a poem, I am absorbed and have plenty of company.

IX.

So! These are my cheerful remarks about the Art of the Theatre; and the fact is that I am fifty-three years old and I have no life in the theatre. *What* am I talking about?

When we talk about the *medium* of an art, we are like Adam in paradise, for the media of art are practical, like the materials to hand in paradise. Except in architecture, media are made of cheap stuff, mud and rock and noise and light and people moving and blabbing.

But when it comes to *practicing* an art, then we are engaged as we unfortunately *are.* The plays in this volume were written in 1941, 1948, 1955, and I am writing this preface in 1964.

To me, writing for the theatre is the only kind of writing that is not lonely, and if I had my choice I would write mainly for the theatre. But I have not had the choice because the theatre has not been willing to have me.

To write for the theatre means to belong to a company for whose known actors I make appropriate speeches that ring beforehand in my ears; at whose rehearsals I swiftly tailor a scene so that they may all shine at their best. I do not have such a company. And the company does not have me.

And the audience and I have fallen into a ridiculous misunderstanding. The ordinary scenes I like are so ordinary that the ordinary audience couldn't care less. And on the other hand, if I use sentences that I think are very true, then they don't know what I'm batting about. I think that I am wrestling with an important problem of my country, and the audience is not aware that such a problem even exists.

Needless to say, the dilemma works in reverse. Most of their plays and all of their movies bore *me.* But I ought to have a better understanding with my neighbors in order to write plays for them.

Yet the audience is right, it is always right, for nobody has asked the playwright to come forward. *Are* the Americans right? It would be strange, since they are so wrong about everything else.

And suppose that *I* am "right"—what good does that do? A play is today and the audience is today.

X.

My considered judgment is this:

Some of my hang-ups are only my own and there is no reason why other people should be interested. For instance, they have their psychosexual delusions and I have mine. That's too bad for me—for I'm in the minority.

But there are other things I have to offer which, if I may say so, are too important and simple for present-day Americans to take seriously. And that's too bad for them as well as me. After a while—after I am good and dead—I stoically count on being a statue in the park.

Worse than either of these difficulties, however, is the miserable *technical* dilemma of trying to say simply, in simple scenes, what probably requires considerable *prior* explanation; and especially to an audience that no longer carefully listens to plain English and that mistakes a glossy format for the art of the theatre. Then I myself fall into every kind of trap of bad theatre. Sometimes I explain too much. Sometimes I impatiently throw the audience the bone of a prosy little essay that kills theatre. Sometimes I forthrightly stay with my own perception and beautifully move myself, my friends and nobody else.

Let me make a comparison with the two living playwrights whom I esteem, Beckett and Genet. These artists deal powerfully with important matters that, it seems to me, *are* available to live Americans at present, for they deal with extremes. But I am out of touch just because I am engaged in a more middle-ground; I have not given up on fatherhood, community, vocation, rational politics, benevolent nature, the culture of the Western world. I suppose there are two opposite reasons for my perseverance or delusion in these things: I think more soundly than those other playwrights, and I am too cowardly to risk as much as they do.

XI.

It is in this unhappy plight that I make a pathetic pitch for community in all my books, and also in these plays. I refuse to concede that our community does not exist. Presumably, if it existed, it would solve my dilemma.

But I'm certainly not getting any younger.

This was the preface to *Three Plays* (1965).

Blue and slow through the gathering violence
the juke-box is turning disks of silence.
That smash hit You Can Hear a Pin Drop
and Hush-a-Bye Baby on the Treetop.
A man with neither will nor whim
has bought a nickel of Interim
and the sweat is standing on Richard's neck
at the quiet Moment After the Wreck.
The eyes I seek with gaze intent
are listening to Embarrassment.
On the house the patrons hear
Time's Winged Chariot Hurrying Near
but few The Silence of the Seas
Beyond the Farthest Hebrides.
The needle grinding in a groove
is spinning out Don't Make a Move
and every one's humming at the San Remote
the popular It Has You By the Throat.

III

MODERN LITERATURE

Advance-Guard Writing in America: 1900-1950

Se quoque principibus permixtum agnovit Achivis,
Eoasque acies et nigri Memnonis arma.
—Virgil, *Aeneid*

I.

An artist does not know that he is advance-guard, he must be told so or learn it from the reaction of the audience. *All* original composition—classical, standard, or advance-guard—occurs at the limits of the artist's knowledge, feeling, and technique. Being a spontaneous act, it risks, supported by what one has already grown up to, something unknown. The action of all art accepts an inner problem and concentrates on a sensuous medium. Obviously if one has an *inner* problem, one does not know beforehand the coming solution of it; and concentrating on the medium, one is surprised beyond oneself. Art-working is always just beyond what one can control, and the thing "does not turn out the way I planned." (In the best cases it is *just* beyond what one can control, and one has indeed learned to control the previous adventures up to that point, has acquired, as the ancients used to say, the habit of art that now again, in act, is in a present and therefore novel urgency.) Thus, whatever the subsequent social evaluation of a work—it may be quite traditional—to the creative artist as he makes it, it is always new and daring, and he cannot be morally or politically responsible for it. How could he be responsible, if he does not know what it will be? And further, the more powerfully spontaneous the working, the more he himself as a moral being will resist and disclaim it; a poet says what he does not wish to hear said. (Of course he is responsible artistically, to let the coming figure form with the utmost clarity and unity.)

For the most part, the products of such countless acts of artistic daring have been acceptable works, not far-fetched at all, but animating or perhaps troubling. The irresponsible adventure turns out to be another proof of the common sensibility of mankind. The "inner problem" accepted with reluctance by the artist is after all some universal problem that now, thanks to the responsible art-working, has new words, a new image, a new facet. The audience accepts the work as genuine art. Sometimes, to be sure, if the effort has been extremely profound or subtle, or the problem has been new or idiosyncratic, the product does not find a ready or large audience. Nevertheless, it is accepted as genuine, but perhaps "not for us," being too deep, decadent, or so forth.

But now there are also these other works that are indignantly rejected and called not genuine art, but insult, outrage, *blague, fumiste,* willfully incomprehensible, or more favorably, with our childlike American docility, experimental. And what is puzzling is that they are not isolated pieces, but some artists persistently produce such pieces, and there are whole schools of such "not-genuine" artists! What to make of this? In this case, the feeling of the audience is sound—it is always sound—there *is* insult, willful incomprehensibility, experiment; and yet the judgment of the audience is wrong—it is often wrong—for this is genuine art.

This seems to be a contradiction. For we defined the art-act as accepting the inner problem and concentrating on the sensuous medium; yet now we speak of a rhetorical attitude toward the audience, e.g., insult, and of an experimental handling of the medium, as still being genuine art. The explanation of this apparent contradiction gives us the nature of advance-guard and tells us its recent history and present direction.

Within the advance-guard artist, the norms of the audience, of "society," exist as an introjected, unassimilated mass; it is their irk that is his special inner problem. It is his spontaneous attempt to vomit up or destroy and assimilate this irksome material that results in products that, as if willfully, offend, insult, or seek to disintegrate these same social norms. ("Introjects" are other people's standards that one is forced to identify with as one's own.) All creative work occurs at the limits of knowledge and feeling, and the limits here are the risky attack on the unassimilated, and perhaps unassimilable, as if to say, "Until I get rid of this, I cannot breathe."

We may distinguish immature and mature advance-guard. If the undigested mass is indeed digestible to those of experience in society as a whole, then the advance-guard offense is not taken as offensive, but as brash rebelliousness which, if the offender is youthful, is considered hopeful and charming. But if the undigested norms are generally really indigestible, though socially accepted—that is, if the standards of society in fact make everybody unhappy—then the offense is insulting and "dangerous," and is met with social sanctions. Having caused offense and being punished, the artist first knows that he is an advance-guard artist. Secondarily, then, he may as a moral and political act appoint himself to this thankless career and engage programmatically in the offense originally suggested by his creative work. Such a vocation of advance-guard is not only insulting to the audience but a threat to established institutions.

Consider as an example how France has been, up to now, the native home of *avant-garde*. (I presume that the military term comes from the disgusted generation of the Restoration after the Congress of Vienna.) A stable land-rooted bourgeois morality, an official "Cartesian" culture of peculiar uniformity, and a sentimental Catholicism were calculated to impress themselves on a growing mind as the norms of all sense, reason, and charm; one could not help swallowing them whole, without criticism. But therefore, if one had any intellect and spirit, the subsequent inner nausea was bound to be early and total: bohemian, antisyntactical, and social-revolutionary. But therefore again, the French *avant-garde* always turns out to be very "Cartesian," with proofs and manifestoes all in order, and a keenness to proselytize and make uniform in the latest cut. The French way of being a very great writer with world-wide influence has usually been to invent a new method or broach a new subject; writers of other lands have had to write great books.

Whenever the mores are outmoded, anti-instinctual, or otherwise counter to the developing powers of intelligent and sensitive persons, there will be advance-guard work. Yet, to repeat, advance-guard is not a direct attack on the inhibiting mores, except secondarily. On the contrary, it is precisely the intelligent and sensitive who, when they were precocious children, most absorbed and identified themselves with the accepted culture, with whatever value it had. It is only afterward that the nausea and anger set in, inwardly, unknown, pervading the creative work. If advance-guard were a direct attack, it would not be genuine art at all, and it would not ultimately become part of the stream of tradition; but as the response to an inner irk, it corrodes and pulverizes with creative work, it suffers the conflict through, and it prepares the integrated normal style of the next generation. Again, if advance-guard were a direct attack, the response of the audience would be angry defense and counterattack, instead of the peculiar "outrage" which indicates that the members of the audience have the same inner difficulty but are unwilling to recognize it; they are somehow "threatened."

Thus, if we want to retain the concept of "alienation"—e.g., to speak of artists "alienated" in having no social status and having dissident values—we must be careful not to mean simply that there are rival warring camps between society and the artists—a sociological absurdity. But we must mean (1) that society is "alienated" from itself, from its own natural life and growth, and its persons are estranged from one another; but most members of society do not feel their estrangement; (2) the artists, however, feel it and regard themselves as estranged; and (3) society responds to them not with snobbery and incomprehension, as to foreigners speaking a foreign tongue, but with outrage, embarrassment, and ridicule, as to an inner threat. "Alienation" is primarily self-estrangement—this is, by the way, how Marx used the term—and the advance-guard tries to disgorge the alien culture.

Advance-guard periods are unsuited for the creation of perfect works "exemplary to future generations," as Kant would have said. The unassimilated culture prevents the all-round development of the artist, it prevents him from achieving a habit, and he spends too much energy in merely destroying what is not nourishing. Advance-guard works tend to be impatient, fragmentary, ill tempered, capricious. (Whether they are not thereby nearer to the human truth is another question.) Perfect works are not fostered, either, by periods of "stability," whatever that means. They are fostered by periods of expansion, for these nourish the ongoing adventurous creative powers. If a period of expansion is followed, as Matthew Arnold said, by a period of criticism that standardizes and popularizes the achievement, then, to the creative spirit, such a period is stagnant and will be followed by a disgusted advance-guard. The only healthy stability is an even growth.

II. NATURALISM

I have set down these academic remarks in order to be able to say something about the American advance-guard from 1900 to 1950. During that period there was a deepening cultural crisis, and a deepening literary response, going from an advance-guard of subject matter to an advance-guard of form to an advance-guard questioning the worth of the art itself and its relation to the audience. By the end of the period, we can see shaping the lineaments of our present writing. (May I ask the reader's indulgence if, in treating so broad a subject, I speak in terms of decades and mention "styles" and symbolical historical landmarks, instead of individual works and real molecular changes.)

The advance-guard of the beginning of the century introduced offensive subject matter, in novels about the seamy side of accepted morals, economics, and politics. Contemporary with these were direct muckraking exposés of the same subjects—so that advance-guard and reform politics seem very close, but their approach is quite different. In an important sense this advance-guard succeeded, for, just as previously on the Continent, the factual account of sexuality and sexual misery, and poverty, exploitation, and graft has become standard literary content. That is, what was achieved was the destruction not of the institutions but of the hypocrisy and reticence concealing them.

What gave to these early works a peculiar passion, quite absent from later stories about this same subject matter, was the passionless and precise reportage, the naturalism of the telling. And contrast these creative works with the muckraking journalism (and novels) of the same period. The journalism was indignant with the infamy. If the novels, apparently having the same aim, had adopted the same tone, they would not have outraged, though they might have been banned as dangerous. For the muckraking tone accepts the same moral attitude as the audience's, saying, "We attack what we consider evil, and this is an evil overlooked by you." If the artists had said this, they would have been worthy moral opponents. Instead they offered the detailed image without evaluation and without the selection and arrangement that, according to the taste of that time, implied evaluation. What was the meaning of this naturalism?

The avowed aim of naturalism is familiar; to attack and reform by letting the facts speak for themselves, without style, as if to say, "There you see our world, damn it!" But of course naturalism is a highly artificial style. Its lack of selectivity is an icy selection from the common speech which abounds in evaluation. Naturalism is an icily hostile withdrawal from the audience; it will not share in their moral sense; it says in effect, "There is the world you have made for me, damn you. *I* abjure it. Put up with it if you can." This is an inward reaction to an introjected moral attitude, as if to say, "To be a person at all, to make evaluations, is to be like you, a hypocrite."

We may see the creative, self-curative use of such a response to an inward pathological situation if we bear in mind that naturalism is fundamentally a detailed stream of consciousness without evaluation. This is the means used in psychotherapy to recover a traumatic image; the detail provides associations, the suspension of evaluation prevents censorship. Now, it seems to me that, far from poets' having a conception of the abuse and attacking it, it was only by their method of naturalism that they were able to call up the scene of horror and overcome the hypocrisy in themselves. Secondarily they added on a program of reforms.

We, who have a different acquaintance with the kind of subject matter they broached, might find it hard to conceive their difficulty. Yet, to give a great example, it is hard otherwise to understand how so masterly an intellect as Ibsen could have hamstrung himself with his theatrical naturalism. It was *only* so, by making the scene real before his eyes, that he could believe the magnitude of his dissent from the mores.

In a Mallarmé, the anamnestic naturalism is pure and wonderfully total; he does nothing but notice and he notices, in principle, everything. Our novelists were more limited in what they noticed; and, more important, they at once confused their noticing with muckracking and moralizing. The reason for this confusion was that they made the assumption that a mere institutional change—sexual reform, socialism, etc.—would heal the inner irk, or, what is the same thing, create a society they could breathe in. Hypocrisy overcome, the truth out, everything good would follow. This assumption, which makes them seem close to the political reformers, was an illusion. The irk that brought them to a naturalistic handling of the subject matter could not be healed by merely altering the subject matter. However it was, even before the First World War, the advance-guard was already shifting away from the offensive subject matter to the offensive form and style, a much bolder effort to a much deeper dismay.

The audience reacted to the naturalistic offense with the specific sanction of censorship, on moral and political grounds. Yet this was obviously not a police measure of defense, to protect the children, but a reaction of outraged sensibility. There had to be spectacular trials to affirm the faith of the audience in itself. If there had been an objective danger, e.g., warmblooded pornography, the sales would have been wider and the police measures more quiet. The naturalistic scenes were socially harmless, the sales were small; but they were insulting, outrageous. That is, the audience felt perfectly well the icy hostility and froze, and rationalized the outrage as best it could.

III. THE REVOLUTION OF THE WORD

The 'twenties, the aftermath of the war, was the golden age of advance-guard, and this kind of art was almost able to transform itself into integrated art. From that time on, the advance-guard has been international. It was an advance-guard of method, form, style.

A golden flowering of advance-guard is a paradox, but the paradox was in the times. People were stunned by the surprising barbarism of the First World War—how far we have come since then! The troubles in Western society, it was clear, were far deeper than could be cured by the intelligent practical reforms of its most social-minded physicians. History had gone beyond the revelations of the naturalists, and an artist could feel that if mankind dared so much, he could justifiably dare much further to solace his inner distress. At the same time, it was a period of hope and buoyancy. There was a general conviction that peace would be permanent—the nations outlawed war as "an instrument of national policy." The world became spectacularly international, and there was, after a short interim of reconstruction, an enormous economic production, scientific innovation, and technological application. It was a period of expansion, calculated, if it lasted, to produce modern masterpieces.

To understand the golden age of advance-guard, we must bear in mind the contrary facets: (1) the profound dismay at the breakdown of "civilization," and the inner disbelief in the previous programs of institutional change; the need to corrode the inner irk with a more thorough destructiveness; but (2) the buoyant hope and material prosperity, and the half-willingness of people in the victorious countries to venture a change—just as the vanquished were driven into a change. The first factor explains the advance-guard; but if we omit the second, we cannot understand the quantity and depth of the experiments, and the almost popularity achieved by the bizarre products. For advance-guard always rouses anxiety, but in conditions of expansion it is possible to tolerate the anxiety and allow the creative excitement to approach an integrated solution.

The advance-guard of the 'twenties was a concentrated attack on the formal attitudes of literature, the vocabulary, syntax, genre, method of narration, judgment of what is real and what is fantasy; everything, in short, that goes by the name Revolution of the Word. This revolution had begun earlier on the Continent, but now all forces joined and came to a climax and a self-consciousness. What is its meaning as a creative response to introjected norms?

The syntax and style of speech convey character, the so-called system of defenses and projections. Consider, as an analogy, the Rorschach test. In this test of "personality-type," the most important indices are not the content of what is seen in the blots, but the form of perception, e.g., whether color is seen or overlooked or there is shock at seeing color; whether color is seen free or in delineated areas; whether large details, small details, the whole are seen, and in what order; whether what is seen is on the periphery, in the center, down the middle line, always on the surface or sometimes in depth; whether the white spaces are seen as well as the inked ones; whether movement is projected, and so forth. It is these formal differences that project the type of feeling, the "personality." And so in literature. It is the formal actions, the structure, texture, diction, syntax, mood and tense, trope and image, concreteness and abstraction, directness and periphrasis, and so forth, that deeply communicate the character. To experiment with these things is the same as saying, "Not only do I disagree with you, but I am trying to make myself a different kind of person from what you made me, or what you are." Considered genetically, it is going back to the time one first learned to speak and be a "person" at all. At the same time there is still the attempt to communicate by using the accepted machinery of communication, orthography, books, publication, as if to say, "Won't you become a different person? Try to understand me if I speak this new way."

Just as the previous naturalism was a kind of recovery of the traumatic scene, the Revolution of the Word was what later came to be called "character analysis." The parallel nonartistic movement of the time was medical psychoanalysis and progressive education, attempts to heal not institutions but personality disorders. And the secondary politics of the advance-guard tended to be the "permanent revolution," the expression of a worsening crisis in a period of expansion.

The insulted audience ridiculed the artists and charged them with bad faith and willful incomprehensibility. This meant that the audience felt that it was being not so much hostilely assaulted as disregarded. And this was indeed a correct feeling, for the artists were not regarding the audience as "persons"; it was the personality they shared with the audience that they were trying to disgorge. Alternately, the audience called the artists irresponsible children and felt that they themselves were bewildered children, and this was indeed the ambiguous nature of the case, for both were experimenting in learning to speak.

Unlike the grimness of naturalism, the Revolution of the Word was playful, euphoric, libidinous, dreamy, barbaric, exotic. To attack the institutions and ideology as the naturalists did, was to be infected with the guilt and punishment of instinct that had first resulted in the introjections. But to "pierce the character-armor" as did the Revolution of the Word, was to release pent-up drives. In principle such release is accompanied by intense anxiety. Nevertheless, as long as the period was economically booming and politically hopeful, it was possible to achieve wide toleration of this anxiety, especially by regarding the innovations as sophisticated (extremely "grown-up") and superficial (not "meant"). However it was, just as the standard literature of the 'twenties and 'thirties accepted the earlier advance-guard subject matter, so the 'forties consolidated much of the Revolution of the Word, especially in poetry, and the 'fifties have played with it still more freely, using it as a lingua franca for dissidents.

IV. SOCIAL SOLIDARITY AND "IRRESPONSIBILITY"

With the Depression and the looming of another war after all, the buoyancy vanished and the general anxiety became intolerable. In such circumstances, surface defenses are tightened and no inward adventure is possible. At once the advance-guard seemed to vanish from the scene. In the opinion of most critics twenty years later, it vanished for good and my history has no further relevance. But I shall show how in this continually deepening anxiety there has always been an advance-guard reaction, begun in the 'thirties and running afoul, and now—at the end of the 'fifties and into the 'sixties—beginning to affirm itself strongly, though not yet hitting on the right course. (If indeed the advance-guard had vanished in the 'thirties, we should have to reconcile ourselves to having no genuine literature at all—as seems to have been almost the case for two decades!—for it is impossible to *accept* the norms of anxiety, a clinging to security, and still create something.) But let us proceed step by step.

In the 'thirties, the Revolution of the Word began to be called "irresponsible"; and its obscurity, which had previously been shared in as entertaining and challenging, was rebuffed as Ivory Tower and of no consequence. To the artist this meant that now indeed he had no social role and he could call himself "alienated" or estranged, with what profound effect we must soon discuss. There was, however, an immediate reaction in the tightened circumstances of the anxious surface.

This was the literary manner of so-called "Socialist Realism"; for the most part it was merely reactive and without creative meaning, but if we carefully anatomize it, we can see that it contained something new. (1) The socialist-realists fully accepted the early-century program of reform, and with a deadly monotony reiterated the naturalistic subject matter. (2) They couched it in a banal dramatic manner, full of standard evaluation, that made the old-fashioned message quite reactionary in effect (as Trotsky, for instance, was quick to point out). (3) With this, however, there was a new sentiment: the solidarity of the artist and audience; that art is a solidary action; the artist is not physically or culturally isolated from the audience, though he may purposely attack it. This sentiment, which still has vitality, went back to such different advance-guard roots as Dada, the theater of participation, and the Bauhaus. But (4) instead of finding a creative expression of solidarity, the sentiment at once degenerated into opportunistic propagandizing of party formulas, first of the minority then of the majority.

The valuable new sentiment of solidarity—which we expect to appear in a crisis of fear, and which did appear—was debauched by the miserable pretense of the art, which renounced the artistic responsibility of inventing something new. It was a pretense, for whereas the naturalists had suffered an illusion, that their society, which they accepted at face value, could be reformed, these artists did not inwardly believe it at all. And outwardly, as it turned out, they eventually migrated to Hollywood or advertising or government service, there to endure ulcers, Stalinism, sinusitis, and such other complaints as come from aggressing against oneself and laying the blame elsewhere. The charge of "irresponsibility" was a projection; it was they who were irresponsible to their own creative selves. And finally, when the Second World War broke out, it was the official spokesmen who used the word "irresponsible" and took up the call for social solidarity.

Let us review the situation as it passed into the 'forties and toward our present day. On the one hand the norms that a young person perforce introjected were now extraordinarily senseless and unnatural—a routine technology geared to war, a muffled and guilty science, a standard of living measured by commodities, a commercial art, a moral "freedom" without personal contact: it is not necessary to go over this familiar ground. Then we should have expected the activity of artists of the late 'forties and the 'fifties to have been more than ever advance-guard. But the general anxiety and their own anxiety were such that there could be no audience recognition of any product of inward daring, if anyone could dare to produce it. (I think some of us continued.) What an artist would say spontaneously would now seem hopelessly irrelevant, likely even to himself, and he would have no means to communicate it, nor perhaps even incentive. This was a clinch. The tendency of some artists would therefore be to fall silent, to accept their estrangement—and this seems to have been the case. (Instead of writers, we got the epidemic "revivals" of Melville, Henry James, F. Scott Fitzgerald, etc., even Nathanael West. This is too pathetic to dwell on.)

But of course the silence—the "silence, cunning, and exile"—is a physiological impossibility. Creative vitality simply expresses itself. The advance-guard action, then, took the form of concern neither with the subject matter nor the method, but with the use, and attitude, of being an artist at all. In the language of the accompanying philosophy, this was the "existential" problem for the artist: not what to think nor what kind of person to be, but how to persist at all, being an artist. (As usual, the advance-guard problem has slightly anticipated the current general problem: how to persist, being alive.) The literary revival—in America it was a discovery—of Kierkegaard made sense, for the age was again very like the Congress of Vienna.

The problem we faced—how to be an artist at all—was different from that blithely tackled by Dada in the early 'twenties, for at that time, in buoyant circumstances, it was possible to decide that art was pointless and to take revenge with irksome acts of anti-art; but in straitened circumstances one cannot allow himself such luxuries.

V. AFTERMATH OF WORLD WAR II

One would not call the aftermath of World War II buoyant and confident of progress. Probably one should not even call it an age of anxiety, as Auden did. Rather, from the clinical point of view, we have seen the phenomena of shell shock, a clinging to adjustment and security of whatever quality, and a complete inability to bear anxiety of any kind, to avoid panic and collapse. For instance, in 1948 I lectured on Kafka to a college audience composed of ex-soldiers. This audience unanimously insisted, with frantic emphasis, that Kafka was a freak whose psychotic vision had no relevance to anything in "real life." Where there was such insecurity as this, as not to allow even the possibility that all might not be well, we could expect little creativity of any kind.

Correspondingly, for at least a decade after the war, the literary atmosphere for the reception of any deep-springing art, advance-guard or otherwise, was miserable. Certainly the literary magazines were never so poor in forty years in this country. In the interest of a secure academism, including an academism of the 'twenties, they printed nothing that could arrest attention (although some things that were fine and solid). Perhaps no new things were submitted. At least the impression was created among young persons, who get incentive from such periodicals, that nothing astonishing was being done and nothing could be done. One felt, indeed, that this was the intention of the editors.

It is the thesis of this essay that advance-guard is only one species of art and is, in principle, not the best art. Yet it comes to be the case that where the literary climate is unfavorable to the destructive elan of advance-guard, there is little genuine creation of any kind. The best period is one in which every new work destroys the convention of its predecessors, yet, advancing to just the next step—the result of an achieved habit and assimilated tradition—it carries its audience along. The possible, and usual, period is one in which the integrated artist employs productively the destructive work of an immediately previous advance-guard—and this is common within an artist's own career, his own youth being his advance-guard. But where the advance-guard dies, the language dies.

VI. NEW DIRECTIONS APPARENT AROUND 1950

Now consider, as we have been doing, the introjection of the norm of shell shock, equivalent to clinging to security. Genetically this takes us very far back, to the infantile fright of total abandonment. The average person feels it as a lack of concern and a passionless going about one's business. (Hannah Arendt has well described this indifference and excessive busyness in the spectacularly guilty and shell-shocked Germans post Hitler; but the ill has been much more universal than she seems to be aware of.) A self-aware person feels the introjected shell shock as his estrangement. The advance-guard artist, however, unwilling to accept this introject as his own, revives from the fright of total abandonment, begins to wail and reach out—to the audience, for a new possibility. He becomes first a cry baby, then an unwanted lover. That is, to persist at all, being an artist, the advance-guard artist tries to create a new relation of artist and audience. The art of the artist is to invent ways needfully to throw himself on the mercy of the audience. By this aggression he saves the audience from its numb shock. To explore this, let me describe three advance-guard tendencies apparent around 1950, and that still are working themselves out. Let me call them the direction of Genet, of Cocteau, and of a writer who proceeds from a remark of Goethe.

(1) Conscious of estrangement, serious standard writers, in their self-portraits and choice of protagonists, have more and more been describing marginal personalities—criminals, perverts, drunkards, underground people—or persons in extreme situations that make them "existent" rather than universal. Their artist no longer considers himself an accuser or advocate, an explorer or a radical, but as one beyond justification, as if to say, "Your judgment is indifferent to me." In plot, the melodrama of the sensational popular writer is now the sober content of the standard writer. The meaning of it is, clearly, the assertion of the repressed vitality in despite of the lifeless or shell-shocked norms, but it accepts the normal judgment and fails to create a new valuation. This is, of course, to give up the possibility of humane synthesis altogether. Therefore, one kind of possible advance-guard action would be to assert the marginal as the central and to prove its justification, thereby demolishing the norm.

This is what Genet has tried. In a famous speech on delinquency, he explains himself succinctly. He says that as a man he has little sense of moral values, they do not concern him. His only contact with life is the act of writing. But when he comes to write about the law-abiding or the esteemed, his pen stands still, his images do not soar, the rhythm limps. As soon as he takes up his criminal types, however, he has plenty to say, his style warms up. Therefore he must, he does, present the criminals in a more heroic light; and therefore he has come to understand that they are the superior people. Genet uses the action of art, that is, his existential role, to find vital norms, necessarily offensive and alone, for him, justifying. (Naturally, they are the norms of his own inner problem, which seems to be a conflict between accepted castration and flaming exhibition. It is interesting to contrast this with the almost similar conflict of our Hemingway, accepted castration and stoical endurance, which has made him the classical writer for the serious young men of the Organized system.)

Genet pursues his prophetic role with a careful calculation of his audience. E.g., in *Les Pompes Funèbres* the chief person is at once introduced as honorably glorying in a masochistic idolatry for a Nazi soldier occupying Paris, with whom he happily performs what the audience will consider the ugliest possible sexual act. Yet Genet manages to keep confronting the reader with such fullness of affection and of desire to be accepted—and profound thought and remarkable language—that finally the normal valuation is indeed swept away, and there is confusion, grief, and contact.

As the shock of the infantile fright of total abandonment relaxes, the first creative act is to wail, "Help! I am abandoned." This puts it up to the listener. What the method says is this, "I have proved we are *both* lost; therefore, instead of your clinging to a false adjustment, let us cling together." The audience must respond to it by trying to annihilate the outcry, as if it had not been heard, or to prevent others from hearing it. The snub that the audience administers is not, then, one of outrage but of embarrassment before a poor relation, as in the joke where the millionaire tells his butler, "This beggar is breaking my heart, throw him out!"

(2) To an academic critic, the later plays and films of Jean Cocteau seem to bear out the rule mentioned above, that an artist's

early work is the advance-guard that is consolidated in his later, standard work. The only problem would be how from such a likely sowing comes such poor fruit. But Cocteau himself has explained his intentions otherwise, and has given his theory of the right direction for advance-guard. We must attend to it, for during this century he has been the advance-guard's chief philosopher.

It is inadmissible, he says in *Foyer des Artistes,* for the poet to allow his audience to be lost to commercial entertainers. The heat of the audience is necessary for the persistence of the artist. Now, what attracts the audience is, in principle, corn, vulgar sentiment. Therefore the artist must at present, with all the honor and truth of genuine art, convey this corn, and so Cocteau has chosen to do. That is, what seems to be curiously stupid standard work is really a daring advance-guard effort to answer the crucial question of how to unmake alienation.

Nevertheless, the works are stupid. "Precisely," the creator might say; "they were not made for you." Perhaps the problem is too hard and the poet is suffering an illusion and undergoing a kind of (profitable) martyrdom. The corn in these works of Cocteau is still alien to himself, he cannot energize it with feeling. To put it bluntly, it is not yet low enough to be quite uncorrupted. (Let me say that in the film *Orphée* Cocteau fortunately gave up the noble program for which he was unprepared, and again made something fine. Plastically and poetically, *Orphée* is by no means equal to *Le Sang d'un Poète* of which it is the sequel, but the grim honor with which it treats its subject—what it means to be the youth-thieving poet now "stinking with money and success"—makes a very poignant work.)

Anyone who chooses this direction, of seducing the audience, must without talking down find a level of subject matter so elementary that he and the audience really share it in common, meaning by it the same thing. There must be such common subject matter, for all of us walk on the ground, breathe, and so forth, and these things are common and not subject to the corruption of self-alienation. Somewhere between this level and the level of shell shock and commercialized sentiment, there must be a border line of subject matter felt by the artist and not quite devitalized in the audience. It is here that the advance-guard must operate. (Is this the intention of the *Nouvelle Vague*?)

As the shock of total abandonment relaxes, the infant reaches out with coaxing and flattery, or with teasing and being nasty, saying, "How can I please you? How can I annoy you?" Trying still to please at too adult a level, Cocteau merely flatters the normal audience without offense. The sanction of the audience against him is to make him a commercial success and appoint him to the French Academy. The advance-guard artist must invent something more direct and childish that will win a smile or a slap of which all are at once ashamed.

(3) But finally, the essential aim of our advance-guard must be the physical re-establishment of community. This is to solve the crisis of alienation in the simple way. If the persons are estranged from one another, from themselves, and from their artist, he takes the initiative precisely by putting his arms around them and drawing them together. In literary terms this means: to write for them about them personally, and so break the roles and format they are huddled in. It makes no difference what the genre is, whether praise or satire or description, or whether the style is subtle or obscure, for anyone will pay concentrated attention to a work in which he in his own name is a character. Yet such personal writing can occur only in a small community of acquaintances, where everybody knows everybody and understands what is at stake; in our estranged society it is just this intimate community that is lacking. Of course it is lacking! Then give up the ambitious notion of public artist. The advance-guard action is to create such community, starting where one happens to be. The community comes to exist by having its culture; the artist makes this culture.

We know that for various moral and political reasons such movements toward community have occurred widely, sporadically, since the war. But no such community can flourish on moral, economic, or political grounds alone, for—whatever its personal satisfactions—its humane integration cannot compete with the great society, however empty it is. As a friend to all such places, I would urge them to attach to themselves their artists and give them free rein, even at the risk of the *disruptive* influence of these artists.

As soon as the intimate community does exist—whether geographically or not is not essential—and the artist writes for it about it, the advance-guard at once becomes a genre of the highest integrated art, namely Occasional poetry, the poetry celebrating weddings, commencements, and local heroes. "Occasional poetry," said Goethe, "is the highest kind"—for it gives real and detailed subject matter, it is closest in effect on the audience, and it poses the enormous problem of being plausible to the actuality and yet creatively imagining something unlooked-for.

An aim, one might almost say the chief aim, of art is to heighten the everyday, to bathe the world in such a light of imagination and criticism that the persons who are living in it without meaning or feeling find that it is meaningful and feelingful to live.

Obviously, if the artist, responsible to his art, commits himself to his bold insight and genuine feeling, and brings it home inevitably to the audience by writing man to man *ad hominem,* the Occasional poetry that he creates is not likely to flatter or comfort. Rather it will always have the following ambiguous effect: on the one hand it is clearly an act of love, embarrassing in its directness, for to give one's creative attention to anyone is a gesture of love; on the other hand, given the estrangement of the aliens from one another, it will always seem, and be, an act of hostility, an invasion of privacy, a forcing of unwanted attention. To the extent, then, that this advance-guard does not succeed in welding a community secure enough to bear criticism and anxiety—and how can a single-handed poet accomplish much?—the sanction against it is absolute and terrible: exclusion from the circle of frightened acquaintances.

VII. THE NATURE, ADVANTAGES AND DISADVANTAGES OF ADVANCE-GUARD

Let me now review the course of this argument as a whole. We started by distinguishing advance-guard as a species of genuine art with a social-psychological differentia: that an important part of the advance-guard artist's problem is the destruction of introjected social norms. This explains the peculiar offense of advance-guard to the audience. Tracing the history of the introjected norms and the advance-guard response, we singled out three phases: the phase of the rejection of institutions by naturalistic revelation and hostile withdrawal of feeling; the phase of the rejection of normal personality by experiments on the language (character analysis), arousing anxiety; and the phase of the rejection of self-alienated adjustment by direct contact with the audience, rousing the embarrassments of offered but unwanted love.

We are now in a position to restate more fundamentally the difference between integrated art and advance-guard. What, psychologically, is the meaning of an art that has a sociological differentia in its definition?

We must say, with Otto Rank, that the action of art asserts immortality against the loss, waste, and death in oneself and the world; and the artist appoints himself to the re-creation—who else will do it? Now the advance-guard artist is essentially concerned with the immortal perfection of the particular society of which he is a member, whereas the more integrated artist, taking his environment for granted, is concerned with the universal human condition as embodied in his own problem.

Here too the usual opinion is just the contrary of the truth. The advance-guard artist is considered as going his own irresponsible way, heedless of his audience, and dwelling in an ivory tower. But the truth is that his relation to his audience is his essential plastic medium—so that he is often careless with the material medium; he is excessively socially responsible. On the other hand, the usual sentiment is accurate, for standard art the audience can take or leave, but advance-guard is irritating and obtrusive and cannot be disregarded; it is a loving and hostile aggression on the audience.

In the little history we have sketched, we have seemed to come full circle: in the beginning it was the naturalistic artist who withdrew, in the end it is the shell-shocked audience that withdraws. But throughout there is the attractive and repulsive tampering of the artist and audience with one another. In order to reconstitute a better society within himself, the artist destroys the existing society. This is naturally resisted. Yet people, too, are dissatisfied with their state and want to get on, and they are fascinated by any new direction.

What are the peculiar advantages and disadvantages of advance-guard? We have pointed out that an advance-guard artist must divert energy to an internal problem that is not constructively his own, but only destructively; this hinders an ease of flow and symmetry of form. (In the best cases the parts of an inner conflict are fused and transformed in the coming solution; in advance-guard there are some elements that are merely to be attacked and destroyed.) On the other hand, there is no doubt that his concern for the destruction and reconstruction of society as a part of his art draws on powerful energies of its own, unavailable to standard artists: both the memory of a very early time of satisfactory interpersonal peace—an "age of gold"—and the present-day revolutionary ferment. It is impossible for any artist to ignore the problem of social renovation. In the best, expansive period, all the agents of society are engaged in the renovation, and the artist need not particularly concern himself with it, it "takes care of itself"; that is, he need not inquire where he is man, where artist, where citizen. In other ages, the advance-guard artist "wastes himself" on the social problem—it is his vocation, for it exists within him; but the standard artist ignores it at the price of losing the glancing brilliance of actual relevance (I do not mean the slick shine of commercial relevance), and he may soon become merely academic.

From the point of view of society, again, it is certainly no advantage to be manipulated "for its own good" by artists, and it is even worse when the aim is to make society into a work of art. Yet there is, in life, an important factor that can be called "the art of life"—concern and distress for the style we live—and in a disintegrated culture like our own, very few are busy with it, and among these is the advance-guard artist. And from the point of view of the artist, again, in a shell-shocked society like ours there is a general estrangement, and the artist is estranged, in the sense especially that he feels helplessly without status. But being more conscious of his estrangement, he is really less estranged than the others, and he is used to inventing means of communication, patterns, irritants, bridges; this is his forte.

An artist feeds on fame. It is only this, to quote Rank again, that alleviates his "guilt of creation" by gaining him accomplices. Here the advance-guard artist is in an ironical situation. More than others, he needs accomplices, not only *post factum,* but as collaborators *in delictu,* in constructing the social art-object in a rebellious atmosphere. Yet his hardly veiled hostility and embarrassing love diminish his chance of personal fame and drive off his collaborators. On the other hand, he is less lonely. He more easily identifies himself, with pain, with the whole social framework; and with hope, with its future in young persons.

In America, as we proceed further into the 'sixties, there seems to be plenty of advance-guard writing again; just as for the previous twenty years there seemed to be none. But these judgments of audiences and critics are pretty illusory: they depend on the degree of the audience's own anxiety. When anxiety is very strong, oblivion is a characteristic sanction of the outraged audience; the advance-guard offense is present, felt, and "annihilated," excluded from the possibility of being real. The artists go underground, and when they reappear they bring with them the underground.

Goodman wrote this elaborate survey and critique during the summer of 1950 while he was teaching (Shakespeare and Creative Writing) at Black Mountain College. It was first published in *Kenyon Review* (Summer 1951); the version printed here is from *Utopian Essays*.

Good Interim Writing: 1954

As we read through anthologies like *The Partisan Reader,* New Directions' *Spearhead,* or the English *The Golden Horizon,* it is gratifying and reassuring to find a large number of perfectly durable pieces of fiction written by my generation. Pieces that have "anthology" written all over them, for they are standard and without serious flaw, and they will be, or already are, at home in collections from all times and places. Of course every one of these works is different, for they are genuine and sound out the individual voices of their authors. If they were not genuine they would not be durable. Yet I think we can by now show a class resemblance in many of the best of them that is distinct from any other literature and makes them stand for a generation as its style. Without mentioning individual pieces, let me explore an important property of that common style.

There is achieved a classical objectivity by maintaining a relativity of points of view, instead of, as in previous classical writing, embodying the cultural norm. (We have no such norm; we have a society of subcultures.) In this style there is always the sense of the possibility of telling what is being told from a number of different scientific, philosophic, or esthetic points of view. The event is explicable sociologically *and* psychologically *and* mythically *and* as an existential crisis of the author *and* it is a phenomenon for naturalistic description *and* an occasion for the nuances of sentiment *and* a plotted drama, etc. These points of view are not felt as clashing, nor as if one were more true than the others; rather, all are equally true and, by composing them, the artist conveys what is. Of course, all are not equally explored by every author; the varying weights of handling give the texture of various pieces.

Now, a first effect of such equi-valence of perspectives is that in the composition of the whole each patch, so to speak, is given purely, with its own color, rhythm, and proper articulation. Sections are often sharply and strongly contrasted. A description, say, of what is on the table will be given as a picture or a reasoned catalogue or an ecological detail, not, or not merely, to set the stage, to create an atmosphere, to indicate social class, or to incorporate symbols. A socio-psychological interpretation will be expert and even professional, but it does not reveal any ultimate secret—there *is* no ultimate secret; nor does it necessarily stir to action or give the sense of scientific analysis or case history. Where there is action, the plotting is good, but it does not carry everything away in its climactic surge nor ever come to a great surprise; it too is a colored line in the composition. Indeed, the analogy I keep thinking of is that these stories are like the classical paintings of the past fifty years, where the colors, without admixture of black or white, are laid on in plain sizable patches; the shadows are also pure colors; there is no chiaroscuro; there is an avoidance of illusory depth; and the composition is lovely.

When such parts compose in good pieces, the effect is clear and animated but not dynamic. I do not mean that the stories are static, but rather factually quiet, as if to say, "There it is." The whole is on the surface, for the perspectives are obvious and even explicit, but the effect is not superficial, for the parts have solidity and value. The tone is not warm or climactic, but it is not cold or pointless, rather dry and bright. The reader is not carried away, yet when he is finished, he does not ask, "So what?" Rather he says, "Well! So that's it."

What is this style accomplishing, for every successful style functions as a workable way of making experience hang together?

Let us contrast it with various achievements of the previous two or three generations. Our style does not allow for character study and the full-blown drama of passion, for it neutralizes identification. It does not evoke a mood and objectify an inner world, for it is not understated or allusive, it tells everything; its "subjectivity" is frankly objectively autobiographical. Yet it has neither thesis nor theme, for its thoughts and depictions are limited in their place and application; they are true and worth-while, but they do not add up to a case, nor is anything on trial. The authors can be neither foolish nor misty nor profound. It is a style weak in sentiment, for it is neither personal nor antiromantically impersonal; rather it gives the personal and impersonal equal valence side by side. It is useless for the pitiless unmasking of naturalism, with the consequent revulsion and indignation, for it refuses to stick to one color and to the lack of evaluation that is a hostile evaluation; it does not disown the subject matter by keeping it "out there."

So much negatively; and we seem to have exhausted most of what serious readers want from stories. But they can't get what they want. Then, positively what do we have? We have an acceptance of any and all factors and the making of a pattern. Now, making of the pattern *proves* that a pattern can be made. But this is an enormously worth-while contemporary achievement! It proves that art still works. For we are notoriously in an age when all assumptions have been undermined, all standards have been demolished, no one is adequate to the fund of knowledge, we cannot cope with the liberation of repressions, ethics (and/or social science) have not kept pace with the advances in technology. I do not doubt for a moment that all of this is so. Nevertheless, these disarmingly unpretentious but tough-textured art-works show that, as ever, an honest exercise of the senses, the feelings, the wits, and the spirit can make a livable experience. This is not the grandest thing in the world, but it *is* something to go on.

It is interesting to see how this style obviates once-formidable problems of content. For instance, frankness; it is impossible in this style to be pornographic, the surface is too astringent. Where everything is told adequately and that's that, nothing is tendentious. The ugly, again, becomes an interesting shape with a certain weight and certain textural relations. One would say of some of these stories as of certain pictures, ''Really very good, but I shouldn't like to live with it on the wall.'' But most astonishing is the vanishing of almost any trace of irony. By making every perspective actual, what starts out as high sophistication ends up as a refreshing naiveness. The fact that the author is contemptuous or is suffering is part of what he composes, it is not the drive of his composition that emerges with the ending. And, as in a psychoanalytic interview, a nightmare is simply another objective datum. But if, by rare chance, the author has hit on a subject matter in which every point of view yields something beautiful, gentle, promissory, or assuaging, then the effect of this flat and ingenuous mode of composition is paradisal, and readers laugh and weep.

I like this style. It has being and unity and is, in so far, good. It is our duty to learn it and study its successful pieces, for they are ours. Its best writers, like good authors of all times, have learning, observation, sensibility, intelligence, and stubborn individuality and integrity. Yet there is something I do not like. The authors are knowledgeable, but the works do not have enough tendency to explode and shatter the veil of the surface, revealing something that nobody knows. The authors of my generation are withholding their strength, they lack daring and absolute aspiration. There is no hint of experimentation in these pieces; rather there is the knowing use of the techniques, attitudes, and subject matters that our predecessors won for us. This is all very well for a brief interim, but I think that the interim has lasted too long.

This omnibus review first appeared in *Book Parade* (1954) and *Kenyon Review* (Winter 1955) as "They've Been Good Long Enough." The present version is taken from *Utopian Essays*.

Underground Writing: 1960

I.

The history of literature is the adding on of new themes and scenes, along with new techniques, styles, and author attitudes. Nevertheless, a special problem is raised by our present tendency to write up, as if in one feverish co-operative effort, everything that is underground and hitherto unmentioned. We apparently want to break down in principle any barrier between underworld and public world, and between what is kept silent and what is literature. Why do we publicize the underworld, why don't we let it remain under?

As with every other spontaneous act in our unsatisfactory era, this effort commences either as a reaction of despair or as a generous gesture of reform; but with astonishing rapidity it is corrupted to the style and effect of the global Thing it means to attack. Because the writers are themselves inwardly betrayed, their frankness rapidly becomes lewd and their impulse to direct action often turns into punk fascism.

To get our bearings, let us recall that in other times the underworld was kept under not necessarily because it was base or shameful. For instance, the ancient Mysteries seem to have been the important community religion of the Greek folk, far more than was the vastly written-up cult of Olympus. Yet they were by no means for publication, so we have few texts from which to learn much about them. From antiquity through the Middle Ages, even in so verbal a subject as philosophy, the highest tradition of certain sects was passed on secretly from the master only to the disciple who had the right character. And of course in less verbal disciplines, apprentices did not learn from books, and there were no books. Socrates and Plato were dubious about writing things down, and in the Chinese tradition, Lao-tse and Confucius, disagreeing on everything else, agreed on this: "We do not speak about the divine."

In most societies there has been silence or reticence also about much of the middle part of life. Concerning Periclean Athens, for example, I should dearly love to have some direct vital statistics, e.g., what were the free and slave populations? At what age (barring plague) did men die? People simply took such affairs for granted and did not write them up. And of course throughout history nothing is said about happy sex or happy married life, although romantic love, sexual failure, and marital failure have been literary topics par excellence. This reticence does not necessarily mean that sex was considered private or that the societies were antisexual. No such conceptions exist in antiquity, not to speak of many more primitive societies. But what is there to write? It is the kind of thing that you *do*. Romantic sexuality is written up precisely because it touches on what you can't do; it is a kind of completing of unfinished situations. (In so far as sex is an art, however, there is a place for speech and writing and even for how-to-do-it manuals; we have some charming ancient ones. But unfortunately, just where instinct is most distorted, there is the strongest drive for "proving" and impersonal technique rather than for culture and art, and I suppose that our own manuals, at least, often cater to this drive.)

At the bottom of the ladder, finally, throughout most of history, illegal low life has, prudently, not courted publicity. It would have been considered a point not of prestige, as with us, but of simple idiocy, for the secrets of a thieves' or addicts' gang to be exposed and written up. One did not blab. The exceptions are remarkable and force us to speculate. There is evidence that Villon wrote his jargon poems for the *coquillards,* the gang, themselves, as if they were a proper community; yet the poems are published and courtly in form, and they merge harmoniously with his lamentations of low life in proper French and with his standard poems about the general human condition. In his own life, we know, he bestrode the two worlds; the fact that he also did so in writing makes us think of the breakdown of medieval culture, the upsurge of the vernaculars, the disasters of the Hundred Years' War. Villon is an interesting contrast to our Genet, an artist of equivalent stature. Villon surveys the scene of his low life from the point of view of universal humanity; Genet finds animation only in his low life and struggles to find in it some universal humanity. Another obvious example is Defoe, in the seamy age of Walpole. Here we seem to get something more like "modern" reporting.

So we return to our own disposition to write up the unutterable, the unmentionable, and the underworld. I want to explore three different general motives for this, so I won't mention any names, since every writer should be treated fairly as an individual.

II.

First, of course, this underground reporting is simply part of our wretched universal reporting and spectatoritis. On the one hand, it is technological. "Objective" reporting of "scientific" data makes no distinction in what it surveys, any more than a camera shies away. In the past history of literature and painting, a new scene, like a new technique, was painfully won to meet a new expressive need; but mechanical reporting eats up every scene omnivorously, and the great presses print off anything that has the format of objective reporting and might sell. The same occurs with the "scientific method" of so-called sociology; any kind of problem "area" is given the works, and the result has no relevance to solving the problem.

Also, we verbalize a lot in this way because active life does not come off for us. It is an easy way of being on the scene without being involved—just as the sociologists can sharpen their tools and work the area without doing any agriculture. In this respect, *Contact* or *Kulchur* or *Big Table,* with their criminal, underground, or Beat issues, are no better than *Life* or *Look*. We substitute journalism for philosophy, poetry, and politics. We regard our existence as though it were already history or nothing better than fiction; and since the essence of existence, its presentness and challenge, is omitted, we get inaccurate history and weak fiction. Thus, far too much gets written, and yet the proper function of letters is neglected or swamped. As part of the popular culture, the scenes of the underworld are like the rest of the chewing gum.

III.

A second motive for the publication of the underworld is more promising, but disappointing in the performance. It is that, since the legitimate world has become lifeless and contemptible, we explore in the illegitimate for vitality. We seem to propose, by affirmation and publication, to make *this* the public world or at least an acceptable part of the public world. The need is pathetic, but beggars aren't choosers. It is no news that, just to live on to tomorrow, many of us have to be illegal. (For instance, I have experienced in a lawyer's office that very few of my friends could apear in court as character witnesses. Though they are fine folk, they could not survive a superficial cross-examination. Certainly I could not.) Thus it is probably a wise course to counterattack ideologically and creatively and get everybody used to the dirty words and the illegal scenes. This is a customary job of advance-guard writing.

We must distinguish two contrasting aspects of our illegitimacy. Given our moronic system of morals and property, it is impossible to live without sinning and trespassing; and in the tight organization of modern society, any spontaneous gesture is a threatening nonconformity. Then to be illegitimate may be simply the continuing defiant affirmation of free love, anarchism, progressive education, and productive work like arts and crafts, that belonged to the bucolic age of Greenwich Village. Our difference is that we have come a further step from bohemianism in honest poverty. It is harder to be decently poor; urbanism and technology are still further out of human scale; civil liberties are harder to defend. The result is that, especially among the unseasoned, a larger number resign from the fight altogether.

But also, given the inhuman pressures and temptations of commercialism, regimentation, and community fragmentation, inevitably there are criminality, flight to the margin, and personality disturbances that are not properly efforts for natural satisfaction in difficult circumstances, but are hostile reaction-formations. Such are the spite, conceit, fantasies of power, and the throwing of tantrums that are the usual tone of hipster letters. The kind of reactive vitality that used to characterize delinquent hoodlums now spreads to middle-class, middle-aged gentlemen who can write books; and naturally it rings bells on Madison Avenue, where there is the same resentment of earnest effort.

Rebellious humanism and reactive hipsterism are by nature incompatible. The positive satisfaction of life; or life striving for satisfaction, being frustrated, and becoming angry—these pay off in a real world of real contacts. There is no need to win "proving" victories, to be one-up in every encounter. Conceit becomes boring and violent methods are rarely constructive. Nevertheless, as the case is *socially,* these two aspects of illegitimacy, humanist and hipster, are lumped together and damned together, and often have to live together. It becomes necessary for a writer to vindicate them together. We who simply want community, productive culture, justice, and pleasure understand that, as Kropotkin said, "So long as one person is in prison, I am not free." Besides, some of us suffer, perhaps neurotically, from a thankless compassion that supports the conceited, wasteful, and violent because they are like sick children.

Unhappily, in the peculiar market of publication, bad writing drives out good. Rebel humanism has an unpopular style; it seems never to pose the "problems" that everybody is talking about—how could it, since the problems are falsely posed? Even muckraking, a proper function of humane letters, e.g., disclosure of police brutality, has a miserable way of becoming sado-masochistic, just as "pacifist" films, on the whole, exacerbate violence. But most fatally, serious humanistic writing really *is* old-fashioned and out of touch. Consider, simply, that a man who for years has accurately understood the worth of Hollywood, the networks, and their related world—which soon includes the whole apparent world—and who has treated them appropriately, that is, with contempt and neglect, such a man will finally have little to say to an audience for whom, perforce, those things have been the *only* world, even though known to be a phony world. One cannot understand, for instance, why Nathanael West is admired, for oneself signed off from California with Aldous Huxley. But the young people must regard that world as important, since it is the only one they have experienced, and it seems that West teaches them a possible attitude to survive by.

The mass public, of course, takes to its heart just that aspect of the illegitimate which is reactive to its own official ideology and mores and which, inevitably, shares the same psychology of power, sensation, and success. The seamy scene of hip literature is an attractive forepleasure, and the acting out of every office clerk's conceit and castration complex provides a relevant thrill. This reportage serves the same function for the philosophy of the mass audience as the bathos of Tennessee Williams does for its sexuality. The poet caters to the tender pornographic side, combining lust with punishment; and the hipster prose writer caters to the conceited power side, combining know-how with putting down. This is utterly boring.

In my opinion, there is something dishonorable and exploiting, queasy-making, about hipster writing—and, similarly, much of the school of Sartre. Life strategies that are brutal necessities for folk who are in clear and present danger, and that precisely would not be written up, are toyed with by intellectuals who evoke fantasy dangers so that they can thrill to extreme situations; and indeed thereby they create unnecessary real dangers, as if life weren't hard enough. It sounds as though they were calling up the underground for spite, as a psychological reaction to blocked creativity—not otherwise than the resentful Stalinists of the 'thirties. The rhythm becomes jabbing and the tone shrill; the fantasy is for the cool to seize power, even via Jack Kennedy. But our real need is otherwise. The case is that our society is in a chronic low-grade emergency. To alleviate this, so that outgoing life can revive, requires patience, fortitude, and music; curtly rejecting anything phony, but having faith in abiding goods and powers. Instead, these writers, lacking the stamina of natural strength, cop out and plunge into the pointless brawl.

IV.

Let me suggest another motive for writing up the underworld that I think is more reasonable. By making all scenes equal, by writing one's situation as it is, whatever it is, writers might hope to get rid of "standards" altogether and perhaps of "writing" altogether. (Unfortunately, the writers who seem to have this motive, e.g., some of the Beats, are both so ignorant and so hopped up, that they don't know what they're after and sell themselves short.)

This is to revive old-fashioned nihilism, to clear the decks. In the nineteenth century, in a scarcity economy, the nihilism was more politically revolutionary and religiously Christian; in the "affluent society" it consists of quitting and being religiously Taoist and pacifist. The aim is certainly not to substitute the underground as a new power, but to form a new community from scratch. I have shown elsewhere that this is a happy direction for an advance-guard.

A nihilist program is a beautifully democratic approach to literature. It seems designed for the millions of the inarticulate who say, "If I could only write, I have a story to tell!" All of the faithful are encouraged to be creative, a very different thing from making whole art-works, the products of a complicated culture. One is permitted to be fragmentary; by learning the trick of spontaneous association, one can achieve exciting poetic moments; by employing the primitive rhetorical devices of repetition, incantation, and crescendo, it is possible to read a scattered page aloud as if one had made a whole poem; and of course by writing "wd" and "cd" and using the slash mark on the typewriter, one is in the swim. Music (bongo) and painting are also Everyman's.

A critic cannot help being bemused, for indeed this Beat art is a remarkable historical product. Consider how the most exquisite efforts of modern art to break free of convention and get back to the elements of expression—one could mention Mallarmé's symbolism, Rimbaud's visions, Pound's and Eliot's fragmentation and pastiche, Apollinaire's and Cummings' ideograms and typography, W.C. Williams' neo-Wordsworthianism, Viennese atonality, Webern's pointillism, Stravinsky's and Varèse's percussion, Bártok's rhythm, polyrhythms from Bali and New Orleans, Picasso's abstraction and collage, Matisse's fauvism, Kandinsky's non-objectivism, Mondrian's and Albers' elementarism, Pollock's action and Kline's gesture—how all of these intensely cultivated sources have met up with the deliberately programmatic realism of Sherwood Anderson, Joyce, Lawrence, Céline, and others, to give a lingua franca to amateur boys. They have a means of esthetically expressing how they are. None of their art is inventive, little of it is any good, yet there is in it a valuable contribution, its very communitarianism, and supported by the sense of a community—the very opposite of the dueling of the hipsters—literature is cultivated as an action on the audience, to increase the community. When they have read their poems at one another, they can barge in for bed and board like Samoans.

Culturally they, and we, are not up to this nihilism. Those who abdicate from the economy and university of the big society become a sect rather than a universal solvent. The "scene" soon becomes a stereotyped subject matter, with monotonous repetition of jejune experiences and standard props, rather than a modest account of just where one happens to be thrown, with its materiality and wonder. Public readings become boringly drunken rituals. And to one's astonishment, the creative community spits with envy at proper writers. The situation is bitterly ironical: on the one hand, we who are cultivated artists and realize how little that's worth (though let me speak no ill of the Creator Spirit) would gladly see our culture relapse into the human community; yet every youth feels thwarted by his writer's block and spiteful because he doesn't know anything.

To sum up: the resigned beatnik publicizes his scene as the only world; the impotent hipster calls up the underworld to put down everybody else; and the technological popular culture makes an amalgam of underworld and public world that is as nourishing as chewing gum. Yet I don't think it is at present possible to return to a classical silence. Our literary task must be to get rid of distinctions altogether and recognize only the human beings as existing.

V.

What are the "human beings"? When there are dominant groups and minorities, legal and underworld groups, the minorities and the underworld are necessarily "in the right," for they exist as a repressed potentiality within the dominating majority, and there is nothing to do with such a repression but undo it. If they did not symbolize something within the preponderant group, there would be no "Negroes," "homosexuals," or "Jews," but only varieties of people; and the underworld would be either citizens or frank outlaws at war with us. Once they emerge into notice as "problems," the minorities and the underworld are a lively revolutionary force.

It is an inner boundary that creates dominant groups and minorities, and the success of a revolution is to eradicate the boundary, to liquidate the problems. It is not to give equal justice to different classes—though justice is always indispensable; it is surely not to transform the downs into ups, which would be simply a compulsive acting-out of the repressed resentment and rebellion. To give an actual social example: for the whites the "Negro problem" is their own psychological problem, to be psychiatrically treated. (For the Negroes, of course, it is also a problem of personal dignity and social justice, to be solved by resisting and fighting.) Now the bother with much underground writing at present is that it is a fetishism of the underground—it does not eradicate the boundary. Base or noble properties are assigned to addicts and addiction, or to breathless violence, or to queer society. This is no different from socialist realism or the religion of Catholic writers. But no behavior or ideology is in fact such a big deal; for only the human beings exist. The literary problem is not to present the scene but to show the man destroyed, fulfilled, or chastened in the scene. Also, unless this is done, we do not even get the scene but only its props, for there is no exploration of causes and ideals. Some writers, sensing this superficiality, treat the scene as symbolic of "real life"; but this gambit is bound to be boring, for it requires extraordinary spirituality to write allegory, and the "real life" of these authors is very thin gruel.

To one with any memory or history, it is evident that the need for prejudice, for inner boundaries, goes deeper than the particular content people are prejudiced against at any time. Right-thinking people were just as upset by tobacco as they are now by marijuana. Reading in popular novels of 1880, one eerily senses the same dismay about marriage across class lines that is now felt about marriage across color lines; and, especially among Jews, marriage across religious lines used to be mourned like death. It is as if people cannot feel they exist except by affirming, with a shudder, that they are different from something that they are against.

But to be rid of it, we must *indeed* do without the boundaries. This might mean, for instance, taking it for granted that a chap (like young Freud), busy with God's work and touchingly in love with a well-bred girl, is also sending himself on cocaine, and that's just how it is; or to give a common example, that a splendid teacher is naturally queer for his students. As might be expected, it is just this matter-of-fact attitude that is shocking to the audience and unacceptable to the publishers, whereas any kind of "underground" writing has become perfectly acceptable. The problem for modern writing is not treating some "underground" property, but simply coping with the facts of life with reason, compassion, learning, and imagination.

This brings me, finally, to the dilemma that, in my opinion, is the most serious that faces an earnest writer at present. This is the fact, which I mentioned above, that especially for younger readers the dominant scene in our society—of role-playing, front personalities, and phony achievement—is the only culture and manners that they think they have experienced, it is the "real world," even though they dissent from it. This simulacrum of life is not worth criticizing in detail, and since literature is the criticism of life, there is no function for literature. With regard to this dominant scene, the only possible literary tone is the apocalyptic one, which of course some writers have hit on.

But the case is not so desperate, for the dominant scene only seems to occupy the world. This phony world stays in existence precisely by the tension of an inner boundary: people conform against their better impulse because they are afraid to be different and excluded; and they compel others to the same behavior in order to protect the image they have invested their lives in. It is a structure of conceit made by the polarity of proving and success versus failure and shame; and its characteristic feelings, if they can be called so, are face-saving and embarrassment. In *Growing Up Absurd* I pictured this world as a Closed Room with a Rat Race as the center of fascination, powerfully energized by the fear of being outcaste. If this is so, the underground writing we have been getting is only one more expression of the same world. But contrariwise, if, as I urge, our writers refuse to take seriously the boundaries, the distinctions between respectable and outcaste, and begin to consider only the human beings as real, then even the younger readers must recognize that they too have had a different experience than they thought.

This idea gives a curious literature—I myself essayed it in *The Empire City*—about a kind of real persons living in an illusory system, with such comic and dreadful adventures as then befall them. They are sane; their behavior seems crazy, but it is society that is crazy; but they bitterly suffer, for one lives in the only society that there is. Or imagine this theme in a more elementary work, say, a film about children: we would show nothing but shots of children, laughing children, jumping children, children bawling beat by mamas in the park, children playing ball, children whose hands are slapped because they touch their genitals, children crying themselves to sleep, children in disgrace because they have pissed in their pants in school, children twisting the arms of other children.

This survey of the current literary scene at the beginning of the Sixties was first published in *The Nation* (March 11, 1960), just after the big success of *Growing Up Absurd.* It provoked an angry letter from Nelson Algren. The version printed here is from *Utopian Essays.*

"The Crime of Our Century"

I.

Here are two recent books about the Leopold-Loeb case which Meyer Levin calls "the crime of our century." It occurred when Levin was in college (1924). James Yaffe is younger and takes the whole matter less seriously. Now the case is always considered the typical crime of the Twenties, and I should like to set against these books for comparison a book of the Twenties, Dreiser's *An American Tragedy* (1925), that retells a typical murder of the time of Dreiser's own youth, the case of Chester Gillette (1906). By this comparison I hope to say something about the Twenties and the Fifties, two decades of expansion.

I am not here making a literary evaluation, yet I must begin from a literary distinction. Of the two recent books, Yaffe's is quite worthless; by bowdlerizing, up-to-dating, stereotyping, and juvenilizing the events and persons of the case, he contrives to lose both artistic probability and any other interest. But *Compulsion* is not a bad book; by its earnest selection of the journalistic, medical, and legal material, often given verbatim, it presents an interesting and believable report; and Levin makes something touching and significant of his personal involvement in the action. Dreiser's book, however, is of a different genre, it is a work of art; not (to my taste) a wonderful work, but a work of art in that it makes itself a world and this world is more important than the "case," it is the real case. The questions that I would ask are these: what would a book about the Crime of Our Century be like if it were worked as Dreiser worked? Would such a work get itself written and received? What, contrariwise, are Levin and Yaffe doing? And what does this tell us about the Fifties and the Twenties?

What strikes one immediately and persistently, is how Dreiser is *in* his story, in a way that our writers are not. He works as though all the motives and behaviors were immediately plausible, *unquestionable by either the author or the audience,* and therefore needing no explanation, only presentation. He may or may not have a theory of causation—we know that he had several—but he does not need one and he does not offer one; simply he shows us how first undeniably Clyde Griffiths did and suffered so and so, and then he did and suffered so and so. Instead of causation and the imputation of responsibility or compulsion, we get a solid and stolid probability that adds up to a real world; that's just how it was, like life only more so. (Dreiser carries this through admirably; the only episode that seems to me sketchy and a little fumbled is the temptation to the murder plan; but the author recovers.) Again, as a doctrinaire naturalist, Dreiser eschews every literary attitude except this narrowly selective "life-like" presentation; there is no perspective, no irony, no wonder, no humor, no wisdom, compassion, admiration or contempt; no symbol, no formal surprise; certainly no sympathy. (But love, the love of undeviating attentiveness.) In all these ways Dreiser is not involved in the crime, but we shall see that just in these ways Levin and Yaffe are, each in his own fashion, involved. They cannot present the case as a naturalistic probability. Levin wisely makes little effort to do so and relies on the documents to move his story (that's how it was because that's how it was reported in the press); when Yaffe tries it, his story moves not at all.

When Dreiser succeeds in his art-work of this kind, there follow two cultural consequences of the highest importance. In the first place he triumphantly vindicates the art act itself, for it is art and art alone that does human justice to Clyde Griffiths (and perhaps to his original Chester Gillette; but that no longer makes any difference). Here Dreiser is perfectly aware of what he is doing;

he devotes his entire dénouement to the varying attempts to understand and be fair to the young murderer: the trial, the appeal, the compassionate minister, the wise governor, the loving and sacrificing mother, and finally the confused boy himself trying honestly to assay himself. No one truly understands what occurred; but the author can say, "Nay, read here; *this* is what occurred." (Indeed, my bother with this good book is that Dreiser does not bring this poignant problem to the forefront soon enough; he does not show us until too far along the *confused* youth, longing to be understood and told what he is. Dreiser shows us always his vacillation and cowardice, but not enough his confused integrity; he sticks so close to what is like that particular life that he misses one transcendent tragedy of every life.)

But even more relevant to our present theme, when Dreiser succeeds in making a probable crime by accepting every usual presupposition, the social effect is revolutionary. If people do not like the outcome, they cannot simply reject it; they must reject the whole sequence en bloc; and since they have been patiently led along step by step, accepting every step as sensible, plausible, and like their lives, they must—must they not?—be shaken in their whole way of experiencing as a viable way of life. See, says the author, here is how *you* make sense, and it is not viable. Something is wrong. At this level, simply to entertain an alternative is to disavow. . . . Historically, Dreiser's works were part of the revolutionary change in the sexual mores. The events of *An American Tragedy* would no longer be probable if retold today; this particular plot would occur today in a soap-opera.

II.

The authors of our books on Leopold and Loeb are not in those events, which are alien to them. There is no shared assumption of author and audience that this is, step by step, inevitable behavior leading up to what is quite unacceptable but must be accepted nevertheless or all our sense rejected en bloc. Yaffe's book is merely manufactured on a causal theory, that such and such parental attitudes lead to such and such juvenile delinquency:

the premises are stereotypes, and the esthetic effect is the frigid one of having established a possibility, for the sake of argument or to get a book written, that such and such might occur; but there is never any probability or internal motion. Levin, much more masterfully, makes the chief thing his own need to find out the cause, a fine theme, not unlike Proust's; but then there is too much about Leopold and Loeb and not enough about Meyer Levin. The esthetic effect of the major bulk, the crime, is the harsh one of unpleasant newspaper reports. Both authors make the philosophical error of trying to present a living process by explaining it rather than by reliving it with us; their causes are *ex post facto;* at every moment the protagonists might do otherwise but don't happen to; afterwards we can trace the trajectory they did follow, as if to say, "there must have been a compulsion"; we are certainly none the wiser about ourselves, or any urgent present matter.

Then there arises the question: What on earth makes two writers devote so much effort to a narrative they cannot get on with, and one of them to call it by such a title as The Crime of Our Century? Why do they treat with it at all? This is a crucial question. They are obviously fascinated. With what? It is fortunate that we have two books, for unlike as they are in most respects, they prove to have a couple of surprising attitudes in common, and these give us the clue to the relevance of these books at this time in the Fifties.

As alien as they are to the case, our authors feel even more alien to the social milieu in which the case occurs. In Yaffe, who up-to-dates the story, the disaffection is blatant from the beginning. He is dealing with what would be normally a gloomy subject, yet with almost every character except the protagonists, his manner is usually satirical and often sarcastic. One father is a frigid ass, the other is a weak fool; one mother is sickly and timid, the other is a domineering club-woman and a fool; the principal is a pompous fool; the lawyer is a vain conniver; the psychiatrists don't care; the judge is a sentimental fool. And as his story reaches its climax, Yaffe hits on the pattern he is after: that nobody is concerned with the one important thing, the case, but this one is interested in his golf-score, that one in his new article, another in his business-prestige, etc. To drive it home, the author runs through the routine a second time.

Levin's disaffection is more touching; it is a slow growth to awareness of how pointless his own career as a man has been. Let me quote from his ending:

> . . . As it happened, I never again reached the intense involvement and achievement—if achievement it may be called—of my first assignment. When something big comes to us early in our careers we have an expectation of exceeding and exceeding ourselves; yet for some this never happens, just as, for some, no later love has the quality of first love. I married, divorced, and during the war I was a correspondent with the Third Army. It was in the last weeks that the case came finally home to me.

Back in America he meets his first love.

> . . . Looking at her, I was thinking, *It could have been.* It could all have been. . . . And I tended my job and married again, and we live in Norwalk.

But the social disaffection of both authors is evident also in their surprising attitude toward the two protagonists. They sympathize with, and admire, the dark funny-looking Jewish intellectual misfit (of course in Yaffe nobody is Jewish)—the one who wears the glasses and loses the glasses—the brooding one who has the fantasies of being a serviceable slave. They yearn to extenuate for him according to their own standards of decency, and Yaffe even contrives his metaphysical salvation. But toward the other, the fair good-looking youth, skilled in sports, dancing, and dramatics, sought after by the girls and boys, both authors are cold and even hostile; he is, somehow, to blame. What does this mean? Our authors look at themselves and at the world and its desirable roles, and they find nothing to admire and love—at most something to envy and be vindictive about—but certainly nothing that adds up to what you could be "intensely involved" in, or to "achieve" anything there. Yaffe, the younger, takes this pretty much for granted; Levin has learned it as he pursued his career and found that he, or it (it makes no difference), didn't come across. But there were those two rich and bright boys back in the Twenties who "had everything," and they were wise to it already. They acted it out—it is fascinating—because one of them seduced the other into doing something spectacularly pointless, for the excitement; they committed the Crime of Our Century.

III.

As is often the case, the opening page of *Compulsion,* before the author has a chance to develop his habitual defenses, tells more about the case and the real situation than all the rest. A professor is giving a brilliant cram-lecture for the morrow's entrance-examination to Law School. Judd, who killed the boy the day before, takes no notes; yet he is paying attention, because he seizes the first occasion to interrupt and bother the teacher and the class with his theory of the Superman; but he feels they don't understand his argument. . . Levin here wants to portray the preoccupied youth, doodling a hawk, and unable to keep away from the area of the crime, and this is very well. But the salient psychological features of the scene are not these "unconscious" ones but much simpler and revealing ones: (1) What would seem to be "objectively" important, the cram-lecture and the examination, is unimportant not only to Judd but also to the other students and to the teacher, for they rush at once into the time-wasting argument; (2) The aim of the young man is chiefly to claim attention, as if starved for attention, and to have something vital to him drawn forth and treated seriously, though not necessarily approved, even perhaps more to be refuted; (3) But since what he offers has no immediate practical content, there is no way to get himself understood. He wants to share his fantasy, which is his only creative act, but it is only a fantasy. We can be sure that, uninterested in the objective business of society—the examination—and unable to make contact with the other persons, he will pour his energy into lush fantasies indeed. (Of course I am not here speaking of Leopold and Loeb but of how they exist as fantasies of Meyer Levin.)

Now let me revert to the first question above: if our author were going to artifice a real world of the case, as Dreiser did in *An American Tragedy,* it is in these scenes of social behavior and how the protagonists are in them, and how they are *not* in them, that half the substance of the work would be. This is especially true for the outgoing, the socially-successful youth (Artie). The author tells us, for instance, that Artie is a fine tennis-player. In Yaffe's book the counterpart is manager of the baseball team. How is he *in* these sports? We get not a word. But Levin in one brief passage lets us know that Artie is impotent. Then we can envisage him on the field, or dancing hot jazz, throwing himself wildly into it for the relieving excitement of the muscular activity; excelling with the need to prove potency, and with the flash of triumph (and contempt) in doing so; but never, never with the total release of orgasm—having always something unfinished and the need, more fiercely next time, to repeat—and with this, the inability to get any of the quiet rewards of activity and success. He can do it and he proves it, but then it doesn't mean anything and he turns on his heel; or—more deeply—he turns on his heel in full flight from the anxiety of losing control and bursting into tears. Levin is concerned with explaining, and he is compassionate; but if he envisaged the real scenes and simply constructed them, there would be no need for explanation—any more than Dreiser explains anything—and the work itself would repair something, make it whole again, and this is the act of compassion.

Now the other half of such a reconstruction of the real case would, I think, deal with the proliferating fantasies, especially of the inward-turning youth. It happens that in our generation, by no accident, writers have learned to reconstruct such masturbation-fantasies as a literary form. Genet is the most masterly, Henry Miller is more pedestrian. The essence of such reconstruction is that the physical and social reality, the "other's reality," enters the presented world with apparent caprice or is there only on the fringes; its meaning and value is the use it plays in beginning, maintaining, and heightening the fantasy. Certainly this is not far from the Leopold-Loeb "case" as told in the books we are considering; but our authors do not stay with the fantasist's world and therefrom lead us to the crime step-by-step as it really was; rather they persist in keeping the social valuation as their structural framework—and then the overt acts of fantasy occur as alien and require a causal explanation. And yet these same authors, as I have said, do not take that social reality seriously at all! Then what on earth are they doing? They are fascinated and they are avoiding.

In order to get something more nearly resembling what Dreiser did, we could structure this material as follows: On the one hand the scenes of the unsatisfactoriness of our social reality, made obvious and probable for us, the final pointlessness of the esteemed roles and careers, of the games and dates, the coldness of the families and fraternities, and the gnawing need to exceed. On the other hand, the rich reality of the fantasy world into which something looms from outside so that there begins to occur overt behavior continuous with the fantasy. It is in this matrix that the events occur that are reported in the newspapers as crime by those who have not gone step-by-step this whole road.

The youths kill a random boy for no reason, that is for a trivial reason that would fit a trivial deed; but of course to them the deed is neither enormous nor trivial but of the order of their other acts; and their reason is not trivial, but to run the risk of being caught, exposed, punished. (It is hard to know what Levin means by "compulsion"—he seems to be saying that the death-wish is compelling; but I think the usual psychological wisdom is that the thrilling excitement, the compulsion, is in the confrontation with the others. This is what the affectless repeat.) Yaffe and Levin seem to be peculiarly moved by the acts. They do not seem to understand how any principle of disaffection or estrangement, continuously operating, will take a person far afield; and not only negative principles, but such positive faculties as healthy lust or common-sense in a crazy world will eventually lead a man to enormities of eccentricity; and the honest artistic need to touch a smug and debauched audience eventuates in dada. But these books keep the enormity of the act in the foreground; the crime is isolated. We continually feel their tug toward the crime as unfinished business for themselves—several times Levin says as much.

They cannot make the agents real and the act inevitable; they are too involved; they must explain it away. To sum up our comparison: in these books it is the crime we are to disavow and not the world of our assumptions; yet that world is not looked at squarely either, but avoided. But in *An American Tragedy* it was not the murder but the whole way of social life in which that murder was an incident that was recreated and since our own experience of life allowed us to regard the sequence of events as probable, we had radically to disavow it, that is, to entertain alternatives.

Yet the book we have proposed in theory, portraying as plausible and probable so radical a disaffection from the accepted institutions and behaviors, and developing with sympathy the fantasies of perversity—such a book could not get itself accepted. People do not dare disavow so frankly our conventionally desirable world, and therefore they would not admit the real scenes to be plausible; nor can they accept the fantasies of desire as what some one indeed might desire. It would all seem far-fetched and repugnant, rather than only too real and inadmissible en bloc. Yet the books that put the crime in the foreground—these exert a fascination.

IV.

Let me now generalize and compare the Twenties and Fifties as two periods of expansion. Both are marked by a booming productivity, much money to spend, a rising standard of living, and also by cultural adjustments to great technical innovations that offer exciting prospects; radio then and television now; flying the ocean and the geophysical year; relativity physics and psychoanalysis then and nucleonics and psychotherapy now. In both decades a vast increase in international travel and cultural exchange. Such things both support and give content to the expansion. At the same time the Twenties and the Fifties are marked by a profound disillusionment and disgust at the way our civilization has recently disgraced itself. No doubt the First World War was a more severe shock to moral preconceptions—we were inured by their experience of barbarism; yet we managed to turn up with crematoria and atom-bombs. But these experiences too foster expansion in those who survive and in whom the shell-shock thaws out, for people are purged, especially if there has been frank vomiting; and then more daring and radical notions can express themselves with a good conscience, since nothing an individual can think of would be so wicked as what everybody thought of collectively.

But there is also a dark contrast between the decades. The Twenties were a time in which people thought (really believed) that there would never be another war. Great nations scuttled their warships according to a formula, and signed the Kellogg-Briand agreement. This element, of security, is of course capital to an expanding mood, for it is the absence of an external counter-pressure.

If we consider the artistic creations of the Twenties, they were indeed such as one would expect and hope for in a time of expansion and disgust. There was a flowering of advance-guard work, experimental, offensive, outrageous, bringing to a large public the esoteric efforts of several decades. And the standard style, as by that time *An American Tragedy* was in standard style, moved with serene self-confidence, immune from the need to explain, as if all the necessary radical positions had been securely conquered. In art as in politics, we had all the three elements necessary for the emergence of novelty: expanding energy, a rejection of the past, and security enough to tolerate confusion and anxiety.

Artistic creation today gives, rather, an impression of being balked, potential but unable to get along. There is a counter-pressure that both opposes expansion and discourages it inwardly. Not only is there no peace, but no forthright effort for it; the international community and even science are not free exchanges; and the increased standard of living no longer pays off in pride and joy, for people are avoiding some risk. There is not enough security, therefore not enough ability to tolerate anxiety, and therefore not enough risk of something startlingly new. At the same time, of course, there is too much disgust with the old, and too much new energy to burn, to allow for great conventional products. Instead there is a balked and teasing flirtation with something different, without daring to affirm it. It is in this ambience, I think, that books like *Compulsion* and *Nothing But the Night* get themselves conceived in fascination, executed defensively, and widely accepted by an audience that will not thereby change. They are widely accepted because everybody is in the same boat. Everybody *knows* better, but few dare to believe it and witness it.

Finally, let me return to the Case itself. The Twenties had Flaming Youth; the Fifties have Juvenile Delinquents. Leopold and Loeb were not Flaming Youth, they were juvenile delinquents a generation ahead of their time, and therefore they seem now to have committed the Crime of Our Century. Flaming Youth is rebellious youth astoundingly careless of the wisdom it rejects, claiming to be grown-up and untrammeled even while admitting it might be making mistakes to which it claims a right; but its aims are positive enough: sex, speed and liquor to relax inhibition, ideal political doctrines, and frank answers in words of one syllable for thorny moral dilemmas. These are kids (they recur) looking for an honest adult to refute them. Meyer Levin's protagonists show some of this zeal, but I suspect that it is Meyer who is looking for the honest adult. Our juvenile delinquents are not rebellious but resigned; and they are trapped and desperate. Since these young people do not know where to try to exercise their energies, they do mischief. The speed and liquor, and the PAL and the fan-clubs, are not the prelude to a quieter good time but to more desperate expedients toward excitement. Their philosophy would be *Existenz* and *L'Acte Gratuite,* except that to philosophize affirms an essence, truth, and it is not an *acte gratuite* but the property of a rational animal.

Dreiser's Clyde Griffiths is a dumb precursor of the rebel; he feels he is deprived, only he does not know how; and he is lovingly portrayed in a decade when they thought they knew what was wrong, and importantly did know, and were engaged in changing it. But our present protagonists "have" everything and it's no good; there is no point in their rebelling against their fathers for *they* don't have it either; and nobody demonstrates anything new for them in the best-sellers.

I am reminded of the Commencement exercises some years ago at one of the superior academic high schools in New York, Music and Art. Senator Javits, then State's attorney, addressed the class and urged them to help combat juvenile delinquency by interesting the tough kids of their neighborhoods in their own cultural pursuits. Abstractly this was not a foolish proposal—even meaty for a commencement-address. But the teen-agers to whom I listened thought it was ridiculous; that the delinquents were much in the right and they were stronger and would influence the good boys rather than the other way around; also—with a certain purity—that music and art should not be degraded to do police-work, for they impugned the State's attorney's motives.

Midstream (Summer 1957) first published this review of Meyer Levin's *Compulsion* and James Yaffe's *Nothing But the Night,* two books about the famous Leopold-Loeb case.

Kerouac's On the Road

I.

In three hundred pages these fellows cross America eight times, usually camping on friends or relatives; and they have kicks. The narrator tends to become saddened by it all, but gives little evidence of understanding why. The fellows seem to be in their middle or late 'twenties ("not long after my wife and I split up")—surprisingly, for the kicks are the same as we used to have less solemnly in our teens, between terms. Mostly they are from the middle class. Many other young men in their 'twenties and 'thirties call this book crazy and the greatest, as if it were their history: they were there. So let's look into it.

To an uncritical reading, *On The Road* seems worse written than it is. There are hundreds of incidents but, throughout most of the book, nothing is told, nothing is presented, everything is just "written about." Worse, the narrator seems to try to pep it up by sentences like, "That night all hell broke loose," when the incident is some drinking sailors refusing to obey an order; "this was the greatest ride I ever had," but nothing occurs beyond a fellow getting his pants wet trying to urinate from a moving truck; "this was exciting, this was the greatest"—but it's not exciting. Soon, when the narrator or some other character says "The greatest," we expect that he means "pretty fair"; but alas, he does not mean even this, but simply that there was *some* little object of experience, of whatever value, instead of the blank of experience in which these poor kids generally live.

For when you ask yourself what *is* expressed by this prose, by this buoyant writing about racing-across-the-continent, you find that it is the woeful emptiness of running away from even loneliness and vague discontent. The words "exciting," "crazy," "the greatest," do not refer to any object or feeling, but are a means by which the members of the "beat generation" convince one another that they have been there at all. "I dig it" doesn't mean "I understand it," but, "I perceive that something exists out there." On me as a reader, the effect is dismay and, since I know some of these boys (I say "boys"; Jack Kerouac is thirty-five), I almost burst into tears.

Last summer I listened to Kerouac's friend Allen Ginsberg read a passage from his *Howl*; it was a list of imprecations that he began pianissimo and ended with a thunderous fortissimo. The fellows were excited, it was "the greatest." But I sadly asked Allen just where in either the ideas, the imagery, or the rhythm was the probability for the crescendo; what made it a sequence at all and a sequence to be read just like that. The poet was crestfallen and furious; this thought had never occurred to him. And yet, during those few minutes they *had* shared the simple-minded excitement of speaking in a low voice and gradually increasing to a roar; it was not much of a poetic experience, but it was something, it was better than feeling nothing at all that night. What Kerouac does well, not just writes about, is his description of the jazz-musician who has hit on "it" and everybody goes wild shouting "Go! Man! Go!" But they cannot say what "it" is. These boys are touchingly inarticulate, because they don't know anything; but they talk so much and so loud, because they feel insulted by the existence of grown-ups who know a little bit.

"You can't *howl* a gripe, Allen. You can howl in pain or in rage, but what you are doing is griping." Perhaps the pain is too sore to utter a sound at all; and certainly their justifiable rage is far too dangerous for them to feel at all. The entire action of *On The Road* is the avoidance of interpersonal conflict.

One is stunned at how conventional and law-fearing these lonely middle-class fellows are. They dutifully get legal marriages and divorces. The hint of a "gangbang" makes them impotent. They never masturbate or perform homosexual acts. They do not dodge the draft. They are hygienic about drugs and diet. They do not resent being underpaid, nor speak up at all. To disobey a cop is "all hell." Their idea of crime is the petty shoplifting of ten-year-olds stealing cigarettes or of 'teen agers joyriding in other people's cars. But how could it be otherwise? It is necessary to have some contact with institutions and people in order to rebel against them. It is necessary to want something in order to be frustrated and angry. They have the theory that to be affectless, not to care, is the ultimate rebellion, but this is a fantasy; for right under the surface, obvious to the trained eye, is burning shame, hurt feelings, fear of impotence, speechless and powerless tantrum, cowering before papa, being rebuffed by mama; and it is these anxieties that dictate their behavior in every crisis. Their behavior is a conformity *plus royaliste que le roi.*

One kid (age twenty-one) visited my home the other night, carrying his copy of *On The Road.* The salient feature was his expressionless mask-face, with the squared jaw of unconscious, suspicious watchfulness, the eyes in a fixed stare of unfelt hostility, plus occasional grinding of his back teeth at a vague projected threat. Even the hostility was hard to make overt, but his lips cracked in a small childish smile when he was paid attention to. "But nothing *can* be interesting from coast to coast, boy, if you do not respond to it with some interest. Instead all you can possibly get is to activate your rigid body in various towns, what you call kicks." He explained that one had to avoid committing oneself to any activity, lest one make a wrong choice.

II.

It is useful to place this inexpressive face and his unoffending kicks in our recent literary genealogy. Great-granddaddy, I guess, is the stoical hero of Hemingway: Hemingway's young fellow understands that the grown-up world is corrupt and shattering, but he is not "beat," for he can prove that he is himself a man by being taciturn, growing hair on his chest, and shooting elephants. He has "values" and therefore can live through a few books. His heir is Céline's anti-hero, a much shrewder fellow: he sees that to have those "values" is already to be duped by the corrupt adults, so he adopts the much more powerful role of universal griper and cry-baby, to make everybody feel guilty and disgusted. The bother with his long gripe is that it is monotonous, there is a lot of opportunity for writing, but not even a single book. The next hero, and I think the immediate predecessor of being on the road, gives up the pretense of being grown-up altogether (a good case is Salinger's *Catcher in the Rye*): he is the boy in the very act of being mortally wounded by the grown-ups' corruption. This terrible moment is one book. But you can't cry forever, so you set your face in a mask and go on the road. The adolescent decides that he himself is the guilty one—this is less painful than the memory of being hurt—so he'd better get going. The trouble is that there is no longer any drama in this; the drama occurred before "*my wife and I split up,*" before I lost my father.

Sociologically, the following propositions seem to me to be relevant: (1) In our economy of abundance there are also surplus people, and the fellows on the road are among them. There is in fact no man's work for them to do. (2) We are inheriting our failure, as an advanced industrial country, to have made reasonable social arrangements in the last century; now when there is no longer a motive to work hard and accumulate capital, we have not developed an alternative style of life. (3) The style that we do have, "Madison Avenue," is too phony for a young person to grow up into. (4) Alternatively, there is an attraction to the vitality (by comparison) of the disfranchised Negroes and now the Puerto Ricans; these provide a language and music, but this culture is primitive and it corrupts itself to Madison Avenue as soon as it can. (5) In family life there has been a similar missed-revolution and confusion, so that many young people have grown up in cold, hypocritical, or broken homes. Lacking a primary environment for the expression and training of their feelings, they are both affectless and naive in the secondary environment. (6) The spontaneous "wild" invention that we may expect from every young generation has been seriously blighted by the anxieties of the war and the cold war. (7) The style of life resulting from all this is an obsessional conformity, busy-ness without any urge toward the goals of activity, whether ideal goals or wealth and power. There is not much difference between the fellows "on the road" and the "organization men"—the former readily become the latter.

> I ate another apple pie and ice cream; that's practically all I ate all the way across the country, I knew it was nutritious and it was delicious of course. (page 15)

On other occasions, they eat franks and beans. More rarely hamburgers, malted milks, of course. That is, the drink-down quick-sugar food of spoiled children, and the pre-cut meat for lazy chewing beloved of ages six to ten. Nothing is bitten or bitten-off, very little is chewed; there is a lot of sugar for animal energy, but not much solid food to grow on. I suppose that this is the most significant observation one can make about *On The Road.*

For nearly two-thirds of this book one is struck, I have said, by the lack of writing; the book is nothing but a conversation between the buddies, "Do you remember when?" and "Do you remember how we?" "That was the greatest!" Here is confirmation that they, like Kilroy, were there; but not much distilled experience for the reader. But then (page 173) there *is* a page of writing, not very good and not original—it is from the vein of rhapsody of Céline and Henry Miller—nevertheless, writing. The situation is that the narrator finally finds himself betrayed, abandoned, penniless, and hungry in a strange city. The theme of the rhapsody is metempsychosis, "I realized that I had died and been reborn numberless times but just didn't remember"—and this theme is a happy invention, for it momentarily raises the road to a plane of metaphysical fantasy. And this is how the passage climaxes:

> In the window I smelled all the food of San Francisco. . . . Let me smell the drawn butter and lobster claws. There were places where they specialized in thick red roast beef *au jus* or roast chicken basted in wine. There were places where hamburgs sizzled on grills and the coffee was only a nickel. And oh, that pan-fried chow mein, etc.

Here, at least in wish, is a piece of reality that is not just kicks and "the greatest"; he wants to *eat* this food. Silone was right when he said that we must learn again the words for Bread and Wine.

Goodman reviewed Jack Kerouac's *On the Road* for *Midstream* (Winter 1958).

The Sweet Style of Ernest Hemingway

It is an exaggeration to say that the language determines the metaphysics of the tribe and what people can think—the so-called "Whorfian hypothesis." Language is checked by unverbalized experience. Language itself is plastic and says new things when necessary. People do manage to communicate across the barrier of language and culture, e.g., I get something out of Homer, Genesis, and Confucius. And in the problems of philosophy, we can usually think away the language of previous thinkers and still find a real problem for ourselves.

But we can put Whorf's thesis in a more modest form that is more rewarding: a style of speech is a hypothesis about how the world is. When speakers adopt a style, they are already saying something substantive. A good style, colloquial and literary, is one that is adequate to cope with, that "saves," a wide range of experience, omitting nothing indispensable. It proves itself as a way of being, it does not break down, it is believable.

I.

This view is similar to the newer philosophy of linguistic analysis that has developed out of linguistic positivism. Instead of treating popular metaphysics as nonsense in which people are stuck, and to which prophylaxis must be applied, linguistic analysis takes common speech as a repository of vast empirical experience of curious matters by the community, just as the common law is the embodied wisdom of the Anglo-Saxon people (such as it is). The philosophical problem is to decipher exactly what is being said; in colloquial sentences, what do people *mean* when they say "mind," "cause," "responsibility," "good," "bad," and so forth?

Literary style is a convenient object for this kind of analysis. It is usually less subtle than excellent colloquial speech, but it is recorded and it provides large coherent wholes to examine. Let us look briefly at a famous modern style, Hemingway's, and single out one of its dominant hypotheses.

It is a passive style. The characters, including the narrator, are held off in such a way—"alienated," as Brecht puts it—that they influence nothing; events happen to them. The actions that they initiate—the story consists entirely of actions that they initiate—do not add up to actualizing them; it is one thing after another. Yet neither do the actions betray and doom them, as in ancient stories of Fate, for that would impart a meaning, a tragic meaning, to the world. Rather, the events turn out to be happenings.

Needless to say, the passivity of people in contemporary society, with its high technology and centralized organization, has been the prevailing theme of naturalistic fiction for over a century. But Hemingway takes the theme at a deeper level. His stories are located in nonindustrial scenes, often in fairly primitive places, and they are about activities that are even spectacularly individualistic and active, dangerous sports, smuggling, soldiers on the loose. The characters come on with a heavy preponderance of active verbs. And the effect is passive. Unlike the naturalists who show how men are puppets of the institutions, and *by* showing it inject their own activity, often political, into the prose, Hemingway contrives by his style, by what he tells and what he avoids telling, to show that happening-to-one is the nature of things. (Psychoanalytically, the passivity has been internalized.)

II.

Here are two passages from *The Sun Also Rises,* published in 1926 when Hemingway was twenty-eight. The first is the end of a description, similar to others in the book. The characters have driven up a high mountain and it is cold.

> The bus leveled down onto the straight line of a road that ran to Burguete. We passed a cross roads and crossed a bridge over a stream. The houses of Burguete were along both sides of the road. There were no side-streets. We passed the church and the school-yard, and the bus stopped. We got down and the driver handed down our bags and the rod-case. A carabineer in his cocked hat and yellow leather cross straps came up.
>
> "What's in there?" he pointed to the rod-case.
>
> I opened it and showed him. He asked to see our fishing-permits and I got them out. He looked at the date and then waved us on.
>
> "Is that all right?" I asked.
>
> "Yes. Of course."
>
> We went up the street, past the whitewashed stone houses.

The other passage is the climax of action of the novel, the bullfight.

> When he had finished his work with the muleta and was ready to kill, the crowd made him go on. They did not want the bull killed yet, they did not want it to be over. Romero went on. It was like a course in bull fighting. All the passes he linked up, all completed, all slow, templed and smooth. There were no tricks and no mystifications. There was no brusqueness. And each pass as it reached the summit gave you a sudden ache inside. The crowd did not want it ever to be finished.
>
> The bull was squared on all four feet to be killed, and Romero killed directly below us. He killed not as he had been forced to by the last bull, but as he wanted to. He profiled directly in front of the bull, drew the sword out of the muleta and sighted along the blade. The bull watched him. Romero spoke to the bull and tapped one of his feet. The bull charged and Romero waited for the charge, the muleta held low, sighting along the blade, his feet firm. Then without taking a step forward, he became one with the bull, the sword was in high between the shoulders, the bull had followed the low slung flannel, that disappeared as Romero lurched clear to the left, and it was over. The bull tried to go forward, his legs commenced to settle, he swung from side to side, hesitated, then went down on his knees, and.... Handkerchiefs were waving all over the bull-ring. The President looked down from the box and waved his handkerchief....

These passages are, of course, artfully different—within the narrow range of language that Hemingway uses. The short, active, declarative sentences of the description are increasingly connected by "and" in the action, accelerating the tempo; finally, there are only commas, speed of speech. In the climactic sentence "Then without taking a step, etc.," the syntax is allowed to break down. The description has a natural randomness, as things turn up, including the pointless dialogue with the carabineer. In the action every sentence is pointed to the climax.

In both passages, Hemingway uses the repetitions that are his favorite glue. But in the description they are more freely scattered and oddly equivocal in syntax: "road," "cross roads," "Cross straps," "crossed," "sides of the road," "side-streets," "leveled down," "got down," "handed down." In the action, the repetitions follow more directly and are univocal, urgent, plangent: "They did not want," "they did not want it over," "he wanted to"; "killed," "killed," "killed"; "directly below us," "directly in front of the bull"; "charged," "waited for the charge"; "handkerchiefs were waving," "waved his handkerchief."

III.

Nevertheless, the two passages have overwhelmingly in common the chief characteristic of Hemingway's style early and mature: the persons are held at arm's length, there is no way to get inside them or identify with them, it is happening to them. (But note that the events do not happen to the prose; rather the prose influences the events. For instance, it is because the driver handed *down* the bags and *ended* with the rod-case that the carabineer came *up* and pointed to the rod-case.)

In a description of arriving in a new place, it is plausible for events to happen to a person; but in the passages of action it is almost uncanny—and this is why this is a remarkable style—how we still seem to hear, "It happened that the crowd did not want," or even "it happened to the crowd that it did not want"; "it happened to Romero that he wanted," "it happened that he profiled," "it happened to him that the bull charged," and "it happened that he met the charge." This has gotten to be the style of "objective" journalism, but it was writers like Hemingway who invented the style for the journalists. The verbs are active and the sentences are declarative, but since the *persons* do not do it, we feel that they do not *do* it. And this is how the author has plotted it in the preceding pages anyway.

The narrator too is mesmerized by what he is telling. The effect is not at all like the impressionism of Virginia Woolf, for she lets us experience the first-person knower, who grows. Rather, as I have said, it is like the Brechtian "alienation," which Hemingway achieves more consistently than Brecht.[1]

That we exist in a meaningless universe—vanity of vanities—is the theme of *The Sun Also Rises* with its motto and title taken from Ecclesiastes; and this novel, though not powerful, is authentic through and through. In Hemingway's later works, the more romantic or adventurous themes are betrayed by the passive style. (*The Old Man and the Sea* has some authenticity, but the style is richer.) Ideally, the style of any work should be the style *of* that work, a unique language saying what the whole work wants to say. But of course with Hemingway and most of us, our style is our way of being in the world in general rather than for just this one book. We are wise to choose our subjects according to what we *can* say. In the best cases, we choose on the borderline and learn to say more. Hemingway played it a little too safe.

IV.

To make my point, let me contrast this passive style with a powerful active style. I unfairly choose a very great passage. Here is the exordium of the opening section of *The Decline and Fall of the Roman Empire.*

For three long chapters Gibbon has been describing and (more or less) extolling the Roman Empire under the Antonines, its extent, its power, its prosperity, its arts, its institutions and civil peace, the occasional beneficence of its rulers. He concludes,

> But the empire of the Romans filled the world, and, when that empire fell into the hands of a single person, the world became a safe and dreary prison for his enemies. The slave of Imperial despotism, whether he was condemned to drag his gilded chain in Rome and the senate, or to wear out a life of exile on the barren rock of Seriphus, or the frozen banks of the Danube, expected his fate in silent despair. To resist was fatal, and it was impossible to fly. On every side he was encompassed with a vast extent of

[1] In one of his aphorisms, Kafka says, "I have long since fallen under the wheels—comfortingly enough." But in his stories he persists in asking why; he feels insulted. The effect is not comfortingly passive but painfully restive.

sea and land, which he could never hope to traverse without being discovered, seized, and restored to his irritated master. Beyond the frontiers, his anxious view could discover nothing, except the ocean, inhospitable deserts, hostile tribes of barbarians, of fierce manners and unknown language, or dependent kings, who would gladly purchase the emperor's protection by the sacrifice of an obnoxious fugitive. "Wherever you are," said Cicero to the exiled Marcellus, "remember that you are equally within the power of the conqueror."

Whether in his enlightened awareness or in his Enlightenment prejudice, there is no doubt that Gibbon is in complete control of the vast scene and appropriates it for the reader. In each sentence he exhausts the alternative situations, the possibilities of action, the geographical space of the world. The ideas are many and not repeated, the motion is rapid for an elegant style, yet he gives us all the balances and parallels and even a chiasmus. Without losing speed, he builds to longer sentences, grander territory, bleaker scenery, and more desperate gloom. Yet, though he has the story in his grip, he is by no means cold or detached; he does not strangle himself. Nearly every sentence has something sarcastic or spiteful—"safe prison," "gilded chain in the senate," "irritated master," "obnoxious fugitive." He is not talking about an abstraction; we are made to identify with that hyperactive, and balked, victim. And in the book the plotted place of this bitter outburst, after the (rather) golden narration that precedes, is like a blow.

V.

Return now to Hemingway and his narrow range. It is not surprising that a succession of short active indicative sentences produces passivity. We turn to each verb after it has struck. There is not enough syntactical leeway for the author or reader to become engaged either actively or contemplatively, or as one who desires, or one who interprets. An advantage of the style is that it is in close contact with the facts being told, since there is no intermediary of indirect discourse, point of view, subordination, explanation. This is its aptness for journalistic reporting. A disadvantage is that it can rapidly become boring, as Hemingway often is, because it is hard to make the bits add up and there is increasing resistance to taking the bits in. When Hemingway is good, he provides glue, repetitions, or leading tones like the rod-case.

But Hemingway certainly also used the style hoping to tell simple, down-to-earth experience, and in this crucial respect the style doesn't work, since it is not how we experience. I have elsewhere made the same point against taking short active indicative sentences as the syntactical kernels of all sentences. The world that is told by them is not primary experience, which is more elaborately and globally structured, and we see that when such sentences are actually spun out, the effect is human passivity. To derive all sentences from short active sentences, as Chomsky does in his basic grammar, must be wrong, because this is not how uncorrupted speakers are in the world, especially children.

VI.

But we must then ask a further question: If Hemingway's style is so persistently passive in effect, how can it cope with enough of human life to be viable? I can think of four ways in which Hemingway countervails the passive effect of his prose.

First, obviously, is the violent *macho* activism of the characters and events he couches in the prose, nothing but bullfighters, warriors, gun-packing gangsters, hunters of big animals and big fish. But this becomes real thin real soon. One begins to psychoanalyze it simply because there is nothing else to do with it. One wishes that the chosen sport was baseball, with teammates, or that he wrote about equally manly tasks like farming or carpentry, so that there could be some product more interesting than a corpse.

Second, he knows better. There is a unique sentence in *The Sun Also Rises* that is a most peculiar development of the accustomed style. The whole passage is a deviation. A man has been killed on the street by a bull being driven to the ring, and a waiter at the cafe comments that it's a stupid kind of fun and not for him. The narrator says,

> The bull who killed Vicente Gitones was named Bocanegra, was number 118 of the bull-breeding establishment of Sanchez Taberno, and was killed by Pedro Romero as the third bull of that same afternoon. His ear was cut by popular acclamation and given to Pedro Romero, who, in turn, gave it to Brett, who wrapped it in a handkerchief belonging to

myself, and left both ear and handkerchief, along with a number of Muratti cigarette-stubs, shoved far back in the drawer of the bed-table that stood beside her bed in the Hotel Montoya, in Pamplona.

This unusually long and uncharacteristically complex sentence is the only spunky sentence in the book, and one of the few in Hemingway's work. It tells of a rebellious, not passive, response: bitter contempt. Once the short active sentences are brought synoptically together, the effect is to write them off, to tell the world off. But though he *knows* this, Hemingway cannot follow it up, so that the passage is merely sentimental—sentimentality is feeling or "significance" more than the plot warrants. Instead he goes on to the bullfight and, as if on the rebound, to the one overwritten paragraph in the book, "Pedro Romero had the greatness, etc.," which is hopelessly sentimental. Instead of taking his own rage as meaningful, Hemingway makes a desperate bid to find a hero, an agent. It doesn't wash.

The rejected theme reappears years later, however, as the rueful message of *The Old Man and the Sea,* that you try like the devil and bring back bones. The later book is not spunky, it rationalizes; but it is a fairly hard look at Hemingway himself.

(Incidentally, the bull's ear that Brett leaves behind with the cigarette butts, embarrassedly in the back of the drawer, is the real literary probability for her walking out on the young bullfighter in the end, and not the lofty renunciation that some critics seem to read. What *does* one do with shitty underwear or a bull's ear, in a hotel?)

A third way in which Hemingway countervails the passive hypothesis of his style is his stoical ethic. It appears not in the subject matter or the prose, but in the plotting: the people are loyal, they endure, they go it alone. This ethic is surely why he was so popular and seemed to be a major writer during his era. He gave people something to live on with, when the conditions were so absurd. But he did not have enough intellect to assert a lasting ethical position.

VII.

My impression is that young people today do not find him "existential" enough. I have heard young people seriously ask what difference it would make if the human race vanished utterly. Hemingway would have been shocked by such an attitude, as I am. Put it this way: normally, we would expect characters in novels, especially toward the end, to do something, influence events. In Hemingway's novels the characters are done to, but at least they *are* done to by the events, they are engaged in them. In many recent novels, however, the characters just "make the scene," they are not engaged in the events but are like tourists. Or they con the scene like hipsters. They seem to have infinite time. Hemingway understood that people get worn out, grow old.

But therefore—yin and yang—in contemporary writing, there is a flood of very personal reporting of *actual* political events in which the authors have taken part. More passionate and reflective than objective journalism, less plotted and universal than poetic fiction, this has become a new genre since it fills the need of the times. So far as I have read, Barbara Deming is the best. Mailer is an interesting transitional writer; he is caught in an ethic partly Hemingway and partly hipster. He gravitates to the new subject matter, but he is not committed to its actions and therefore he becomes decorative. (Reminds me of Carlyle.)

In my opinion, Hemingway's work will last, not because of his stoical ethic but because of something in his style. It is sweetness. It appears more frequently in books later than *The Sun Also Rises,* especially in *A Farewell to Arms.* When it appears, the short sentences coalesce and flow, and sing—sometimes melancholy, sometimes pastoral, sometimes personally embarrassed in an adult, not an adolescent, way. In the dialogues, he pays loving attention to the spoken word. And the writing is meticulous; he is sweetly devoted to writing well. Most everything else is resigned, but here he makes an effort, and the effort produces lovely moments. The young, since they read poorly, do not dig that *writing* is his "existential" act. As Spinoza would say it, for a writer his writing is intellect in action, his freedom, whereas the themes he is stuck with, his confusion, his audience are likely to be his human bondage.

This essay appeared first in the *New York Review of Books* (December 30, 1971); and in another version as a chapter of *Speaking and Language.* The earlier printing is followed here.

Preface to Kafka's Metamorphosis

In the simple fables of the ancients, the beasts act like men. In the sentimental animal stories of modern times, the beasts act as themselves, but most often in situations related to men and exemplifying passions and virtues interesting in men. Only the great naturalists study the beasts merely as themselves. There is also a kind of satire in which men act like beasts.

It was the rare gift, and heavy curse, of Kafka to be able to describe his beasts in all these ways at once. This is because he makes an identification of man and beast. Kafka's animals are *totems*; to find the analogy for them we must look in the religion of the primitives, in folklore, and in the animal phobias that haunt the dreams of children.

Now, the totemic identification of beast and man is both symbolical and literal; unless we keep in mind both these aspects, we cannot understand the play and nightmares of children nor the wonderful tales of Kafka. Symbolically the beast is a symptom of unconscious conflicts, mostly those centering round the hostile and castrating father and the son's identification with him; the son's surrender to him; perhaps, most deeply of all, the child himself as the devourer, destroying mother and father both, at the age of his omnipotence—and now he can never make amends! The reader of

Kafka is well acquainted with these gnawing, devouring, and bloodsucking little beasts: moles, moths, jackals, mice, and vermin.

But, literally, the beast is in his own person a true friend and communicant, another self. For the primitive, the child, the profound artist like Kafka, the profound sociologist like Kropotkin have not forgotten that there is a community of all life and a continuum of the libido. So in this story of *The Metamorphosis,* hearing his sister play the violin, the bug pathetically asks:

> Could it be that he was only an animal, when music moved him so? It seemed to him to open a way toward that unknown nourishment he so longed for.

Now, we know that Kafka himself, the man, abhorred music; it drew round him a wall, he says, it made him "otherwise than free." But Kafka as the animal—yes, even as a loathsome bug!—is laid open to this language of living feeling. Shall we not say that the bug is better, more oneself, than the commercial traveler or the official in the insurance office?

Clearly the literal and symbolical identifications are related: without love of beasts there would not be totemism; without totemism the adult would not return passionately to the beasts for an escape from his ego into nature, freedom, and community. Kafka's beasts are both totems and literal friends; then we see that it is not that an animal is likened to a man, but a man is acting out some animal-identity in himself. I do not mean that man is satirically "reduced" to an animal, for the animal-identity is deeper than the ordinary human being and his behavior, it is nearer to the unknown deity; it is a totem. Likewise the treatment is realistic, the animal acts as itself—often observed with stunning accuracy—but just for this reason it abreacts the human complex, it furnishes a release, because the animal is a literal friend and lover closer to guiltless nature. Again I do not mean that there is a sentimentality of the "happy primitive"; it is an understatement to say that Kafka had a vivid sense of "nature red in tooth and claw"; but there is a release from moral delusions and conventional defenses, a return to living ethics both communal and self-regarding.

One more note that is indispensable for the reader of *The Metamorphosis*: in the famous Letter to his Father, Kafka puts in his father's mouth the following remarkable reproach against himself:

> I admit that we are fighting each other, but there are two kinds of fight. There is the knightly battle—and there is the struggle of vermin which not only stings but at the same time preserves itself by sucking the other's blood. Such are you. You are not fit for life, but in order to live in comfort, without worry or self-reproach, you prove that I have taken away your fitness for life and put it all into my pocket.

Kafka did not flee from the reproach, as we others do; he dragged it into the forefront of consciousness. Shall we not say that he was—our Knight?

In 1946 Vanguard brought out a new translation of Kafka's famous story, and Goodman, whom they had been publishing for several years, wrote the preface. That same year he was working on *Kafka's Prayer* for Vanguard.

The Real Dream

I.

In *Description of a Struggle,* a dreamy narrative that Kafka wrote when he was twenty, he is already adept and committed in the humoristic vein of post-romantic capricious fantasy, one of the manners of Heine. This capricious tone, as it gets to be expert and weary, is most associated with, I guess, Vienna. Richard Strauss is its best voice; and certainly it is what Musil, another fine Viennese humorist, makes us understand as the appropriate tone of Franz Josef's empire. Keeping this background in mind, it is interesting to see with what slight alterations Kafka in a few years transforms it into his high and original style. I want to call attention to a key passage in this early piece.

Description begins as a realistic account of an erotically-tinged intimacy leading rapidly to embarrassment and the fear of rejection; soon the humorous fantasy takes over, with the kind of sign-language of incest and castration that the young man could still write unconsciously in 1903 (though the content is almost the same as in *The Judgment* and *The Trial*, ten years later); finally, in traditional caprice-style, the humor broadens into fantastic horse-play, expressing one's own victory, and the section ends, "I left him there on the stones (with a wounded knee) and whistled down a few vultures. . . to guard him." The second section then begins as follows:

> I walked on, unperturbed. But since, as a pedestrian, I dreaded the effort of climbing the mountainous road, I let it become gradually flatter, let it slope down into a valley in the distance. . . . Because I love pine-woods, I went through woods of this kind, and since I like gazing silently up at the stars, the stars appeared slowly in the sky, as is their wont. . . I caused to rise an enormously high mountain whose plateau overgrown with brushwood bordered on the sky. I could see quite clearly the little ramifications of the highest branches. This sight, ordinary as it may be, made me so happy that I, as a small bird on a twig of those distant scrubby brushes, forgot to let the moon come up. It lay already behind, no doubt angry at the delay. . . . And suddenly the moon itself appeared.

This passage is remarkable and startling. What has happened is that the young man has suddenly invented for himself surrealism. In the beginning section, working in the framework of a purely literary and not very interesting "real world," he tried to liven it up by constructing fantastic and humorous events. Now suddenly he has turned to a real actuality, oneself fantasizing and willing the fantasies. He rings the changes on this, and soon he sees that the real fantasies have a will of their own, they even get angry. And finally they begin to act on their own, whether he wants them to or not. This is the method of surrealism.

> From the interior of the forest, I heard the approaching crashes of collapsing trees. Now I could have thrown myself down on the moss to sleep, but since I feared to sleep on the ground, I crept up a tree—the trunk sliding quickly down the rings formed by my arms and legs. . . . I went hastily to sleep while a squirrel of my whim sat stiff-tailed at the trembling end of the branch.

It is the stiff-tailed squirrel, which is actually willed, that makes us see by contrast that the scene is a compelled fantasy, it is surreal. Now this is one element in the manner of *The Trial* and *The Castle*: he cannot help dreaming out this dream, even though he is inventing it step by step.

II.

There is a contrasting element of his high style that is also illustrated in this book of sketches and fragments. Consider the little piece about "Poseidon": the administrator of the waters is so occupied with keeping his books and accounts that he has never had time to sail and has hardly seen the oceans.

Paraphrased thus, this is another stale variety of fantastic humor: sophomoric satire; indeed, give him buttons and call him a Count and he is a rear-admiral of the Dual Empire. And one can have fantastic fun with bureaucracy, in the manner of the Captain of Koepenik. Yet this is not at all the effect of Kafka's "Poseidon." Rather—remarkably, for he eschews any description—what we carry away is a sense of the vastness of the earth's waters, and touchingly, that one would have to be a very busy and great man to keep account of them. Just so, in two long novels, in "The Great Wall of China" and a dozen other pieces, like "Blumfeld," "The Refusal," and "The Conscription of Troops" in the present collection, Kafka delineates the unbelievable features of bureaucracy, yet there is no "satire." Rather, he convinces us, first, that "the disharmony of this world is mathematical," and very immense it is; and then, that the bureaucracy is in us, it answers to our deep needs, for we are dogs—even the young women from remote villages come in their best finery to the hour of conscription, though they are only beaten and rejected for their pains. As if he said, "Who can afford the luxury of making fun of it? We are too engaged." Lofty satire attacks its target from a position of inner security and indignation that Kafka never enjoyed; humorous mockery strikes its spiteful blows safely cowering, but Kafka was too earnest, and too loving, to take cover in humor.

(Of course I do not mean that Kafka is not comic. From the point of view of eternity, all disharmony is comic and people are ridiculous; and Kafka often had a good glimpse from that point of view. We know that he used to become hilarious when reading some of his little paragraphs; his readers generally wear a quieter smile, for it's not so rich as all that.)

So in the fantastic humor of the post-romantics, Kafka again doggedly recovers the actuality of the real world. Yet it *is* very like a dream; it is like the compelled dream that the surrealist finds when he exercises his method. Then we may say that it is by combining these two opposite ways of handling the humorous that we can reconstruct the high style of Kafka: first, the humorist turns upon his real action of fantasizing till he comes to that in it which he does not will but which wills itself, the dream he is compelled to dream; and second, he finds that the content of this absurd fantasy is your actual world, in careful detail. Maybe sometimes he starts with the second, by worrying a small detail of reality, and then he finds that he is having a terrible bad dream, wide-awake too.

Critics have said that Kafka starts with a fantastic premise, and once that is granted, everything follows with a meticulous realism. But that cannot be, for the effect of it would be fantasy-and-science-fiction, not Kafka. The case is that the premise is not fantastic but actual—man *is* a bug, a mouse, a dog; and the great Ape in captivity *is* a man—it is all meticulously realistic; and oh Lord, the *whole* of it is an absurd fantasy. Hilarious.

III.

Let me follow one further step this tack of Kafka's relation to his fantasizing. It is evident that in him the normal function of fantasy was both very powerful and tightly reined in. (One would say that he reined it in, not to go off altogether.) He cannot allow his freakish symbols to live their own life and go their own way; he must check them back soon, and finally continuously, to the actuality. Now I think this explains why there are almost no Kafka stories that are simply fictions, with self-standing *personae,* and moving with the easy-going good-enough probability of free fictions. To Kafka that probability is not good enough; he needs it also to be more *true,* in the sense of more actual. But then he is fascinated and frozen by the actuality he finds in it, and he cannot lightly think away from it to the next episode.

Here we have one more explanation, I think (I have elsewhere given several others), why he left so many fragments, so much discontinuous in the middle and unfinished in the end. The fantasy image becomes too actual and he becomes fascinated because something is still concealed in the actual; yet it is only the actual, it is boring, and he leaves off. The present volume has again several fragments, as well as some beautifully finished small pieces. "Blumfeld" is typical: the original fiction is delightful, probable, profound, psychologically true—an elderly orderly functionary is lonely, and he suddenly finds he has the company of two neat jolly bouncing balls. He is embarrassed by them, he squelches them in the closet, and when he goes off to the office, he tries to use the neighborhood kids, who are also difficult to handle, to get rid of them. At the office there are, again, his two worthless and bothersome assistants. But they are too close to the actuality; Kafka bogs down in describing their tricks, and drops the whole story. Meantime, the proper next episode: confronting the results of the plan to get rid of the balls—this he never gets to. To be sure, the present narrative, as it is, conveys a salutary truth, namely "There's nothing different after all"; but this newsy gospel it conveys too dryly.

On the other hand, Kafka's close-checked handling of fantastic humor does give his lovely prose one of its finest and quietly stunning forward motions: we are bobbing along in the flow becoming diffuse, a little vague, a little wandering, of fantasy and fantasy-confabulation, and we quietly drop the infinite distance to what is only too real.

Goodman reviewed Kafka's *Description of a Struggle* for *Midstream* (Winter 1959).

Between the Flash and the Thunderstroke

All these poems have a uniform versification, so we can take it this is an achieved norm for Williams, and let me devote most of this review to discussing it. It is repetitions of the triplet

```
        ----------------------------
              ----------------------------
                     ----------------------------
```

where each dash is a beat of meaning that may contain from one to about ten ametric syllables, one to six or seven words. By a "beat of meaning" I mean any word or group of words that can momentarily, and relatively to its sentence, be attended to in itself. Pauses fall most frequently at the end of the first or second dash, but only sometimes at the end of the triplet: the versification is such as to keep you running on.

Now to understand this meter, we must at once observe it is laid across a serious nervous common speech given just as it might actually be spoken, without inversion, compression, or other alteration by which poets tailor speech. For instance, omitting the versification: "I should have known, though I did not, that the lily-of-the-valley is a flower makes many ill who whiff it." "This would be a fine day to go on a journey. Say to Florida where at this season all go nowadays." "She fed the King's poor and when she died left them some slight moneys under certain conditions." "In the name of love I came proudly as to an equal to be forgiven. Let me, for I know you take it hard, with good reason, give the steps if it may be by which you shall mount again to think well of me."

By "actual common speech" I do not mean prose. It is more profitable to regard common speech as the matrix from which both prose and verse are formed (and back towards which certain species of prose and verse aspire). You can hear this when you listen to Eliot or Gertrude Stein or William Carlos Williams and then notice that people sound like that when they talk. Stein more catches overheard voices, Eliot both social conversation and musing to oneself; but Williams gives you mostly the speech of a man explaining to you, perhaps over a cup of coffee, how it is with him, and trying to be accurate, clear, quick, and modest.

Here are some verses:

Once
        at El Paso
                toward evening,
I saw—and heard!—
        ten thousand sparrows
                who had come in from
the desert
        to roost. They filled the trees
                etc.

I think this versification has a twofold genealogy and is a fairly viable compromise of the conflicting demands of both lines.

(1) These are the three beats of meaning to a line of normal English blank verse. (As in blank verse, Williams occasionally has two beats and occasionally four.) Quite often Williams' triplets are perfect pentameters: "cannot surpass/the insistence/of his cheep"; "more than a natural one./His voice,/his movements"; "keen eyes,/serviceable beak/and general truculence"; "does it portend? /A war/will not erase it." There is, I choose quite at random, a pervasive blank verse with the usual variations. And with the poetic program of achieving the actual common speech unaltered, the most direct way of writing blank verses is to keep the triplets of meaning but to give up the pentameter meter, rather filling each beat with whatever is required, ametrically. This is just what Williams does. Thus Milton, in the sonnets also employing a nervous earnest style very close to speech, writes

to serve therewith/my Maker/and present
my true account/lest He returning/chide;

but Williams allows also

I cannot say/that I have gone to Hell/for you
but often/found myself there/in your pursuit.

(2) If, however, we consider the blank verse

throws back his head
and simply—
yells! The din

we see at once the other genealogy of this versification: each beat of meaning is to be if possible taken also in isolation, as an image. Such brief bursts are the direct heir of the imagist poetry of the beginning of the century, and especially of the Chinese influence. Compare, e.g., Florence Ayscough's translation of Tu Fu, where the attempt is made to keep the ideograms intact (so that the couplets of ideograms can be read both vertically and horizontally). At the start of his career, to be sure, Williams was concerned with the common objects, generally pictorial and generally static, and he used to construct them handsomely with these isolating phrases. Or we can take these little bursts as a kind of pointillism, every spot a color, every color a spot; from this beginning Cummings and Pound went off in their own directions—to bursts of surprise, shapes of words, glancing references and fragmentary allusions, etc. But Williams has taken up a program of actual common speech that does not fragment into little entities in exactly this way; he has accordingly tried to get back to a regular underlying flow, in which the sudden accents and turns and digressions can sound out more like the actuality of talking.

This versification does manage to give Williams an imagist blank verse serviceable for his purposes. I question its widespread utility. In the first place there is a difficulty of breathing. The bread-and-butter virtue of pentameter blank verses—or alexandrines or Greek iambic trimeters—is that each verse is one breath; this is the modulus for dramatic recitation, and to maintain it poets have been willing to make large alterations of what is actually spoken. By contrast, many of Williams' lines have to be rehearsed, or contrariwise, there is the temptation to disregard the versification altogether and recite straight on, a very sweet melody but swifter than he intends. But secondly, and more important, it is very difficult to make these cut-up ametric little units flow and grow into true paragraphs, the way blank verses grow with power and intensity into large wholes.

This makes little difference here, for mostly Williams is interested in a more glancing and unimpassioned effect, darting from aspect to aspect, shifting his point of view. But this versification too can achieve paragraphs of power and intensity. For example: "It is ridiculous//what airs we put on/to seem profound/while our hearts//gasp dying/for want of love./Having your love//I was rich./Thinking to have lost it/I am tortured//and cannot rest./I do not come to you/abjectly//with confessions of my faults,/I have confessed,/all of them.//In the name of love/I come proudly/as to an equal//to be forgiven" and so forth. Here the gasping, the interruptions and the turns, that are in the verse are in the situation itself, and you cannot arrange the words better.

So much for Williams' versification; but finally let me add a few remarks about *Journey to Love* as a whole. I find it a disturbing book. As he tells us frequently in these poems, Williams is now seventy years old; and the case is—whether he likes it or not (my guess is that he would both like it and not)—he is a sage. For that's what a sage is, a person who keeps growing and producing and nevertheless manages to live a long time; as Rilke said, the point is not to be happy but to persist. A sage has got the trick of it; we open our ears and say, tell *us*.

He has curious things to say about eyes and looking; here are some passages: "To a look in my son's eyes—/I hope he did not see/that I was looking—"; and "we dare not stare too hard/or we are lost./The instant//trivial as it is/is all we have"; and "He kept looking at me//and I at him . . . His eyes/which were intelligent/ were wide open//but evasive, mild. . . . my father's/face!" Is this, then, the trick of it? Look and see, but do not let on that you're looking, and you daren't let on to yourself that you see. Elsewhere he projects this feeling onto the Others: "It would be/too much//if the public//pried among the minutiae/of our private affairs.// Not/that we have anything to hide//but could *they*/stand it?" The motive here, to spare the Others, sounds like a rationalization; certainly at least poets first blurt it out to the Others and then find out what it is we mean to say. Williams knows this, of course, and his advice seems to be, "Don't give yourself away too far (to yourself); take it easy and you'll live long."

You can see it in a structural device that recurs half a dozen times. He starts out with a forthright picturesque excited affirmation; then suddenly he stops and asks a question, much weaker, and doubtful: "What is she/but an ambassador/from another world?" or "And who but we are concerned/with the beauty of apple-blossoms?" or "Are we not most of us like that?" or "What was he intent upon/but to drown out/that look?" Frankly, I cannot help feeling that these questions are spurious, they are smoke-screens. He doesn't ask because he wants to know, he asks because he knows something *else* too well and he is changing the subject; or closer, he has trapped himself into saying something that makes him suddenly feel very lonely and unsafe, and so he covers up with a modest question to get back to the animal warmth of agreement.

The most excited and affirmative poem in this volume is "The Sparrow," dedicated "To My Father," and a very fine poem it is. And what a busy, sexy, decisive, truculent, and independent bird that sparrow is! even though he does end up the dried-out victim of a female. As a figure for himself, however, our poet chooses a flower. "The Pink Locust": "I'm persistent as the pink locust,/ once admitted/to the garden//you will not easily get rid of it." And this is a fine poem too; but the ending of it has a certain doctrinal abstractness, and I, at least, can't help asking, "Who's he kidding? and why is he kidding himself?" Also I give myself the answer, "Say! who is supposed to know the trick of persisting, you or he?"

The longest and most ambitious poem in this volume is "Asphodel, That Greeny Flower." This is a curious poem, much too elaborate to explore here in a few words. But it seems to be founded on a simple enough premise: the old poet is seeking for forgiveness from his wife and reinstatement in her affections, since this love is after all the main thing in life. (What the devil sin did he commit anyway?) Now if this *is* the premise, I'm damned if it's a sage one. If at the age of discretion we are still making this particular Journey to Love, it's too bad, it simply isn't worth it. But I don't believe it (and I don't think he believes it).

This review of William Carlos Williams' *Journey to Love* was published in *Poetry* (March 1956).

The Abundance

I.

Poems 1906-26 is a translation into the original rhyming meters of *Gedichte 1906 bis 1926,* collected from the remains and manuscripts by Ernst Zinn. J.B. Leishman's valiant effort is here, as in his other renderings of Rilke, occasionally successful; and his Introduction is an admirable exploration of the poet's inner biography during these years of his highest development. The German and the English collections are differently arranged. Ernst Zinn gives us these hitherto uncollected works in the following series: those scatteredly published by Rilke or expressly indicated by him for publication; those written as gifts and dedications and therefore certainly meant for some audience; and whatever else was left in notebooks etc. of poems, fragments, projects. This arrangement makes sense for the lover of poems as works of finished art: we get the polished work first and all together. But Mr. Leishman chooses to give us all these pieces in the strict chronological order of their composition; and this arrangement remarkably makes us see the continuity and transformation in how that poet was in the world, and it casts bright light on the interrelation of the various Rilkean themes.

In whatever arrangement, the salient fact is that here is this new treasury (more than 600 pages of German text!) of one of the three or four great poets of our century. As a reviewer with a limited space I am at a loss how to cope with my task. Then rather than say nothing or something vague, let me offer some rough notes on one particular question: "What is the peculiarly *Rilkean* effect? what were its vicissitudes during these 20 years?"

Consider a few phrases: "As twice a year the flocking birds are thrown," "the black landscape of distance pushes into the undecided town," "surround the tree with retention," "departures patrol (stroke?) the streets," the palm is a "sole that no longer walks except on feeling," "Sad big nearness weighs me down, that incurable human weight," "but not to remain is the essence of swinging," "as a colonnade bears its arches, you your joy, yet that also rests on something." Everywhere there are examples: how the ball lets go and flies, how odors stand in the alley, how the doves dive up from the valley of swooping. Now what strikes one first here is that the object of experience is not something out-there but how-the-thing-is-had. In recent philosophy this way of notating is called *phenomenology,* and the phenomenal object is momentarily bracketed-off (in Husserl's phrase) from both the "subject" and the "environment." Such concrete notations are the raw materials of Rilke's poems. "I linger but all my boundaries keep precipitating themselves outside and are already there": this sounds like technical phenomenology, just as Husserl uses the Rilkean word "horizons."

Let me say the same thing in another context. Rilke was of course intensely concerned with paintings and plastic arts. Now consider the passage: "Slowly recall it: sea on sea heavy with itself, blue out of itself, empty at the edge with a green ground, and suddenly, breathless, the cliffs racing from so deep that they don't know where their steep climb will end." This is a pictorial analysis exactly in the manner of Paul Klee, with the emphasis on the values in the plane and the directedness of attention. Or the God Horus: "And where from the overfull block the neck slowly to the cheek turns, reveals the fertility of youthful locks the face that full-gazing stands" (word order as in the original). Here again, it is not directly the feeling of the poet nor the fact or symbolical significance of the thing that is given, but the experience of having-the-thing, from which both feeling and meaning spring alive.

In a very important sense, Rilke did the same thing as Wordsworth. Unlike as these poets seem and are, they are working the same raw material of actual moments, and they therefore turn out to have many of the same themes: that the world is too much with us, but it is not the unworldly but the concrete, the happening, that can save; such were the gods of the pagans; and in our childhood we lived so; poetry is recollection in tranquillity, "the very fact that you're not there is warm with you and realer and more than a privation"; the early dead have a special immortality. (It is a fascinating study to compare and contrast Rilke's "Requiem on the Death of A Boy" and Wordsworth's astounding "There Was a Boy.") Wordsworth has one enormous advantage over Rilke, for he never overlooks the most concrete thing of all: that when he is making a poem he is indeed having-making-a-poem, secure in it (by grace). Then his relived actual moments have a solid permanence. But Rilke, never quite secure in *that* moment, of re-creating, feels the remembered contact as always slipping away, never "quite" achieved; he harps on its momentariness, its eye-blinking; he over-estimates its immensity; he is more sentimental than Wordsworth and allows himself to say, what is poetic nonsense that "undefined and without all utterance remains what inly makes us." Wordsworth is humbler; like Cezanne, he does not try to catch the real world but to reconstruct it; this is Resolution and Independence. But let me hasten to say that even here Rilke has the virtue of his defect: he can say, "from having forgotten, rises time"; he is not a "waster of griefs," for lapse, loss, and helplessness are "our winter foliage."

A third poet for this comparison is Mallarmé: and like the Frenchman, Rilke is a great poet of the actual moment after the event: "the silence of screams is ashing endlessly downwards from the arching vault." "In the air polished by gymnasts and trembling from the going of victors."

II.

Now given the raw material of such notations of the actual phenomenon, we can define the Rilkean effect and trace its vicissitudes. First, an example: "Look, the god has now determined on me: a road reels out of him, and now rush toward me his horses—" That is, the phenomenology becomes drama; the actual awareness turns into stage, properties, actors. "Only the noise as he breaks the next piece of muteness off from the mountain of silence." This is simply miraculous. *When* it occurs, and it occurs frequently for it is implicit in his data. "People depart. The distance flees and flows." "Column of Wedlock! you rise to receive domes." "Weight falls from the sleeper like liberal rain from a cloud." (Isn't that gorgeous!) The bird at the fountain "adds the gift of its tranquil meeting to that quivering overflow." This effect, of the bracketed off phenomenon coming into action, is the Rilkean effect quintessentially.

Chronologically earlier, more primitive, and of course less unique, is for the environmental object to be transformed by the subjective mode of perception. Let me give an example from a lovely early poem, "The Valley": he is watching the stars come out and, with them, the lamps' existence; "I take them seriously (ernst) as stars, I know that most make a little circle, and no two shine alike"; but *therefore,* "I saw the railroad-station's little constellation pale." That is, he now knows what stars *are,* and lamps are stars. Here we see psychology and description turning into phenomenology. Such are the poems that make up a picture-book.

On the other hand, a subsequent development of the Rilkean dramatic effect is for the phenomena to become metaphysical entities. Sometimes he states this quite academically: "Meaningful word, 'inclination,' would we were aware of it everywhere—a hill, when it slowly, with gathering growth, inclines to the welcoming field." (The thought is Aristotle's things-seek-their-proper-places! but of course Aristotle was also a metaphysical phenomenologist.) "Can that be the redthorn, which presently our feeling will have to bear?"—this is taking the phenomenon seriously as a metaphysical entity, and what a typically odd Rilkean effect!

We come by an immediate step to Rilke's mythology, his Angels, his Early Dead, Saints, Animals with open eyes that look into eternity as brooks run on. Where he kept in touch with the dramatic moment, this mythology is deeply important for us (it is evidence for ethics), and it makes for the magnificent speech of the

Duino Elegies. Grandly: "Angels' loving is space . . . we in the wrestling nights fall from nearness to nearness." Every word seems abstract, and not one word is abstract. "The Poet fetches up in Heaven with a start." "The small bird's liberal flight making a future unneeded. All is abundance."

But then he tends to become abstract and create Platonic ideas which must then be manipulated in the manner of Shelley. Explicitly: "Now they've been so long known, let House, Tree, Bridge be differently dared." "Let us make a constellation on high out of the semblance below." (Alas, he no longer takes them seriously as stars!) And there is still a final stage: a kind of scholasticism of the phenomena in which, like Caroline conceits about roses, we get "Take now from a branch the sign that it's greeting you or saying see you again . . . nothing is lost, all gives out further." To my taste this is frigid, it is based on private abstractions that communicate very little.

(There is an alternative to a metaphysical-mythological development of a phenomenology: namely the psychoanalytic effort to get under the ground of experience. And to one's astonishment, Rilke indeed started on this tack, late 1913 and early 1914. The *Poems to Night* hover on the psychoanalytic—there are thoughts about sister and incest—"the questioning child"—"the endlessly older sister bending over the sister in me." What is psychologically interesting is how these poems follow on the accepted agony of the poems of the end of 1913: "If pain is where you plunge into another layer, is not pain good? O sure and swiftly guided plough!")

But then remarkably, toward the end, 1925, he emerges into a new world, a world not centered in the phenomena at all, and not centered at all, but just as it is and as it comes. The sound of it is the inharmonious Gong: "Sound, no longer with ears to be measured." "No lullaby—Gong! gong!" "No longer for ears, sound which like a deeper ear hears us. Reversal of spaces—storm in the column that bears—Gong!" It is as if he were throwing away all his darling experiences; certainly it is a critique of that Orpheus mood of hearing and praising. "Wanderer's plunge into way!" It is remarkable how sagely he sees through everything he has believed and achieved: "The praising bird-calls promise a little self-will, a little sadness, and much promise-making filing at the half-unlocked future. We hearkening heal the silence they are breaking." And with this a yearning for Full Power: "Out with hunters at dawn, hot with their youthful power, shouting above the barking. That was what we were meant for!" (June 1926.)

Let me say, finally, a word about the wonderful lines on his dying, *Komm du, du letzter.* The thought is that at last the wood is burning up in the fire it feeds, "so pure, so planless free from all future." "I snatch no memories within—O life! life! being-outside. And I in flame. No one that knows me." But then follow four lines that he crossed out; and what they contain *is* a memory, a typical Rilkean memory: that illness in childhood was not like this, it was a "subterfuge for growing. Things called and whispered promises." Obviously he crossed out the lines because they contradicted what preceded and dulled the effect; he had said that in this agony he snatched no memories, yet here he was recording a memory. And what else could a poet do? How beautiful and pathetic are these crossed-out lines and the crossing out of these lines!

This review of two new Rilke volumes, in English and German, was published in *Poetry* (December 1958).

Thee God we praise for this complete
book that overwork and doubt
and pain could mar but not prevent
because Thy spirit still was sent.

Such as it is, this now belongs
also among the created things
whilst I relapse, Thy dying fact
more spent, more sullen, and more racked.

IV

SELF CRITICISM

A Decade of Writing Projects

GUGGENHEIM FELLOWSHIP APPLICATION 1941

I have been composing imaginative works for 12 years, and in that time have produced about a hundred stories, 4 novels, a dozen short plays, 2 long plays, and very many short poems. These works have first begun to find publication in the last year or so. In subject they deal mostly with the social framework, the religious personality, and the life of desire. For the most part the characters are taken not at their surface appearance, but, as best I can, at the springs of their behavior, sociologically, psychoanalytically, or in the creative order. It is impossible to say more without giving an item catalogue, for I try not to say the same thing twice, or at least not three times!

In method, (1) I began by using a realist method modeled perhaps after Maupassant; when I write realistically at present the tendency is rather toward the causal-realism of Balzac. (2) In psychological subject-matter, especially the aspects of the libido, I have always followed Proust, tho generally with a more elaborate psychoanalysis and (of course!) a briefer description of the sentiments. (3) Both in objective and psychological subject-matter, I have always also been symbolist: the objective symbols resulting in the creation of social myths, the psychological symbols in dreams. (4) Lastly, for the past five years or so I have tried to break down much of the symbolism into cubism and scientific expressionism.

By expressionism I here mean that in place of activating individual characters as either representative or symbolic of their causes, I activate the causes working in them directly. By cubism I here mean an attempt to organize a pattern of the prose-structures appropriate to each subject; but unlike Miss Stein, I do not restrict myself to mere rhythm, sound, and at most pictorial description, but attempt to pattern the larger structures of hypothesis, rhetoric, journalism, dialectic, etc.

Perhaps I may make a certain exception to the above list with respect to my plays. Two other influences have often overborne the above in these: namely Racine and the Japanese Noh-drama.

To illustrate some of the above remarks: (1) *The Break-Up of Our Camp* (1935) is a novel describing with a certain realism the departure of a camp of Jewish boys at the end of summer, and the attempt of enough of the counsellors to remain to form a congregation for the recitation of mourner's prayers. This realistic plot is thruout treated as symbolical of a general social break-up and the withdrawal of Spirit. Incidentally the attempt is made to explore certain sociological phenomena abstractly. (2) *The Grand Piano* (1940-1) is a comedy of humors of persons who have found some device to alienate themselves completely from society: e.g., a little boy who does not go to school because he was able to destroy the registration-card before it was copied, and now he is educated from the headlines; a financier whose aim is to turn everything into exchange-value which he sums as endless zeroes without an integer; a girl on relief who regards herself as the proprietary coupon-clipper of an Empire, etc. There is no symbolism in the characters (tho the story and the Grand Piano are symbolic); they are rather presented as the asymptotic points of actual living situations. (3) "Tiberius," "Saul," "Orpheus," "Ravel" (1936-1940): these are "heroic portraits," where the hero is regarded as the embodiment, and tragic result, of some operative cause: but the portrayal itself is cubist. (The fact is that I cannot at all describe these.)

1. Project of Jonah

Jonah will be a "Biblical comedy with Jewish jokes culled far and wide."

There is no doubt that the Bible story itself is comic in its inspiration. The prophet's insistence that he has a "right to be angry even unto the death'' meets a deliciously playful treatment at the hands of the Almighty.

I present the prophet as about 60, shrewd, perhaps with a little pot-belly, joke-cracking, highly irascible, superficially vain. Perhaps he has a Jewish accent; his speech is homely, but he is capable of a dry eloquence and an extreme theology absolutely without unction. The foundation of the Bible story is the unexplained motive of Jonah's flight (it is not necessarily a defect in the Bible that there is no explanation, because at the end of the story it is quite clear that Jonah doesn't know what he wants!) I provide this motive as follows: Jonah's prophecies have always been bad, ''cryings out against'': but he is a humanitarian and his heart is wrung; besides he has gotten to be called a Jonah and his feelings are hurt. But the *fact* is—and this comes out when he is enraged because Nineveh is not destroyed—that he has become convinced, perhaps aided by an unconscious motive of aggression, that this bad luck is the divine order. The Lord deals with this attitude by means of the gourd really not differently than with Job!

Jonah is to be a study of Non-Commitment (a state of mind that belongs to some of us cerebrals as a kind of birthright!) The prophet is convinced of his truth; but why should *he* express it. Jonah is the prophet of the philosophy that the Jews call *Nebichism:* a synthesis of *nil admirari* and the conviction that ''everything goes from bad to worse.'' It is in this aspect that I will introduce many a famous Jewish joke.

The action will have 5 scenes:

1. Jonah at home with his wife and baby—trying to get some sleep—trying not to answer the Angel's knock—slapstick fight with the angel—mysterious profound acquiescence—subtile dialectical carping against the Angel, etc.

2. Jonah at sea. Storm. Character study of the sea-captain, skilled in his art, profoundly skeptical of its efficacy. The humane refusal of all the good people to allow Jonah's sacrifice.

3. Jonah in the whale. This is to be a combination of the Joseph's Pit of Mann, where one is purged and reborn, and the womb as the place of ultimate security and escape.

4. Nineveh. An imperial city of wealth and vice which has, however, gone so far in both that it has freed itself from illusions as

to their true nature. (The analysis will be in the manner of Mandeville's *Fable.*) It is therefore very near to prayer.

5. Jonah waiting outside the walls.

Jonah will be my fifth biblical play. The preceding are *Jacob at Shechem, The Tower of Babel, Cain and Abel* (these last two have now been published), and the full length play *Hagar and Ishmael.* If I turn to the Bible stories it is fundamentally, I believe, because these present heroic and public episodes which I know to be symbolically of the profoundest truth, yet toward which I have no religious scruples to prevent my handling them with free art and even playful dialectic.

2. *Project for* Don Juan

This will be a novel. It is impossible to give the plot and structure, however, because the nature of the materials and the appropriate technique require that the structure be given in the actual thinking and handling of the material. Perhaps, I can say something of the genesis and scope.

My last novel, *The Grand Piano* (to be published in December), was a study of Alienations in society, and in fact of a society constructed of a system of alienations. Into this structure I allowed, for the most part, no personal-psychological elements to enter: desire, family relations, etc. were introduced only in so far as they could be discussed in committee and decided by parliamentary procedure. (Such scenes are frequent in the book.) The technique of the whole was therefore a kind of realistic expressionism: the social status of the individual is set in motion as the agent, but as best I could I copied this off from what I see.

Now I present a "modern Don Juan." By this I mean a systematic explorer and gratifier of the aspects of the libido. Now *he* is just the alienated individual presented externally in the other work. Until we turn to him, there is no resolution for *The Grand Piano.* But turning to and thru him, perhaps we might come out somewhere: this I can by no means predict.

The technique of this portrayal must consist of speculations, meditations, dreams, and flashes of bright lit external experience. And all this must be organized into a pattern not unlike Picasso's *3*

Musicians. The 3 here are the Don, the Negro, and Mynheer (instructor of the 5 senses and the intellect).

These 3 in some way constitute a mental state.

The Negro has been brought to a pause because the idealization and intensification of desire, which he sees at the movies, must be transferred in his imagination to the black women he loves: this indirection has brought him to a pause.

There is also an old man, a Smoker, who hopes to cure himself by discovering what lust it is that the smoking is a surrogate for. (The Don encourages him in this delusion of endless symbolization.) But it is just the Tobacco itself that his body desires.

Again, physiological signs: postures of walking, varieties of stuttering and their cure, pitches of the voice. And the physiology merged in a space constructed in detail of the Vortices of gases, wherein all the animals are flexible Tubes.

Yet, toward the end, all is frozen fast in certain Habits. . . .

GUGGENHEIM FELLOWSHIP APPLICATION 1942

My project for the year 1943 is a work of fiction to be called *The Art of Fiction.* It will consist of variations on a well-known story, presenting, by different literary methods, its deepening motivations, proceeding in general from the secondary to the primary and infantile environments.

I have discovered, both in my own experience and writing and in the analysis of classical works, that there is a variation of literary handling with the variation of author-attitude toward the subject-matter, and ultimately with the variation in the source of energy of the writer's experience. By variation in literary handling I mean, for instance, naturalism, symbolism, expressionism, cubism. By variation in author-attitude and the experience of the writer I mean, for instance, the struggle in the secondary environment, the adjustment of the primary and secondary environment, the infantile archetypes. By the pure primary environment I mean only the infantile life prior to the formation of the ego by anxiety (taking the "ego" as the part of individuality and consciousness formed by deprivation). The life of adult sexual pleasure I take as the activity par excellence of the ego mastering its secondary environment under the urges of forgotten infantile longing. The secondary environment is the public world. The spiritual world of art and truth I take (after Rank) to be the effort of the ego toward immortality, attainable only by analyzing away its own anxieties and illusions and drawing on its deepest sources of energy.

My plan is to re-state, first in a purer naturalism than in the original, the story of Balzac's *Les Illusions Perdues,* Lucien in Paris. Then to re-state this story in its deeper causes in terms of the family relations that Lucien left behind in the provinces. (So far there is no doubt that Balzac himself saw the duality of his subject and treated it, in different sections, with appropriate differences of method.) Then to re-state the story again at the level of the sources of the relationship of Lucien and his sister in the family constellation. And then again, asking: what *is* this creative desire of Lucien, and what are his "illusions" which he is later to lose?

The story will be Balzac's (it is a universal story), but I shall attempt to retell it as of our times.

In these re-statements, and in several in-between parts reflecting combinations of the others, it will be necessary to run thru many (even most) of the methods of fiction that by now have classical representatives; and the whole will therefore be a kind of Art of the Novel.

This work is the third of a series of which *The Grand Piano*—a pure expressionistic-naturalist study of the secondary environment—and *Don Juan*—a symbolist and mythological treatment of the primary environment—are the first and second.

GUGGENHEIM FELLOWSHIP APPLICATION 1944

1.

The last part of the book whose first two volumes were *The Grand Piano* and *The State of Nature.* The novel as whole is an attempt to assay the social values. *The Grand Piano* dealt with commercial peace, *The State of Nature* with war. The last volume must seek to describe the kind of sociolatry toward which, by many signs, we are headed, and to describe and praise the social inventions of fraternity and natural unanimity. The scenes of *The Grand Piano* are for the most part laid in rational committee-meetings and the tone is satirical; the scenes of *The State of Nature* represent the emergence of single latent thoughts among random crowds in crisis, and the tone is ethical. The last volume I mean to be natural and spiritual and its scenes will represent strokes of "magic" in the sense of the Tao: the creation of somewhat from the vacuum when once we set aside our distractions.

Horatio, whose social education I am depicting thruout, is now presented as bereft of many of his old friends and exemplars; but he is accompanied by "the presence of their absence," and this characterizes his action among the post-war social arrangements. As to his age and other physical traits in this part I am not yet clear, nor as to those of Laura, Emilia, Mynheer, Lothair, and the rest. But the locale will again be the Empire City and will include set views of New York—but I have not yet hit on just which views.

2.

A new play after *The Life of Richard Savage* by Samuel Johnson. This astounding narrative of the mother-rejected and mother-hounded poet—with on the one hand the strange ambiguity of the mother's motives and on the other the pathetic but transparent reactions of the man—seems to me very closely to describe the place of man in Nature. Johnson's telling is admirably dramatic and divided into convenient episodes (the mother before Parliament, the Duel, the Trial, the Mother before the Queen, etc.) The great puzzle is: what do these episodes mean? As in *Jonah* I shall try to make a synthesis of the different perspectives of interpretation.

GUGGENHEIM FELLOWSHIP APPLICATION 1945

I intend to write the last volume, *The Holy Terror,* of the series whose first two parts were *The Grand Piano* (Colt 1942) and *The State of Nature* (Vanguard 1946). The whole is a kind of educational romance of Horatio, whom I endow with natural powers, strategems, and luck so as to make plausible his freedom vis à vis the social roles and ethical standards of the other characters. In *The Grand Piano* he is at the top of childhood wisdom; in *The State of Nature* he is adolescent; in *The Holy Terror* he will be a young man.

The Grand Piano describes the basic peacetime conventions of our money society carried to the extreme. The tone is comical in a rather genial way; the chief figure is the perfect financier Eliphaz whom Horatio sets up as his model hero. *The State of Nature* treats of war, a condition in which something at least must be taken seriously; the tone is so sardonic as to be hardly comic. Eliphaz, a spirit of reason (after his fashion) dies at the beginning and his place is taken by Horatio's brother Lothar, a political man who finds himself in a state of Nature and is presented as out of his senses. But at the end of the book, with the resumption of an uneasy peace, the spirit of Eliphaz returns and threatens a regulated, "high standard of living" sociolatry, penetrable by no serious or comic word, and doomed to burst when the suppressed life gathers too violent a potential.

The problem of *The Holy Terror* is to explore in this "perfect" system for the loopholes where surprising life may emerge. The tone will (I think) prove to be comical in a rather mystical and parabolic way. In any case there will be scenes of apparent magic, the blooming of natural institutions in unlikely places. Horatio is continually accompanied by the "presence of the absence" of his dear friends dead in the war. Besides, in a recounting of several celebrated modern court-trials, there will be a testing of what nature there is in the conventions (for obviously it is because there are natural as well as coercive conventions that we manage to exist at all).

GUGGENHEIM FELLOWSHIP APPLICATION 1946

Theme of a Novel [Parents' Day]

An account of a progressive educational community, regarded as a unity of home, work, and growth, in the world as it is. In principle such a community is not far from an ideal family—especially for the children whose parents are the staff. In actuality, in an American boarding school, both the staff and children have backgrounds, and characters, of broken families.

It is a good school; all are devoted to it and well-intentioned to do the best job; continually, hard problems are solved by a creative unanimity, the wisdom of the group transcending the limitations of the individuals. The individualities are strongly marked, even eccentric, but all the stronger is the inventiveness of their unanimity.

On the other hand, there is a fatal conflict between these injured characters with their persistent pasts and the growth in the living present. This flaw is pervasive thruout the staff, thruout the boys and girls. There is also a conflict, ever in evidence, between this good educational practice and the mad mores of the war-torn big world. The injured character-structures and the war-torn world are closely related.

These teachers, parents, children are engaged in a task really beyond their wisdom and available energy; the results are dubious. But this is not to condemn the effort, because in fact *only* these persons are alive to what is worthwhile.

In manner this book marks a change from my fictions of the past ten years. The delineation is naturalistic, rather than expressionist or symbolist. I attempt to dispense altogether with the pervasive irony of my other novels. I try to muster the courage to make absolute judgments of value, after (and by means of) analyzing the motives prompting me.

GUGGENHEIM FELLOWSHIP APPLICATION 1952

Plan of Work

I intend to work on the fifth volume of the novel *The Empire City*. As a whole this is the educational romance of a boy freed from the social conditions by having stolen the records and then seeking to appropriate the society as his own. He is appropriately called Horatio Alger. In *The Grand Piano*—period of the '30's—he is ten or eleven years old; in *The State of Nature*—war—he is in his adolescence; in *The Dead of Spring*—post-war anxiety—he confronts the problem of how, these days, to be in love; in *Holy Fright*—presentness—he takes the case as it is and how he is; and I now wish him to perform an epic exploit. (Horatio is now, perhaps, in his early thirties.)

But tho this is the thread, the other half dozen characters who persist are equally treated and each volume has a different protagonist: Eliphaz the financier who purifies the commercialism of the world by testing what use-value can be turned into exchange-value; brother Lothar, who returns to the more natural war and champions the pigeons and the bears; the intellectual Mynheer who serves *noblesse oblige* and weeps blood out of his eyes. In *Holy Fright* I have introduced St. Wayward at the age of six, and I foresee that he will loom very large in the next book—one thing he will do surely is mount and liberate the Unicorn caged in the tapestry at the Cloisters in Ft. Tryon Park.

In narrative manner, I find that *The Grand Piano* lays great emphasis on the committee-meetings of rational folk; the next book on the emerging irrational idea when a crowd is stunned; the third on the erotic ideas of fraternal community; and the fourth on the rituals of natural functioning, digestion, sexuality, recognizing and welcoming, dying in due time. I will know what the manner of the new book is when I am writing it.

In tone, correspondingly, the comedy has moved from a light irony to a sardonic and savage comedy and then, in the fourth volume, to a sad simplicity, without irony (tho perhaps with a certain amount of fun). I would wish, as I go on—but I do not know if I can do it—to have the syntax and vocabulary explode in keeping with the fantasy. I say fantasy—but the idea is that our *Argo,* with its unashamed accomplices, is truth-worthy, and truth-worthy does not founder on facts; it tries to reach what is not foreign to the created world, but yonder of it, what occurs on the *next* Six Days.

Account of My Writing

Since my twentieth year I have been writing rather more than a book a year—stories, novels, plays, criticism, sociology, psychology, and poetry. There are now about 25 volumes, of which I guess more than half is in print. My use has been to alternate a work of fiction, exhausting the imagination, with one of non-fiction, theory and empirical observation.

My theoretical essays have been mostly in the analysis of the background conditions of humane achievement, e.g., the city-plan, the community relations, pedagogy. In my novels correspondingly, e.g., *The Break-Up of Our Camp* or *Parents' Day*, a study of a school-community, I have been excited to show the foreground flowering or new presentness in a pattern whose social and psychological conditions are strongly at work. My long novel, *The Empire City,* is growing from the society in general—including its contemporary history, for the volumes have been evenly spaced since 1940, and each one takes the scene at the time of writing, and how the characters cope with it.

I have always been regarded as one of the "advance-guard" artists—but this not so much because of any experimentation in my style or manner, but because I persistently treat what is on the edge, whether of doubt, confusion, anxiety, or hope.

Goodman applied eight times for a Guggenheim with letters from such luminaries as W.H. Auden, James Farrell, Dwight Macdonald, James Laughlin, Richard McKeon, John Crowe Ransom, Hannah Arendt, and Isaac Rosenfeld. He never got one. The selections printed here are accounts of his career and plans for work that he submitted with his applications.

Preface to The Grand Piano

Lest we neglect to add
a little more confusion—

The Paris-International Style languished during the thirties; and its political counterparts, promising at first to compensate at least in action for the lost exquisite edge of spirit, sank into the calamitous retrenchment whose end (I am writing in August 1941) is not yet. But these things had been the hope of our young lives;—to me at least, habituated to the ancient poets and philosophers, it seemed that here also was a similar directness and childlikeness and no scruples about irritating at every moment the *vif,* quick of the soul. We loved those cubist musicians, painters, and architects with no close scrutiny, but God forbid that we should dare to scrutinize them yet! (To our surprise they will yet thru centuries of praise outface those who do not love them now.) When, therefore, June 1940, put an historically official seal on the coffin of this death, I was struck with dismay for my witty friends, and I was allowed a momentary feeling of careless contempt for the well-known social arrangements. For luckily I enjoyed private ills, not symbolically unrelated in my feelings to the general disaster, which energized anxiety and mourning and let me assume for a spell an attitude of simple animosity.

This comedy was written in that dismay; I was able to compile a whole Almanac of Alienation, instead of the piecemeal efforts I had been accustomed to. I trust that certain readers will enjoy a pleasure appropriate to mine. I trust there is nothing fundamentally unobjectionable.

Let me contrast the *method* here with that of the master in this sociological kind, Balzac. (By "sociological" I mean a poem in which the probability is given by the characters' social roles.) Now Balzac poses his actions in an environment of humane "unsociological" values and characters, and in this setting the sociological vices, e.g. Accumulation, wreak their havoc—actions immensely dramatic and pathetic, and almost tragic. (Why do they fail to be tragic? Most often because the good Catholic characters seem to be sheep without adequate social armor of their own or even the personal satisfactions that come from love or sanity in a capitalist world.) Omitting the sociological limitation, this is the dramatic formula of Shakespere.

But *The Grand Piano* is a comedy of sociological *humors,* modeled rather after Ben Jonson. The method is to extend each social role to infinity and give it rein; and everybody has such a role. Fixed completely in their attitudes, the characters clash only superficially—for each gets the satisfaction that befits him, and the Empire (we see it every day!) is great enough to house them all. Therefore the tone and action are comic and even cheerful. But in fact, the framework of their Empire being what it is, none of these persons is aspiring to any good thing, so the tone and action are sarcastic and even dismayed. *The formal structure of such a combination of cheer and dismay is that the persons proceed unobstructed to an impasse and no miracle is prepared to relieve the impasse.*

(What I say here does not apply to the boy, whom I have freed by a trick. His action is a simple educational romance in the manner of Horatio Alger Jr.)

This work is a sociological *abstraction* in that no motives of personal psychology here have weight. Love, art, and family affection are such that they can be promoted by a committee and discussed according to the rules of parliamentary procedure. To most readers this has made the persons seem cerebral and unreal.

Allow me to differ: there is no unreality in attributing to persons the motives according to which we daily see that they act or wish to act; is it my responsibility if our life resulting is arid and schematic?

Again, a certain abstraction comes from the style. I try to present only such surface appearances as are given with their social causes (or more rarely, their causes in the family-constellation). The chief words of vitality and color are thus "because" or "inasmuch as" or "the fact that. . .this made him"; or especially the divine formula of Proust, "Soit que (c'est à dire parce que)"— "Despite the fact (that is, just because)." I say especially this one because the explanation of the characters is dialectical and progressive thruout; perhaps the chief element of suspense is nothing but the question, "What will he be next?"

The kinds of causes I have of course borrowed from Marx (more modestly, in this work, from Freud); those who know, e.g., the 24th Chapter of the 1st Volume of *Capital* will see that I have hooked whole paragraphs. I have rather vainly aimed at the kind of humor in which Marx is an incomparable master. And in my protagonist Eliphaz I have even humorously tried to turn the tables on the master by demonstrating the holiness, if not the morality, of the accumulation of exchange value. Mynheer is a Dutchman because of the beautiful colonial system that the Dutch have enjoyed. Laura is the laurel-crown given by the present at its best moment. Lothario is introduced with a page of psychoanalysis in order to make *plausible* that mystery of mysteries, the reformist radical.

I am a native and a poet of New York City, tho unluckily I have inhabited and love other parts. I say this boastfully because, to be frank, we are sick and tired of the witty visitors who say, "It's nice to see but I couldn't live here"; but they will never know the lovely compounding of intelligently sectarian light-industry; a world seaport and its refugees and sailors; Jews and the *nebichism* which seems to be (alas) our present-day prophetic message; paper-profits; and the entertainment-business, baloney so pure that there is place everywhere for isolated strokes of art, as it is said, "I have a joke, let's write a musical comedy." I am a regional poet of the

Empire City—an empire that will *soon* come to be or not.

Lastly, I leave it perforce to the reader's invention (my publishers refusing to cooperate!) to heighten the ending of *The Grand Piano* to a work of Practical Dada, of Post-War Art, of Bombism, as explained in Chapter 6. I am thinking of nothing lethal, but of fire-crackers or simply sizzlers.

When he published all four volumes of *The Empire City* in 1959, Goodman revised the earlier ones to make the style of the whole more uniform. Among the things that disappeared was this lively preface to the original *Grand Piano.*

Preface to a Collection of Stories Never Published

Concerning the works in this volume I should like to make two points: they are affirmative heroic portraits, and the handling is somewhat cubist.

I.

They are affirmative in that I found myself able to present these characters and their motives without hedging, without irony or ambiguity, or at least without pervasive irony and ambiguity. I do not mean to say that they are uniformly optimistic; on the contrary most of these little pieces tell the tragic story that such and such a motive leads to a bad end, or even is a bad end in itself, for instance that the music of the composer is the same as bouncing the ball in the little courtyard of the asylum. But these motives are treated as if they indeed are the motives of the characters and the characters are indeed what they are presented as; and this is far different from calling precisely this into question, as I have been forced to do in so many works. I do not mean, again, that the motives and characters are definite, in the sense that they can be expressed in a proposition; on the contrary the presentation is always dialectical and the meanings must be discovered in the changes of apparent meaning. Nevertheless the dialectic here at least proceeds in one direction; there is no suspicion, or at least very little suspicion, that at every step the reverse of the argument would be perhaps even more true—a way of writing that I have unfortunately had to employ again and again elsewhere.

It is easier to maintain such an affirmative attitude in writing of heroes that are mythical or are so long dead that they are almost mythical, like Saul or Tiberius, or that belong to the future, as in "A Ceremonial." The absolute power of Saul, to "do as his hand should find," for instance, I for one have found it impossible to describe in a contemporary scene, as in *The Grand Piano,* without humor and sarcasm. Without the classic example of Tiberius as a support, I should not be able to present my own little pleasures with a straight face. And even in this present volume, those characters who are closest to our actual present find their fates clouded over with a certain dubiety, as: the hero of "Azazel" could on the last page hardly know what to think of it all, and the ending of the composition "Beginning with some movement, etc." lets one down even before the beginning. The elegiac futurity of "A Ceremonial" is the tip-off on them all! But against these, when the subject is purely mythologic as in "Orpheus" or "Phaëthon," there is a bland confidence. (I am not saying this in either self-defense or self-castigation, but merely as an explanation how it is with these stories.)

In all these pieces, the object of imitation is not an action nor again a sentiment, nor—least of all—an argument (I assure the reader that I can argue more coherently than these samples). It is rather a more or less abiding way of life, that is in the old psychology a *habit* or system of habits. I suppose it is therefore inappropriate to call any of these pieces "stories." I should prefer to have them regarded as "heroic pictures" in the sense that many seventeenth-century French mythological paintings and tapestries present heroic pictures. The details, then, are selected not to advance a narrative but as anything conventionally or naturally appropriate to lend color or extension to the whole. The problem then arises: How, if not by imitating a sequence of events, is a unified sequence to be found among the details, in a medium whose unity must at least have a beginning, middle, and end, whatever more it may have? This problem I have tried to solve in different ways, for instance by various patterns of dialectic: by a straight upward way in "The Detective-Story," going in four hasty steps from earth to heaven, or by a set of antitheses and sytheses in the "Composition"; half the time, again, I have used a "story-framework," like Phaëthon's ride or the travels of Orpheus; sometimes I have relied on whatever progress can be discovered in mere rhetorical proprietary, as in "Ravel," or literary devices, as in "Saul" and "Tiberius." But perhaps I can explain this better under the second heading.

II.

The essence of literature is in *signifying* sound. "Abstraction" in literature—as we speak of abstraction in painting as the reduction of objects in perspective-space to shapes in the canvas-space—must mean the reduction of significances to the means of signifying them and to the signifying relations of these signifying parts. The world of significances, objective, imaginary, or ideal, is shared by literature with painting and indeed with all arts. The means of signifying peculiar to literature itself are such things as sentences, similes, dilemmas, sounds with exclamation-points, conversations. There is no doubt an appropriateness of certain of these means to certain subject-matters, for instance of short adjectival phrases to surface appearances or of syllogisms to natural causes; but by and large the poet also has a choice among his literary means, and his exercise of this choice is perhaps his Style. To abstract is to concentrate on this choice; it is not, directly, an operation on the subject-matter at all. Still less is it to reduce the signifying to the mere musical sound! an error so widespread that even the classic prosody is analyzed in units of music rather than in units of signifying. (But if from the feet and the verses a signifying whole is to be reconstructed, we must start from units of signifying.)

Now by literary *Cubism* let us here understand not an abstraction from subject-matter, but in the presentation of subject-matter an accompanying emphasis and independent development of the signifying means. And in effect this means, if the work hangs together, that the relations of the characters, thoughts, and acts will seem to be partly advanced by the mere literary handling, apart from their natural or imaginary relations. In a scientific work this is of course a dangerous fallacy, the "literary fallacy"; but in literary works it give a literary, formal quality to the subject-matter which is to my taste excellent. The classical ideal is so to merge the subject-matter and the literary means that nothing is obvious but the world presented, but this "world," on analysis, proves to have no properties beyond what is useful to organize the literary medium. In recent times, minor literature, for example detective fiction, is still true enough to this norm; grand letters, like the works of Joyce, as always overcome all limitations; but the enormous middle literature, of prize novels, is hardly literary at all (I do not mean to say that it necessarily has other merits).

The handling of most of the pieces in this volume leans away from the classical in the cubist direction. Thus, the minutely varying repetitions in the last part of "Ravel" are a cubist expression of that subject-matter; the syllogisms in the "Composition" are a cubist expression of the particular kind of resolved feeling; the reduction of Saul's chase to algebra is cubist; the nonsense-syllables in "Orpheus" are cubist; and so forth. For the most part, unlike Miss Stein or e.e. cummings who analyze especially the elementary parts—words, spelling, punctuation—I rely mainly on the larger means of signifying, the sorites in the "Composition," the dialectic in "The Detective-Story," the eristic in "Tiberius." (The 6th and 4th parts of "Tiberius" are parodies of Bradley.)

Let me make a few remarks about the chronology of these pieces. The earliest of them is "Phaëthon." This is nothing but a mythological account of coming to know something; the temporal sequence of awareness is equated with the sequence of Phaëthon's ride, and apart from this initial device there is little use made of purely literary means in unifying the whole. By the time I came to write "The Detective-Story" I was prepared to organize the entire structure by a formal device. The great advance, however, came with the writing of the "Composition" (1936), for here not only the whole but also the parts underwent cubist analysis, and it was therefore possible to find a beginning, middle, and end not merely in a dialectic of objective ideas but partly in a progress of literary methods, as from continuous exposition to discrete fragments to jokes to syllogisms. "Tiberius," "Orpheus," "Ravel," and "Saul" are simply further explorations of what I discovered in the "Composition." But the latest piece here printed is "Azazel" (1941), and here I seem to be regressing in an ordinary narrative of events, tho I hope having learned something on the way.

After agreeing to print *The Grand Piano* in late 1941, the publisher suddenly got cold feet and asked Goodman if he didn't have something else instead. Goodman promptly put together a volume of short stories, for which he wrote this preface, but the publisher then regained his confidence, *The Grand Piano* was published, and this preface went in the drawer.

Preface to The Break-Up of Our Camp

Preparing this old work for publication—it was written in 1935 and 7 years is long in the work of a young writer—I see that I could not now write in this manner of symbolic realism, yet there is a relation between the way I now write and the way I had to write at that time. And whatever may be the value of the works, either then or now, I think that this relation itself is worth describing in a few words, because it is real and it reveals the attitude of an author and this attitude is likely representative of more than one.

In many works of the last years, and preeminently in the novel *The Grand Piano,* I employ a method of expressionistic realism. By this I mean that incident and motivation are taken indeed from actual society and mentality, but they are presented not as they appear actually but as roles in a sociological analysis and a psychoanalysis. And since the emphasis is on this *causal* interplay, the original acts and characters are presented almost as if materially constituted of these causes, as X-ray pictures, as little rules. Their handling is therefore expressionistic, tho, I hope, without mythology or abstraction; I hope. that is, that they are scientific X-rays and add up to the world we have.

But in *The Break-Up of Our Camp* and other stories contemporaneous with it, I find everywhere what must be called symbolism: that is, in the very description of actualities appear other meanings, other possibilities of interpretation. It is not that I am writing in metaphors, using the appearances to indicate something else; for I hope that I am concentrating directly on what I see; nor again am I writing in allegories, using the visible relations to explore the invisible. But it is simply that in describing an actual scene I find it impossible (I at that time found it impossible) to content myself with saying "it is merely this," but I felt "it must surely be something *more* than this!" and "it is after all also this other."

I think I understand well enough how I proceeded from this symbolism to that expressionism. Thru this change breathes the spirit of a progressive alienation. This alienation was stirring in the symbolism; in the expressionism it is triumphant and complacent. By alienation I do not here necessarily mean revolt—tho I should hope it would be accompanied by both humility and revolt—for these works of art are empty enough of persuasion.

When I wrote as a symbolist, my attitude was as follows: Here in fact is my world and I shall organize it into a work of art. But I feel uneasy in this world; surely it cannot be what *they* think it is; that would be intolerable, God would not tell such a flat joke. Ah, I see that there is something else in what appears—(and here I begin to reach out toward the contexts of my uneasiness; not towards the causes, but towards the contexts of the causes. If I incorporate these other meanings into the appearance, and in fact they do appear there to me, I shall be able to discover in the actuality the satisfactory unity of a work of art.

At least here I still take this actual world to be my world; it is my point of view; it enlists my interest, curiosity, apprehension, ultimately my anxiety. Tho perhaps I am forced, as in *The Break-Up of Our Camp,* to *end* by a systematic withdrawal, trying manfully to interpret also this withdrawal as an aspect of the believed-in actuality! It is amusing how many of my stories of that time incorporate bus-rides, canoe-trips, and hitch-hikes, and in general a man going on his travels.

But when I come to the expressionist stories, I find the following attitude expressed: Look! *there* is what *they* think the actuality is—yes, that error, that America 1940. But we see that for what it is, compelled this way and that, and comically compelled, by rules that in themselves embody no especial value. Far from having a larger significance than those people suspect, these incidents have even less significance than they believe (and they are feeble believers). But we—thanks be to God and our ill-luck—are sufficiently withdrawn to portray those things in their proper little places in the reality in which we have our secret faith!

Now, God willing, I shall not indefinitely continue my career as an author as an expressionist of that kind. (I have been able to compose cubist and pedagogic works of quite a different expression, and little prayers.) At the same time it is not because it would be convenient to write in a different way that an author can change the attitudes on which style feeds—tho I would not deny that *disgust* of a style is a powerful life-sign for an author. But it is by change in himself and the world. I pray that *soon* there could be rational grounds for such changes—to a style self-contained and cheerful or self-contained and tragic.

In re-working *The Break-Up of Our Camp* I have been struck by the character of Ostoric, the "stout untidy counsellor of arts-and-crafts." This fellow I had treated in a careless, a cavalier way; but if I were to write this story today I think he would occupy the *center* of the scene rather than that canoeist of dreams or that counsellor of dramatics "who doesn't know what he wants; I've met that type before."

The Break-Up of Our Camp was mostly written in 1935, during the period when Goodman was spending his summers as dramatics counselor at a Zionist boys' camp where his friend Meyer Liben had gotten him a job. He rewrote the book twice—first in 1942 (see "Literary Method and Author-Attitude") when he wrote this preface for it, and again in 1947, when he added a final chapter and finally found a publisher for it. The preface was never published.

Preface to The Fire (*i.e.*, Parents' Day)

This book is about the most important, because the most hopeful, subject that there is: the freedom of children. The creative spirit of children. If there is to be peace and freedom in the world, it must spring from the children's growth in creative freedom. Every other formula for it is imposed and mechanical and will not work.

But the nature of the subject has laid on me, as an author, a painful necessity: to account for myself, for my relations to the children and to the child I am. For if I did not try in good faith to show myself in the action, the subject would be seen thru my dirty glasses without its being shown that I had on, have on, dirty glasses. Therefore the character in this narrative named "I" is drawn as biographically as the author has been able. The other characters are, of course, fictional combinations adapted to the plot.

Those who have at heart the cause of progressive education will not, I am sure, be offended at this ambivalent account of progressive education. We somewhat know ourselves and the fix we are in. But to others I have to repeat (what the book says on every page) that I write here in committed love for this cause, not censoriously from outside it. Our fix is this: that the task is important and indispensable and that precisely we who are willing to undertake it are unfit for it. Yet the work must be done and we shall continue to do it.

In its first draft (1947-8) *Parents' Day* was titled *The Fire,* a reference to the catastrophic event of its plot, which actually occurred at Manumit School during Goodman's year as a teacher there (1943-4). When he finally published it in 1951, both the title and the preface were dropped.

Preface *to* Our Visit to Niagara

I suppose my stories and novels are, finally, myths—my people turn into nature spirits, genii of the place, or angels. I can't help it, it is how I see (and ineptly behave accordingly). Unfriendly critics have claimed that this makes my fiction "inhuman"; but in my experience, if people are not somehow greater, more portentous than human, they are not human at all, not even human. I am not sure I have ever met any of these plain folks, though I mix in the city a good deal, just like anybody else. People are either remarkable or batty.

In principle there are two opposite ways of making mythical stories: to start with the American scene and find the mythical emerging from it; or to start with an ancient foreign myth and discover that it is familiar to oneself. (These are, of course, similar to the alternative possibilities for romantic poetry that Wordsworth and Coleridge divided between themselves: to make the commonplace fantastic or to make the fantastic real; not that either stuck to the bargain!)

In collecting my stories of the last ten years, I was astonished at how they fell into these two groups. In the American stories I could not keep Jeremy Owen or the lifeguard or the attendant at Niagara Falls from turning into mythical figures. Yet when I drew from ancient Greece and China, or the Bible, or from Art, I found there my daily business and intimate anxieties—just as I feel that Sophocles, Milton, or Hawthorne are more my personal friends, alas dead, than the literary people I know.

In between these two groups, in this collection, I have put three nostalgic "Community Pieces," to portray those conditions, of community, love, and found identity, under which it is not a problem whether or not Man is greater than man.

This brief preface (1960) was one of the few that Goodman published, though he wrote many for his books.

An Interview on The Empire City[1]

M.G.: You recently said that you wrote fiction from the first sentence to the second and on without an over-all plan, paying more attention to the music of the language than to the meaning...

P.G.: In each sentence you worry about what you're saying. I didn't mean necessarily sentence. I mean also paragraph, but certainly not more than a page.

M.G.: Then you had no plan...

P.G.: For this book? No, not when I began. I started this book when I got fired from Chicago. There I was and I had to make a living some way. So I said, "I'll write a novel." I went to the public library to write, because at home the kid made too much noise, and I started out this book and by about the fourth page I'd kind of priced myself out of the market. I said, "Well, there it is!" No, I had no intention of writing later volumes until I thought I was finishing the first one (*The Grand Piano*). When I wrote the

[1] On May 29, 1964, my wife Barbara, an English Instructor at the University of Wisconsin-Milwaukee, Jerry Berndt, an Anthropology student, and I questioned Paul Goodman, visiting Knapp Professor of Urban Affairs at UW-M, about *The Empire City*. Though other students were present who were familiar with Goodman's ideas and some of his books, Jerry was the only student who had read this novel. Excepting two or three questions that I had jotted down in advance, the interview was spontaneous. Lasting three hours, it could not be transcribed completely, but I have selected highlights. At the end of it, Goodman read "Good News," from the fourth volume of the novel.—Morgan Gibson.

second volume (*The State of Nature*) I had no feeling of writing a third volume. The second volume was strictly a reaction to the war. Now when I wrote the third volume (*The Dead of Spring*), on the other hand, I thought that I would have a fourth one (*The Holy Terror*).

M.G.: What begins in Volume V (*Here Begins*)?

P.G.: That's all done by Steve Zoll, my editor. It was absurd to end the book with that episode of St. Wayward and the Laughing Laddy. It was obviously the beginning of something. So we cooked up the notion of making the new book begin with it. In my original operation, though, the last chapter he has there ("Spoiling for a Fight") comes as the ending of *The Holy Terror,* and "The Mission of St. Wayward" was written after, and I meant it to be the beginning of another book. But he said, "You can't end without your hero," so he talked me into ending with "Spoiling for a Fight." It doesn't make a bad ending, because of the prayer, but stylistically it's wrong, because the style belongs to the previous section. Also, there should have been seven chapters in the third part of *The Holy Terror,* because Beethoven's Arietta has seven variations, and that was the form I tried to keep.

M.G.: So there's more to come. Do you have any idea of how to finish the whole work?

P.G.: No, I don't get the idea of finishing. You really mean go on rather than finish. The problem there is to find out something that Horatio can fight with. The fact is that growing up absurd really is the thing that he would fight with, but I don't have it as a dramatic scene. It's clear that he can't find a tangible enemy, but as a matter of fact the organized system is the enemy, the intangible enemy. You can't write a novel, you know, about an intangible enemy. But in fact that's what he's fighting. No? And in a way that whole organized system junk that I do is *that* except there's no action involved. It's a series of disjointed little acts in there, not a clear action. If I only saw a clear action—I don't mean it's got to be real, of course, but even an imaginary one—then I could write it. That's the difficulty with Mynheer. Towards the end of this book there's some talk of his going to fight the Horned Dilemma and he's going to be killed in that fight and I dig that. That's some business about Existentialism and rational philosophy and in fact the difficulty is insoluble. Mynheer would not sink into a solution like Camus'. . . and as a matter of fact would get killed in the fight, because you can't win that one. Him I can understand. That's a logical and philosophical thing. But Horatio's got to have a tangible enemy to fight with.

M.G.: Does society have yet to create this antagonist?

P.G.: No, no, the antagonist is there, but what I can't see is how to get at the society. It's that he can't think of the thing.

B.G.: What if he were in SNCC or CNVA, jumping on Polaris submarines?

P.G.: That doesn't seem to me to attack the organized system. SNCC doesn't either. SNCC is better, but it doesn't feel right, and it's got to be the way it feels like to me.

B.G.: By the organized system do you mean a character that personifies it?

P.G.: No, not personifies it, no, that's no good. No, it's got to be the real thing.

M.G.: When you started *Making Do,* did you feel that it might become the conclusion of *The Empire City*?

P.G.: No, that book was like no book I'd ever written. It had a literary conception—something I was trying to do in the novel and actually wrote down beforehand. I had chapter headings written down, I rearranged them several times, and wrote down little details, a sentence or two, what kind of episode I'd take up, I kept rearranging them. And once I got a plot I sat down and wrote it. But that was the only thing I've ever written that way in my life. That book comes out of doing a number of reviews of novels where each novel dissatisfied me more and more because the characters were always making the scene and it gets so boring. You know, I wanted to write a novel about people not making the scene but people who really feel they are the world, you know, such as it *is.* That was strictly a literary idea. I'd planned to write a book, a novel, which wasn't *Making Do*, of which "Jeremy Owen" (in *Our Visit to Niagara*) was the first chapter, a book about somebody like Jeremy Owen, see, a character who copes, who is a hero. In *Making Do* they're all fuck-ups. There's no hero character. See, Jeremy Owen's no different from the *Making Do* people except that Jeremy can cope. He obviously can take care of himself.

There's a chapter after that where he's going to go back to the town and he was going to—this was before I was on the school board—he was going to get on the school board and really turn things upside down. The sense that Jeremy Owen has—kind of nutty but really quite solid. And when I'd figured out three or four more episodes like that I'd have a novel. I like Jeremy Owen. He's my favorite character.

M.G.: Why did you write in our copy of *Niagara* that it's your best book—and not *The Empire City*?

P.G.: That's the book I think is lovely—*Our Visit to Niagara*—I just like it, everything in it. That last story—"The Galley to Mytilene"—it's enchanting. I love to read it. But I think the best writing I've ever done is in *The Dead of Spring*—the best, say, hundred-page stretches.

M.G.: I was wondering about the metaphysics implied by style, which you were talking about in one of your lectures. It seems to me that there is a lack of unity in the style, an unevenness that implies an uneven metaphysics—in this sense, that the narrator intrudes with his rationalistic analysis of various characters—like you the essayist.

P.G.: That's mostly overdone, and it's mostly impatience. There's much too much talking about.

M.G.: But the impatience implies that you're not confident in the action working itself out.

P.G.: That's right, I don't want to be doing that, but it's necessary in order to make things clear to the readers. The narrator, by the way, also participates as a person and generally is a kind of innocent who is the historian of these people and who takes part in the activities.

M.G.: The characters are all profound but the narrator.

P.G.: I don't know about profound. He's kind of matter of fact. Like when he goes to visit this rock that this guy's brought back from the other planet. "This is a very good sample of a rock. I have a rock just like that." That's the way he is. It's true that there's a lot of jumping around in the style. I let myself go. But there is a rather persistent change in the style which I think has some structural value. For instance the last volume is much simpler in the writing than *The Grand Piano*. The argumentativeness in *The*

Grand Piano is the style of committee meetings—a lot of dialectical interplay indicating that that's the condition society was in. But in *The Holy Terror* where you're dealing with just a little friend group, it's more conversational. In *The Grand Piano* all the conversation is that of parliamentary meetings. When Eliphaz addresses his son it's as if he's saying, "Comrade, the situation is this." In *The Dead of Spring* things tend to be much more rapturous. So there is a consistent change in the writing and each time I felt it differently, I was in a different speech milieu because the relations between people were different.

M.G.: Did you think of the relations between speech and society when you were writing?

P.G.: Oh I did, yes. What is the style appropriate for certain kinds of interpersonal relations—oh yes, yes.

M.G. Would you say that the influences on you have been less literary than sociological and philosophical?

P.G.: No, I wouldn't say that. Obviously in this book Cocteau is very important—that whole business of taking the mythological and using it as if it were matter of fact.

M.G.: Did Kafka influence you?

P.G.: Not in this book. Kafka hasn't influenced me much at all because he's not my dish of tea. I don't feel like Kafka. I'm much closer to Proust.

M.G.: Why did you write a book on Kafka?

P.G.: I explained that at the beginning. I'm fighting with him. He's a great writer, but I don't like it. I think that as a theologian Kafka is correct. The trouble is that as a man he's all bitched up. True theology and confused personality defines his novels, just that confusion.

B.G.: What's true about his theology?

P.G.: Well, he understands that we're damned not because we ate of the Tree of Knowledge but because we didn't then go and eat of the Tree of Life. You have to go on to that next step. And that in a certain way, at that moment, you still could. In fact, you don't, now why don't you?

M.G.: Let's get back to *The Empire City*. What kind of book is it? It's not a novel of ideas as Huxley defined it, in which you have grotesque characters because they don't connect ideas with life. The ideas of this book are in the activities of the characters.

P.G.: I regard it much more as a comic epic. It's something like *Orlando Furioso*, no?—that comic epic stuff they were doing in the Renaissance. And in fact one section of this is taken from *Orlando Furioso,* the one called "Horatio Mad," in *The Holy Terror*. And there's one in *The Dead of Spring* taken from the Greek story, Longus' story, about Horatio and Rosalind. It's almost an imitation, episode by episode, of Daphnis and Chloe. You know, these two, a little shepherd boy and shepherd girl, kind of play around and after awhile they get the notion—they get a strong sexual desire. They don't dig how to make love. There's a hilarious scene, they're trying to figure out what they're supposed to do. They can't figure out what to do. Just when they figure out, the pirates come and kidnap him. Then he has adventures with the pirates till he gets back home. It's the same plot as my story. Of course, my people know what to do physically, but they don't know what to do psychologically. When they learn that, just then he gets arrested. It's the same story. Then in *The Holy Terror* Horatio blows his top, he goes off his rocker. But this kind of comic epic stuff—obviously the whole tone is epic, all the characters are conceived as slightly bigger than life, and in a way they're not persons with emotions, they're more virtues, you know, the way Achilles is. The characters in epics are not like characters in tragedies, who are people. The characters in epic stories always have something in front of them, like "the pious Aeneas" and "the brave Achilles." You're perfectly sure he's always going to be brave, it's impossible that he wouldn't be brave. All these characters are types. But they're not expressionistic. They aren't merely the virtues personified, but they're people with strong dispositions of some kind. That's what makes epic.

M.G.: Are all of your characters literary conceptions—projections of your various interests—or are some derived from people you know?

P.G.: Both, both. What does happen in this book, though, probably because of the way it was written, is that the characters started out much more as comic humours, epic comic humours, like in a Ben Jonson play, and I became interested in them as people as I went on. At the beginning I'm not at all. At the beginning they're like cartoon characters. As it goes on I begin to feel sorry for them, or admire them, whereas in a book like *Making Do* they start off right away as people I'm interested in. In *The Empire City* the characters are not so much ideas as Weltanschauungen. My feeling when I'm writing each one is that he's absolutely right. I don't think I've ever written about a character who couldn't beat me in an argument in the sense that I couldn't refute him. Because it would be boring to make a character stand for something that I knew better than. You know?

M.G.: There are no minor characters in the book, really. They're all treated seriously.

P.G.: There are auxiliary characters.

M.G.: But even they are pretty tricky people.

P.G.: Umm.

M.G.: What's behind the characters' names? Horatio is Horace, Eros, and Hilarious Archer...

P.G.: Horatio is named Horatio because my original conception when I was writing the first page was to do an imitation of the Horatio Alger stories. He got to be Horace because in writing dialogue it's better to have more than one name for each character. Eros is a pun which happened. Eros is a character in a whole slew of Anacreonic poems I was writing at that time. The Eros that you write about in an Anacreonic poem is ten or eleven years old like Horatio. I had no model for him. Except snotty kids, New York street boys.

M.G.: What about Eliphaz?

P.G.: Eliphaz is one of Job's visitors. The name is very fortunate because it gives that elephant pun during *The State of Nature* scene when the elephant comes out and tramples Lothar and Lothar says, "Eliphaz!" Gee, that's terrific. That was luck. I didn't plan to do it. If I'd thought of it beforehand, I would have named him Eliphaz to get that pun, but I didn't do it that way. Now Laura is named after a laurel wreath—the prize you get when you win. No reason for Arthur. He's not King Arthur. "Likely" is my daughter's middle name.

M.G.: I tied up various characters with different books—for example, Lothario and *Drawing the Line,* Mynheer might have written *Utopian Essays*...

P.G.: No, no Horatio's much more likely to have written *Drawing the Line.*

M.G.: But Lothar did draw the line.

P.G.: Not at all. He's a typical conscientious objector. And *Drawing the Line* isn't about conscientious objection. On the contrary, it's about avoiding that whole issue as an unnecessary issue. *Drawing the Line*'s about draft-dodging. That's why I wrote the book. You know, I wrote it during the war as a series of essays for an anarchist publication I was on—*The May Pamphlet* part. And our line was to draft-dodge. The magazine consisted of rather ill-concealed advice on how to draft-dodge. And that's not Lothar's style at all. It's very hard to think of anyone taking the *Drawing the Line* line and, unless they're very unlucky, ending up in jail. Of course you're likely to have bad luck. You know, they catch up with you, and that's a rough go. But the attitude of *Drawing the Line* is that you live in a society like a beast in the jungle and that you are obliged morally to use force or fraud—but at no point to sacrifice an ideal. Conscientious objection assumes that the state's laws are just...

M.G.: Or that it's expedient to obey them up to a point.

P.G.: Well, no, that they're just—the whole framework, though a particular law's no good.

B.G.: Like writing to your draft board and telling them you're not going to register for the draft.

P.G.: That's right, and this is the stupid thing I did, which I could have kicked myself for ever afterwards. I should never have done such a thing. You know, rather than stall up until the very last minute and then when the chips are down come up with something, with some solution; but as a matter of fact I could have gotten out of all the trouble, because it happened that the chips never would have been down if I hadn't written the stupid letter.

B.G.: But you don't seem to have the beast in the jungle philosophy any more.

P.G.: Oh yes, oh yes, I do, but then I have other lines which are incompatible with that. I have a line also that there is such a thing as our natural right to citizenship and my line there is that they have taken away my society. This is what Horatio comes to in the end of this book. Remember that business with Antonicelli at the end, about my president. I have the right to my president just as everybody else does, but they've taken away my right to have my president because they never give me a candidate I could vote for. That's not just. I certainly have that philosophy. Isn't that my attitude around the university? I say that the university is great, it's terrific, it comes right from Abelard. But who is this Klotsche? [Chancellor of the University of Wisconsin-Milwaukee.]

B.G.: This seems like the opposite of the beast in the jungle.

P.G.: It is, it is, it's quite incompatible. The beast in the jungle attitude is something, I think, which befits youth.

B.G.: Isn't it almost the hipster bit?

P.G.: No, no, because the hipster is aggrandizing himself, whereas the beast in the jungle is aggrandizing natural law. The hipster is very little drawn to natural law. Mailer, say. Isn't that true? You know, words like Truth, Loyalty, Justice would be meaningless to him.

B.G.: Well, Freedom wouldn't be.

P.G.: Oh, Freedom. Of course they would have that in common. Freedom. Mailer's philosophy, by the way, is best expressed by Stirner. *The Ego and His Own*—a very good expression of the whole hipster philosophy. A boring book, but it's very sound. Very interesting book.

M.G.: Wasn't he a nihilist?

P.G.: No, no, he's a hipster. No, that's right, there's no other way to describe what he does. There's a group that follows him that call themselves individualist anarchists, but they're not anarchists. It's no anarchy, it's Mailer's position thought through to how you could have a society consisting of guys like that. That's the problem, of how to have a society consisting of hipsters. That's not too easy to think through, and Stirner does make a real effort to do it. But that's not my position, no. No, my position is Hobbes' or Rousseau's. Hobbes' natural law position. You know, before the social contract. The notion is though that Hobbes kind of sells out, that once you've made the social compact there it's got you, whereas with Rousseau you get the feeling that it's always kind of in abeyance. At every moment you can say, "Do I abide by the social compact?" Well, the answer to that has got to be, "Is society abiding by the social compact?" If society abides by it then I'm obliged to abide by it. But society isn't abiding by it any more. It's put me in jeopardy, as Horatio says, of life and honor. Society has abrogated the social compact and I'm returned to the jungle. That's a perfectly good view, but that's a different view from the citizenly view—namely, that we all have a right to a country, a community, or that this is a human thing, that it's human to make up these kinds of laws and so forth and then what right do they have to give me such a dope for president?

M.G.: When society violates the social contract, then does anything go for the individual?

P.G.: No, no, what goes is what follows natural law. The individual then has honor, common sense. The individual can't act irrationally if the society abrogates the social contract because if he does then he becomes less human and diminishes himself. There's a natural law, and then there's a social compact.

M.G.: Yeah, but *can* he act rationally? It seems to me that one of the important problems in *The Empire City* is that if you conform to a sick society you're sick and if you don't conform you're sick too.

P.G.: That's right. I keep running that dilemma. And I think it's a real dilemma. I don't think it's at all just a trick I have. You know, I handle it kind of comically. But it's a real dilemma. That is, if you're not a part of the Lakeside Community Council, or UW-M, as a matter of fact you really can't act very importantly in the neighborhood. On the other hand, if you are, you're a dead duck.

M.G.: Your social criticism in *The Grand Piano* is the most Marxist in the entire *Empire City*. Eliphaz's theory of converting all use value into exchange value...

P.G.: That's right, Eliphaz is a Marxist.

M.G.: A Marxist capitalist. And Lothar's alienation...

P.G.: No. Lothar obviously starts out as a Marxist, but then he very soon begins to get himself into anarchist ideas, you know, like for instance the non-buy campaign. The point that I'm making here is that the society that Marx was talking about is vanishing.

M.G.: When you kill off Eliphaz in *The State of Nature* the society has moved into state capitalism from free enterprise.

P.G.: That's right, you no longer have that kind of capitalist.

M.G.: But before you leave *The Grand Piano*—when you wrote that "our society is like a grand piano and also like a mechanical piano," did you treat the abstraction as you treated language in one of your lectures? You said that language is not a system to which you are tied but like a musical instrument on which you can play. Do you think that society is like an instrument on which one can play with variations?

P.G.: Yeah, but the trouble there—see, what I meant by the grand piano was that society ought not to be that way. In a way that is a belittling of society, but in fact it's like that. Calling a society a grand piano means that something's wrong. Society is supposed to be a community of the people making the society, and that's not a musical instrument. See, the notion of regarding life as an art, there's something wrong with that. Life isn't an art and when it becomes like an art then something's wrong. See what I mean? *The Grand Piano* is a sarcastic, satirical title, and that's why after that comes *The State of Nature.* You've got to blow up that piano. When you blow it up you're in a state of nature. Great! What are they doing? Fighting a war. Is that so great? So when they finally begin to constitute a community it's a crazy community: they're all absolutely out of their heads. In *The Holy Terror.*

J.B.: Would you say something about your second generation characters—Lefty, Droyt, St. Wayward . . .

P.G.: Well, Lefty is the left hand and Droyt is the right hand. Their mother, Laura, has two hands. She's an architect, a maker, and she has two hands. At first they're just helpless. Later, in the camouflage scene, they're the ones who pull down the roof. She's nutty, she's engaged in the war. Then the hands won't play, they run away. Then, when these hands have run away, what kind of life do they have? When you next begin to hear about them they come back, they fly. Now Wayward . . . I had a chapter about the Laughing Laddy which isn't in here, it isn't included in the book. Wayward and the Laughing Laddy have an episode that takes place in Venice in which Wayward keeps making fun of the Laughing Laddy because he's so naive. If there were another volume, Wayward would be a very important character. He's a saint, he's got extra-sensory perception.

J.B.: How could he be a saint after killing his father?

P.G.: That wouldn't be terribly uncommon in a saint's life. You read the lives of the saints. They're generally hectic little bastards. They wouldn't necessarily knife their fathers, but that wouldn't be out of the way. They go through tremendous spiritual events. That's how they arrive in the remarkable state they are. They're not quite human. They're saints! They have unusual powers. They can perform miracles and all that stuff. Where do you think you get that from? From not knifing your father?

M.G.: When you resort to miracles, aren't you despairing of society?

P.G.: No, no, heavens no. I would never resort to miracle that way in my writing. I think miracles are one of the things that there are. If you *resort* to them, then there's something wrong.

M.G.: You mean deliberately.

P.G.: Yeah.

B.G.: Miracles are one of the things that there are, where?

P.G.: In the universe. If you once begin to rely on miracles then there's something very wrong. That's very bad.

B.G.: Like what miracles?

P.G.: You could do some strange thing and bring somebody to life who's dead, something like that.

B.G.: Can you?

P.G.: Well, people who can perform miracles can.

M.G.: You're more Aristotelian that I thought—positively medieval.

B.G.: Where are they?

P.G.: For instance, in the Catholic conversions at . . .

M.G.: Lourdes?

P.G.: No, no, at the University of Chicago. I used to ask Herbert Schwartz who later became Brother Schwartz—he was a musician—what was a typical miracle. Mozart's music.

B.G.: Then you just mean something extraordinary. But a miracle is supernatural.

P.G.: It seems to me be a superstition that scientific causation, natural causes, are the only possible ones. I'm a naturalist not because of the scientific evidence but because of the moral reason: what's the good of having ideals if there's no causal process to do something about them? We want naturalistic explanations because they make the moral life possible.

M.G.: *The Holy Terror* is the most miraculous volume. What's going on there?

P.G.: *The Holy Terror* starts with a set of anthropological rituals. What I'm trying to do is to say, "Let us have a simple community." And a simple community is nothing but a religious act. It has a religion. That's what we mean by a community. OK? We'll invent an anthropology for it. I give them rites, with prayers. How do they eat, how do they dance? They go through these rituals until Lothar gets killed. He's buried, according to their ritual. And then Horatio blows his top. When he recovers from that, then you have this community again, this time without ritual. Then odd things happen. A little child goes to sleep in a maze. Then there's this guy with this rock, the uncarved block. Lao-tse is really hilarious. He says, "The uncarved block is greater than anything under the heavens." OK, let's have an uncarved block . . .

J.B.: But why did you kill off Lothar?

P.G.: Because Lothar is killed, Horatio blows his top, and when he finally gets out of being insane . . . See, Lothar stands for him as the one who is really working very hard to make sense of this stupid country. Horatio's no revolutionary. He didn't believe in it. It didn't make him happy to believe in it. But Lothar is the revolutionary and Lothar gets killed.

M.G.: Do you mean that's the end of radicalism? Is that an historical comment?

P.G.: No, it means the end of that kind of radicalism. That's right.

M.G.: 1952.

P.G.: That's right, and that in fact it's killed off by Wayward, who is just above that whole game. Consciously I didn't mean that when I was writing the book. If you're going to be radical in the old fashioned way, your political opponent has got to be respectable. It's some moral error that he's pursuing and you're going to fight him about it. But what if he turns into an Eisenhower or Jack Kennedy—why bother? You know, it's like a clothing dummy. It's what I call the "World of the *Herald Tribune*." Then the radicalism becomes much more apocalyptic. So Wayward. It's nothing but what Mailer would say—in a very dark and savage way.

M.G.: You don't get rid of Lothar in yourself by killing him off in the novel. It seems to me that you have his kind of earnestness in opposition to Wayward's coolness.

P.G.: That's right.

M.G.: But what *is* the holy terror?

P.G.: The holy terror means confrontation with a simple reality. It casts everybody into utter fear and trembling. I have a play about this called "The Young Disciple," which is a retelling of the gospel of Mark. If you look at the gospel of Mark you see that He's acting like an ordinary Joe, you know, without any illusions, and people are absolutely terified out of their wits. There is this scene where He calms the waves. All the disciples are frightened out of their wits. The Greek words are fantastically strong. Obviously it's not the storm that's frightening them but this guy calming the waves. The scene where it comes up most is where Droyt is describing Lefty in San Francisco.

M.G.: "Good News"?

P.G.: Yeah, "Good News." So the great miracle is that he meets this girl in the bar, and he comes back and he gets the hots for her, and when he comes back the next time and she's there. So when he tells this, everybody is just stunned. Things worked out too much. He makes a song, it's a very nice song and people come to hear him, and the cops *don't* close the place even though there's no entertainment license. I think that's the most touching chapter in the book. Horatio concludes at the end of it, "You've told us a remarkable story." Can you imagine being in love with somebody and wanting him to be happy? It's fantastic. Whoever heard of such a thing? I don't think there's so much difference between that and a miracle.

B.G.: Let's hear it.

This interview was published in *Kulchur 18* (Summer 1965).

An Apology for Literature

I.

Statements in literary works are taken seriously and men of letters are invited to confer with experts as if they had something useful to contribute. They are not scientific statements. They are grounded in something, but in what? It is not exactly evidence. What kind of statement *is* it that men of letters make? What is their warrant for making it? I think the warrant is in the literary process itself.

There are innumerable books on works of literature and the lives of their authors, and there are many books on the philosophy of art. But to my surprise, I cannot think of a comprehensive study of the literary process—what it is to write books—drawn from what men of letters do. Like language itself, literature easily attaches to any subject-matter, yet it is less free-floating than language; criticism deals with whole concrete works. (In this respect, literature is not like grammar, rhetoric, and logic, which are ''universal arts,'' as Aristotle called them, that are used for every purpose.) And literature has its own specific discipline, of writing the essay *through,* with a beginning, a middle, and an end.

Let me spell out these characteristics of literature and compare them with other disciplines, and see if they add up to a warrant for stating anything meaningful and true.

Like everybody else, a writer has a day-to-day life; but unlike any scientist or almost any professional, a writer's daily life and course of life are relevant to his special work and may at any time appear in his sentences. He may say, "My experience has been that . . ." or "For instance, yesterday I had a quarrel with my daughter and . . ." I can think of only pastoral theology and psychotherapy as professions where this would not be out of place, since they deal face to face with their clients and speak *ad hominem.* If a social scientist uses such sentences he is at once identified as a writer (and dismissed).

A writer certainly does not deal *ad hominem* with his unknown readers; yet his readers may take it as if he does and send him letters and so forth.

A writer objectively observes, and so is like a scientist. His method is best compared, in this respect, with natural history or anthropology. A young writer is well advised to learn the geography, botany, and animals—a good model is Hardy—as well as the people and institutions. A writer's method is naturalistic; he does not intervene experimentally or with questionnaires, though like other naturalists, he may station himself to notice what he needs to know.

But then, unlike scientific naturalists, he focuses on the individual case with its unique characteristics, like a painter painting just this scene, or a physician treating just this patient.

He brings together his personal life and the objective subject matter, and the general class and the individual case.

Writers rely heavily on memory, the mother of the muses, both their own biographies and the cultural tradition. Only law, philosophy, and history itself draw as much on records of the past decades, centuries, and millennia. The faculty of bringing together memory and learning with present observation and spontaneous impulse is a remarkable service for human beings. Man is the animal who makes himself and the one who is made by his culture. Literature repeats the meaning and revives the spirit of past makings, so they are not a dead weight, by using them again in a making that is occurring now.

I would not like to distinguish literature from philosophy, if we take philosophy to be the collecting of wide-flung concrete experience, in principle all the experience there is, and saying what is central in it. There are various methods of philosophizing, for instance logical analysis, phenomenological description, grounding and harmonizing the different sciences. Literature could be called philosophizing by making and experimenting with language.

Writers are linguistic analysts and know the folk wisdom and superstition that exist in common vocabulary and grammar. As general semanticists, they are critical of the rhetoric of the street, the mass media, and official institutions. They understand, more than most people, what cannot be said, what is not being said though it ought to be, what is verbalized experience, and what is mere words. They can detect when there is really an idea and an argument rather than a cloud of phrases. They can date a passage and show a forgery. As psychologists of language they are sensitive to how people come on when they talk or write, the ploys they use, and the postures they strike. They can hear the personal character that is expressed in habits of syntax, and the personal inhibition or freedom that are told by the breathing and rhythm of sentences and the quality of metaphor. They can judge the clarity or confusion or spurious clarity in an exposition. They are sociologists of language and can recognize the social background in vocabulary, pronunciation, and routine formulas.

At the same time as they know all this, however, in their own writing they must let their speech come spontaneously; it is free speech, though they monitor it critically. It pursues tangents that they did not plan, produces metaphors that surprise them, uses word order with an emphasis they did not know they had, argues in a way to contradict their theses, and says ideas that they themselves judge to be unpolitical or immoral. But they do not censor or control this wildness, but do their best to assimilate it and keep going. Sometimes the whole must be torn up because it has fallen apart. For writers, these wildnesses are like the phenomena that must be "saved" by the empirical scientist. There are different ideologies to explain the necessity not to control—it is inspiration, it is unconscious contents emerging, the unconscious contents are the return of individual hang-ups, or they are images from the depths, the spontaneous is the voice of the people, or universal man speaking through the writer. Whatever the ideology, a writer writes at the boundary of what he knows.

Not to censor is an act of moral will, a commitment. At some point early in his career a young writer must come to it, like a kind of Hippocratic oath. If he can think something, he will say it; if it says itself, he will not strike it; if he can write it, he will publish it. The writing does not belong to himself.[1] The refusal of censorship and self-censorship is, of course, essential for the use of writing against lying and oppressive regimes; but it also makes a writer a thorn in the side of his own political cause: he gets nice about the slogans, he can't say the half-truth, he states the case of the opposition better than is convenient, and so forth. A writer might be a fine citizen in a perfect community, to which he would lend animation; but he is an unreliable ally, he is "unrealistic," in actual politics.

The spontaneity, the free origination, of writing is one aspect of a writer's disinterestedness; he does not will it but he is present with it. The other aspect is as follows.

He writes it *through,* from the beginning through the middle to the end. This is a writer's chief moral virtue, it is an act of will and often requires a lot of fortitude. It is what distinguishes a writer from a dilettante. A young writer is well advised to start on things he can finish and not get bogged down in long novels. By finishing, you learn the habits that work for you and can then set up a bigger structure.

To make a whole work, each sentence follows from the sentence before with "literary probability" and advances the whole, until nothing more follows. In the course of a fairly long work, there are bound to be impasses. The writer must backtrack and choose other alternatives, observe more, and sometimes have bad headaches till he invents something. Here lies the distinction between a good writer and a bad writer. A good writer does not fake it and try to make it appear, to himself or the reader, that there is a coherent and probable whole when there isn't. If the writer is on the right track, however, things fall serendipitously into

[1] An interesting problem arises with regard to copyright. In principle, what is authentically written is not a commodity bought and paid for, but is in the public domain like air and water and natural growth. Yet as a citizen I object to my writing being exploited for somebody's profit. So I try to set the following conditions: if anybody wants to reprint my writing for non-commercial purposes, they can do so gratis; if the State wants to use it, they must give me safeguards; if a commercial enterprise wants to use it, they must pay the going market price.

place; his sentences prove to have more meaning and formative power than he expected; he has new insights; and the book "writes itself."

At the end of this process, somehow, the finished work will have been worth doing. If it is a long poem, it will have the kind of meaning that poems have. If it is a prose essay, it will say something true about its subject matter.[2]

This last is, of course, simply an act of faith, but it is no different in kind from the faith of all who work at the boundary of the unknown, the faith of a physician that, if he pursues his method, nature will heal the patient; or the faith of an empirical scientist that, if he pursues his method, the nature of things will reveal a secret. Or for that matter, the faith of a child who runs across a field and the ground supports him. If they fail, they do not give up the method, because they have no alternative way of being. When they succeed, they get a passing satisfaction and go on to another work.

Finally there is an odd and revealing unilateral contract that a writer makes with his readers. Some writing, of course, like a political tract, an entertainment, or a popularization, is aimed at a particular audience and always keeps them in mind; but much serious writing, perhaps most, is written for no particular audience; and fiction and poetry for an "ideal" audience. Nevertheless, the writer is always under an obligation to make it "clear." He will explain references that an ordinary literate reader is not likely to know, he will fill out the argument, he will avoid private or clique information, even though his ideal audience would hardly need such help. But "clear" does not mean easily comprehensible—consider Mallarmé, an exceedingly clear and logical writer, but one who cannot sacrifice the conciseness, texture, and immediacy of his

[2] Schopenhauer or Nietzsche—I no longer remember which; either is possible because both were snappish and down-to-earth—advises looking first at the last chapter and asking, "*Was will der Mensch?*—What's the man after?" He is after where he ends up. But has he *gone* there? If so, you have to go the way with him. My own usual experience is that I do start out with him frankly on his way; but somewhere along he fakes something, or he doesn't know something that he ought to know; and then I find it hard to continue. My experience also is that one can usually easily recognize the writer who is really in there pitching, suffering, doing his best, finding new things—at least new to himself, and not just working a sewing machine. To him one allows any number of mistakes and gaps.

style just to be easily understood by readers, so you have to figure it out like a puzzle. My opinion is that, in most cases, the writer is not thinking of a reader at all; he makes it "clear" as a contract with *language.* Since it is the essence of speech to have a hearer—even though he intends no hearer—the correct use of speech is to be clear.

Let us go back to the question I started with. How do these traits and powers of literary writing add up to a warrant to make true statements, in the sense that scientific statements are true? They don't. *But there is no alternative.* There is no other discourse but literature that is subjective and objective, general and concrete, spontaneous and deliberate, and that, though it is just thinking aloud, gives so much attention to speech, our chief communication.

Philosophers have always quoted literary texts as if they provided another line of proof, a special kind of evidence. As a writer, I do not judge that I provide evidence. But I do go through the literary process to produce the text.

Men of letters have definite virtues. They do not wear blinders. They are honest and do not omit the seamy or awkward side. They are intolerant of censorship and skeptical of authority. They work hard to write it through. They disinterestedly lose themselves in what they do and are innocently in love with the product.

But it is not so definite what is the use of their ethic. They are not committed, like scientists, to find confirmable and replicable truth. Politically, they are usually inept at finding ways to realize what they advocate. They are not trustworthy as pedagogues or curers of souls.

Perhaps, in the social division of labor, they are the group to whom it is assigned to make sense. One is reminded of Nestor, the orator of the *Iliad.* Nestor's honeyed speech at no time dissuaded the Greeks from their infatuation, but it was no doubt a good thing for them to go to their doom with open eyes.

II.

It has been argued, however, that literature is simply outmoded in modern times. One clamorous line of attack has recently been coming from the champions of multi-media. In my opinion it is nonsensical. They say that writing, and indeed all speech, is "linear," it pays out its meanings one after another like signals in an unrolling tape. But in fact, speech can be amazingly contrapuntal, more so even than orchestral music with all its voices and timbres. In colloquial speech, the phonetics, grammar, and lexicon can simultaneously have meaning, either reinforcing or shading one another, and to these we must add non-verbal signs and attending to the respondent. Writing, which is more deliberate speech, lacks the non-verbal and the respondent, but it adds contrapuntal voices like a system of metaphor, systematic irony, allegory, subordination of clauses in the framework of an independent clause—consider a paragraph of Proust. In poetry it is usual for three systems of rhythm to be heard at the same time, the meter, the beats of phrasing, and the period or paragraph. Good colloquial conversation or the complex-word of a poem can keep globally in touch with almost every aspect of a situation.

Speech rises from within people; they reach out to say it or to hear it, even when they are reading. My observation is that people are rather passive to multi-media. Multi-media have their own quality, of surrounding the audience spatially and sometimes breaking down defenses, but they are not a substitute for saying. It is possible—I doubt it—that future technological and cultural changes may put writing and reading out of business, but other media will not then do the same job as words. It is hard, if at all possible, for non-verbal means to syllogize, define, state class-inclusion, subordinate, say a subjunctive or even imperative or interrogative, to distinguish direct and indirect discourse, to say I, Thou, or It, etc., etc. Film, music, and space-arrangements have to use indirect means to communicate these simple things. On this subject, people like McLuhan don't know what they're talking about, though they have other useful things to say. If they would try to write through a book, they would have to make more sense. A written argument won't hang together unless it copes with at least the obvious objections. Putting in a picture doesn't help.

A different objection is to deny that literature as such is relevant, to say that writing is made honest only by its workaday and community use. In its philosophical form, which I remember hearing during the 20's (e.g., *Gebrauchsmusik*), this is a profound doctrine. It is close to Goethe's great sentence that "Occasional Poetry is the highest kind"—the poetry of weddings, parties, funerals, and dedications. Street theatre and *commedia dell'arte* are the utopia of every playwright. Music and plastic art—though literature less—have certainly flourished in service to religion. It is a doctrine of happy communities.

Since the 30's, however, and very much nowadays, the irrelevance of literature has gotten to mean that the right use of literary speech is political action, like protest songs and guerrilla theatre—we simply don't have the community necessary for celebration, occasional poetry, and *commedia dell'arte*. That is, the process of literature is not used in its natural power to find meaning and make sense, so that we can act in a world that has meaning and sense. It is claimed there is no time for this, there is too much suffering and injustice. And only by engaging in revolutionary action can one produce new thought and lively words. But in practice I have found this comes to not questioning slogans that are convenient for an immediate tactic or a transient alliance. The writers tell half-truths. "Action" becomes idiotic activism. The vocabulary and grammar are pitched to a condescending populism, about at the level of junior high school, including the dirty words. The thought is ideological through and through.

There is, finally, a famous analysis of the history of poetry and human speech that in principle makes literature now quite irrelevant. On this view, poetry was the inevitable and appropriate speech of primitive ages, as the only available way of saying reality when not much was known and before the division of labor; these were ages of myth, when people living in a fearful and uncontrollable environment could not distinguish between magic and science, saga and history, dream and empirical experience; the poets were the prophets, historians, philosophers, and scientists. In the course of time, poetry was replaced by philosophy and history; and these in turn have given way to special physical sciences and positivist sociology. In our time, literature can be merely decoration or entertainment or exercises in emotional noises. This was the line of Vico (on one interpretation) and of Comte. And prophylactic empiricist languages, like Basic English or positivist logic, carry it out as a program.

Apologists for literature have tended to regard exactly the same development of language as a devolution rather than an evolution. In his *Defense of Poesy* Philip Sidney argues that history and moral philosophy are ineffectual to teach the man of action and the warrior—he comes on strongly as the Renaissance scholar-poet who is also soldier-statesman. History tells us only what has been, poetry what should be; moral philosophy is dry analysis, poetry motivates to emulation and action. Sidney would certainly not have been happier with the "value-neutral" language of present departments of sociology. In its high Italian form, Sidney's argument goes so far as to deny that scientific or philosophical sentences are true at all; only Eloquence is true, for truth resides in right action, not in propositions, just as Nietzsche holds that the only true science is the *Gaya Scienza* that makes you happy if you know it.

Shelley, in *Defence of Poetry,* takes the same tack. He sees the world of his time as fragmented, quantified, rule-ridden; it is only poetry that can liberate and bring the parts together.

> We want the creative faculty to imagine that which we know—our calculations have outrun our conceptions. . . . The cultivation of those sciences which have enlarged the limits of the empire of man over the external world has, for want of the poetical faculty, proportionately circumscribed that of the internal world. . . . The great secret of morals is love, or a going out of our own nature and an identification of ourselves with the beautiful which exists in thought, action, or person. . . . A man, to be greatly good, must imagine intensely and comprehensively. . . . Poetry enlarges the circumference of the imagination by replenishing it with thoughts of ever new delight, which have the power of attracting and assimilating to their own nature all other thoughts.

In my opinion, there is a lot of truth in this—it is grounded in Coleridge's post-Kantian epistemology. It *is* odd, however, that as a philosophic anarchist after Godwin, Shelley should end his *Defence* with the fatuous sentence, "Poets are the unacknowledged legislators of the world." What does he intend? That they should be acknowledged? Then what would they do?

Depressed by the passing of Faith, Matthew Arnold—in *Literature and Dogma, Culture and Anarchy,* and the debate with Huxley—deplores the language of the churchmen, the Liberal and Radical economists, and the scientists, and he turns deperately to literature to give a standard for "Conduct" for the majority of mankind. Astoundingly, this view has condemned him as an elitist—in a speech by Louis Kampf of MIT, the President of the Modern Language Association! But Arnold is explicitly drawing on the Wordsworthian doctrine that uncorrupted common speech, heightened by passion and imagination, binds mankind together, whereas the utilitarian speech of the Liberals or the ideological speech of the Radicals destroys humanity.

Nearer to our own times, bureaucratic, urbanized, impersonalized, and depersonalized, Martin Buber could no longer rely even on literature, but went back to face-to-face dialogue, the orally-transmitted legends of the Hasidim, and the experiences that underlie the text of the Bible. And we see that, in the present deep skepticism about special sciences and scientific technology, the young do not trust speech altogether, but only touching or silence.

In this dispute about the evolution of positivist language or the devolution to positivist language, both sides exaggerate—as usual. It is for quite reasonable human purposes that we have developed languages that are more accurately denotative and analytic and simpler in syntax than poetry. But the broader function of literary language, including poetry, also remains indispensable, because we are never exempt from having to cope with the world existentially, morally, and philosophically; and there is always emerging novelty that calls for imagination and poetry.

Consider the worldwide unease about the technology, the social engineering, the specialist sciences, and their positivist value-neutral language. Suddenly, the line of dissent of Blake, Wordsworth, Shelley, William Morris, the symbolists, and the surrealists no longer seems to be the nostalgic romanticism of a vanishing minority, but the intense realism of a vanguard. I have found that I can mention even Jefferson and ruralism without being regarded as a crank. To try to cope with modern conditions by the methods of laboratory science, statistics, and positivist logic has come to seem obsessional, sometimes downright demented, as in the game-strategies for nuclear warfare. As in a dream, people recall that technology is a branch of moral philosophy, with the forgotten criteria of prudence, temperance, amenity, practicality for ordinary use; and they ask for a science that is ecological and modestly naturalistic rather than aggressively experimental. But one cannot *do* moral philosophy, ecology, and naturalism without literary language. It was only a few years ago that C.P. Snow berated literary men for their ignorance of positive science, and now it is only too clear that there is an even greater need for positive scientists who are literary. Unfortunately, since men of letters have for so long let themselves be pushed out, we don't have relevant literary language and topics to say right technology and ecology; our usual literary attempts are apocalyptic, sentimental, out of date, or private.

A physician, for instance, is faced with agonizing dilemmas: euthanasia when novel techniques can keep tissue alive; birth control despite the destiny of a human being as a parental animal; organ transplants and Lord knows what future developments; the allocation of scarce resources between the vital statistics of public health and the maximum of individual health, or mass practice and family practice. How does one spell out the Hippocratic oath in such issues? How can anyone by his own intuition and individual ratiocination, usually in crisis, possibly decide wisely and without anxiety and guilt? Yet there are almost no medical schools that find time for the philosophy of medicine. And we do not have the linguistic analysis, the reasoned description of precedents, the imagined situations, in brief the literature, for such philosophy.

The social sciences have been positivist only during my lifetime, though Comte talked it up a hundred and fifty years ago. Marx was still able to say that Balzac was the greatest of the sociologists. Comte himself was energized by a crazy utopian poetry. Sir Henry Maine, Maitland, Max Weber, and so forth were historians, humanists. Dewey and Veblen were practical philosophers. Freud and Rank came on like novelists and fantasists and posed the problems for anthropology. It is, of course, a matter of opinion whether, after so many lisping centuries, the brief reign of mature positivist sociology has been brilliant.[3]

[3] A recent study captained by Karl Deutsch, emanating from the University of Michigan, points to the great advances in recent years made by big teams of scholars heavily financed; and it refers sarcastically to those—namely me—who claim that we don't know much more than the ancients did about psychology, pedagogy, politics, or any other field where they had adequate empirical evidence. When I look at the list of great advances, however, I find them heavily weighted toward methodology and equipment; stochastic models, computer simulation, large-scale sampling, game theory, structural linguistics, cost-benefit analysis, etc., etc.; in brief, an enormous amount of agronomy and farm-machinery and field hands, but few edible potatoes.

My hunch is that, despite a few more years guaranteed by big funding, it is moribund, done in by the social critics and the politically engaged of the past decades, who have had something useful to say. As one of the social critics, I can affirm that we are *philosophes,* men of letters.

Humanly speaking, the special sciences and their positivist language have been deeply ambiguous. At their best—it is a splendid best—they have gotten (and deserved) the pay-off of the theological virtues of faith, selflessness, and singleminded devotion, and of the moral virtues of honesty, daring, and accuracy. At their worst, however—and it is a very frequent worst—specialist science and its value-neutral language are an avoidance of experience, a narrow limitation of the self, and an act of bad faith. They are obsessional, an idolatry of the System of Science rather than a service to the unknown God and therefore to mankind. Needless to say, such science can be easily bought by money and power. Its language is boring because what the men do is not worth the effort, when it is not actually base. Being busy-work and form-ridden, it has no style.

III.

I have written forty books. Evidently, to make literature is my way of being in the world, without which I would be at a loss. If I here examine and write the Apology for this behavior, I find that it is not very different from the older Defences of Poetry, but I do not need to make their exaggerated claims since I am just describing my own situation—maybe it is simply that Sidney and Shelley were thirty years old, and I am sixty.

I have a scientific disposition, in a naturalistic vein. I get a continual satisfaction from seeing, objectively, how things are and work—it makes me smile, sometimes ruefully—and I like to write it down. But I do not exclude how I myself am and work as one of the things, unfortunately an omnipresent one in my experience. (I can occasionally smile at this too, but I am happier when I am not there.) God is history, how events actually turn out; but history includes also the history of me. God creates the world and I am only a creature, but I *am* a creature and He takes me into account, though He doesn't always know what's good for me and I complain a lot. Thus, my objective naturalistic sentences are inevitably colored by, and likely distorted by, my own story and feelings. They turn into literature.

I cannot take my wishes, feelings, and needs for granted and directly try to act them, as many other people seem to be able to do. I have to try to make sense, that is, to say my feelings and needs to myself and to other people. It is no doubt the sign of a deep anxiety; I cannot manage the callousness of healthy good conscience, though I do not feel much conscious guilt. I have to justify my needs with meanings. Conversely, I try to translate into action the meanings that I say, for, as with everybody else, much of the meaning that I know is unsatisfactory and something should be done about it. This combination of action and meaning also results in a lot of literature, rhetoric, social criticism, psychoanalysis, pedagogy, and press conferences.

Whether by nature or long habit that has become second-nature, I have that kind of personality that first says and then initiates what it wants, and then knows what it wants, and then wants it. Before saying, I feel just a vague unrest. With most people, it is wise to take seriously what they do, not what they say; their words are rationalizations, pious platitudes, or plain hypocrisy. But writers' words commit them, marshal their feelings, put them on the spot. I make a political analysis because I have a spontaneous gift for making sense; I then have to go through with the corresponding political exercise, unwillingly not because I am timid but because I am lousy at it. I tentatively say "I love you" and find that I love you. Or very often I have said what seems to me to be a bluff, beyond what I know or want, and it proves to be after all what I mean. Like the Egyptian god that Otto Rank mentions, a writer makes himself by saying.

I am in exile. Like everybody else, I live in a world that is given to me—I am thankful for it. It is not made by me—and that too is very well. But it is *not* my native home—therefore I make poems. "To fashion in our lovely English tongue a somewhat livelier world, I am writing this book"—*The Empire City.* In order to appropriate this unfeeling bitter place where I am a second-class citizen. I was no happier when I was young, and I wrote poems; it is no bed of roses when I am toothless and have failing eyes, and I write poems. I never was a beauty, to get what I wanted sexually, but now I am also too tired to seek for it. But even worse than my private trouble is how men have made of the earth an object of disgust, and the stupidity and pettiness of statesmen tormenting mankind and putting additional obstacles in the way, as if life were not hard enough. It does not help, either, that people are so pathetic, the apparently powerful as much as powerless. To pity is another drain of spirit. But it helps me to say it just as it is, however it is.

Also, I am good at thinking up little expedients of how it could be otherwise. I tend not to criticize, nor even to notice, until I can imagine something that would make more sense. My expedients are probably not workable in the form I conceive them, and I certainly do not know how to get them adopted—they are utopian literature—but they rescue me from the horror of metaphysical necessity, and I hope they are useful for my readers in the same way. When they are neat solutions, they make a happy comic kind of poetry. Maybe they are all the more charming because they are practical, simpleminded, and impossible. It is the use of comic writing.

Meaning and confusion are both beautiful. What is chilling is great deeds that have no meaning, the stock-in-trade of warriors and statesmen, but my radical friends also go in for them. What is exasperating is positivistic clarity and precision that are irrelevant to the real irk. A value of literature is that it can inject confusion into positivistic clarity, bring the shadows into the foreground.

Ancient and modern writers are my closest friends, with whom I am in sympathy. They are wise and talented and their conversation sends me. Maybe I am lonely more than average—how would I know?—but I need them. Books and artworks are extraordinary company—one does not need to make allowances!—and in the nature of the case, they speak more clearly to us writers and artists because we respond to them most actively; we notice how he does that, and if it is congenial we say, "I could do something like that." Despite its bloodlessness, the tradition of literature is a grand community and, much as I envy the happy and the young, I doubt that they have as good a one. (How would I know?) Freud said that artists, giving up animal satisfaction and worldly success for their creative life, hope by this detour to win money, fame, and the love of women. He was wrong—I never had such a hope—but I have thereby entered a company that has given me many beautiful hours. Often, talking to young people at their colleges, when I quote from great writers whom I evidently treat as familiars, they look at me with envy because I have a tradition which they lack, through no fault of theirs, but I do not know how to pass it on.

And what a thing it is to write English sentences!—rapid in thought, sometimes blunt, sometimes sinuous in syntax. When writing, I take my syntax and words from my colloquial speech; I strongly disapprove of the usual distinction between "standard colloquial" and "standard literary." I will write the slang that I consider worth using when I talk, for instance in the last few pages I have written "he comes on strongly," "their conversation sends me," "I am lousy at it," "he talked it up." I have no doubt that my voice can be heard in my writing by those who know me face to face. Lecturing, I just muse along and think aloud in a conversational tone, referring to a few notes I have jotted down. When I read verse aloud, I again use a conversational tone and follow the ongoing prose sense rather than the sonority, meter, imagery, or drama. I do not try to be portentous—

> Say my song simply for its prosy sentence,
> cutting at the commas, pausing at the periods.
>
> Any poetry in it will then be apparent,
> motion of mind in English syntax.

On the other hand, though I follow the sense, I am *not* intent on conveying any truth or message, but just the beginning, middle, and end of a whole literary work. I will strike whatever impedes or detracts from the whole, regardless of the "truth." For what I communicate must, in the end, be not anything I know but how I do in getting *rid* of the poem, putting it out there. Afterward, God help me, I am left so much the less.

I use the word "God" freely when I write—much less freely when I speak—never when I think or talk to myself. I don't know clearly what I intend by it. I cannot pray in the usual sense, though I sometimes use the awareness-exercises of psychotherapy which, I guess, is my religion. But in writing of the fundamental relations of my soul, mankind, and the world, I find the terminology of St. Thomas or Karl Barth far more congenial and accurate than that of Freud or Reich, who are either too "subjective" or too "objective," they do not say how it is. To say deliberately just how it is with me is apparently how I pray, if I may judge by the language that comes to me. Especially when I am at a loss for grief, confusion, gratitude, or fear. In moments of impasse—but only when I have earned the right to say it because I have tried hard—I have written "Creator spirit, come."

Maybe it is that when I think or talk to myself, I am embarrassed, but when I write I am not embarrassed. I now remember that I fell on my knees and said a prayer when I had finished writing *The Empire City,* and indeed the ending of that book is very good.

When I write public themes—urbanism, psychology, delinquency, the school system, the use of technology, resisting the draft—I of course try to be honest with the facts, to "save the phenomena," but again I rather obviously put more trust in the literary process, the flow of saying my say, than in statistics. I take the statistics seriously when they contradict me; I modify my line or make a distinction, or I explain how the statistics are an artifact or haven't asked the right question. I like using abrasive material to work with and I have no impulse to sweep difficulties under the rug. (Sometimes, however, I am simply ignorant.) But when the "facts" run positively in my direction, I do not argue from them but treat them literarily; 85 per cent becomes "a good majority," 60 per cent is "in very many cases," 35 per cent is "an appreciable number of cases," 20 per cent is "sometimes it happens that." A single individual situation that I judge to be typical and for which I can provide a global, literary explanation to my satisfaction, weighs more than all the rest, because it is for real and must be coped with politically and humanly. Except for rhetorical effect, I usually don't make generalizations anyway, because I don't care about them—when I do make them they tend to be outrageous because I am outraged. I do not understand a cause or a reason as a correlation, but animally, as continuous with a muscular push or a perceptual *Gestalt.*

But when I rely on the literary process, the flow of saying my say, this does not mean that I say what I *want* to say but what *can*—strongly—be said. The work has its own discipline, to be clear, to make sense, to hang together, to go from the beginning to the end. For instance, I do not allow myself the usual concessive clause, "Although some cases are not so-and-so, yet the majority of cases are so-and-so." Such a construction is stylistically feeble. If there are well-marked exceptions or a single outstanding exception, it is better to find the distinction that explains the exception and to *affirm* it rather than concede it. The difference will then strengthen the explanation of the other cases; it will provide a new reason. Often it provides the best reason, the one I hadn't thought of till I had to write the sentence. A strong and scrupulous style is a method of discovery.

Commenting on this, an unfriendly critic might say, "You mean that it is true if it sounds good." To which I would reply, in an unfriendly tone of voice, "Yes."

My reliance on colloquial speech and the process of literature is certainly closely related, whether as cause or effect, to my political disposition. I am anarchistic and agitational, and I am conservative and traditional. So is good speech. Insistently and consistently applied, any humane value, such as common sense, honor, honesty, or compassion, will soon take one far out of sight of the world as it is; and to have meaning is one of the virtues that is totally disruptive of established institutions. Nevertheless, meaningful language and coherent syntax are always historical and traditional and always have a kind of logic. Speaking is a spontaneous action of the speaker, and he speaks only in a community, for a hearer. Colloquial speech cannot be regimented, whereas even perception and science can be regimented—perception because it is passive, science because they can put blinders on it like a directed horse. But the vulnerability of colloquial speech, unfortunately, is that its freedom is limited to where the speakers have initiative, eyewitnessing, and trust, and these limits may be made narrow indeed. The literary process expands these limits by historical memory, international culture, and welcoming the dark unconscious which common folk prudently inhibit. Common speech can be pretty empty and aimless, whereas to write you must know at least something and try to be clear—it is a profession.

Slogans can't last long in either common speech or literature. In revolutionary situations, the new people, making bad literature (and sometimes even writing it down), have to recall ancient languages, as the Reformers picked up the Hebrew patriarchs, the French Revolutionists picked up Marcus Brutus, and the hippies pick up various Indians and Amerindians; but the good writers ridicule these too.

Thus, my Apology for the literature to which I have devoted the years of my life is very like the others over several centuries, and it is noteworthy that they are all similar. Possibly if we had a very different kind of community, we would say something different; but possibly it is the human condition—how would I know? Literature confounds the personal and impersonal, meaning and beginning to act, and thought and feeling. In this confusion which is like actual experience, it makes a kind of sense. It imagines what might be, taking account of what is. Using the code of language, it continually revises the code to cope with something new. It is more conservative than science and more daring than science. It makes the assured and powerful uneasy, if only out of powerless spite. It speaks my common speech and it makes human speech noble. It provides a friendly community across ages and boundaries, and cheers my solitude. It is the way I pray to God and patriotically revere my background. It is legitimacy and rebellion.

This essay was adapted from the final chapters of *Speaking and Language,* and printed in *Commentary* (July 1971) before the book appeared. Goodman had already had his first heart attack, and the essay represents his last word on his career as a man of letters.

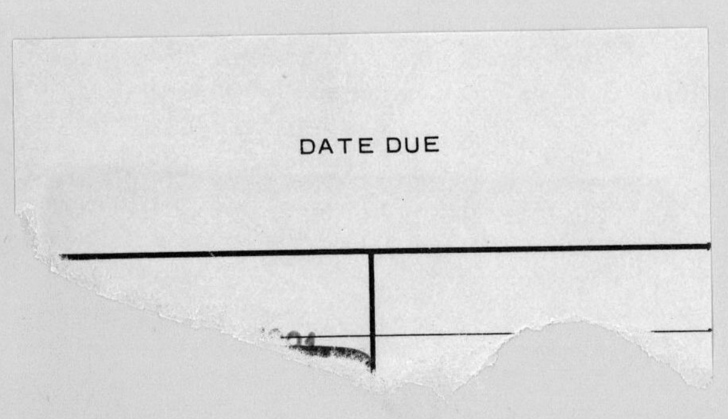